REVOLUTION OF CONSCIENCE

REVOLUTION
OF CONSCIENCE

Martin Luther King, Jr.,
and the Philosophy of Nonviolence

———◆———

GREG MOSES

Foreword by Leonard Harris

THE GUILFORD PRESS
New York London

TO MY SPOUSE,
PAMELA KAYE HARMATIUK

———•◆•———

Portions of the following works are reprinted by permission:
   Where Do We Go from Here: Chaos or Community? by Martin Luther King, Jr. (copyright 1967 by Martin Luther King, Jr., copyright renewed 1995 by Coretta Scott King); *Strength to Love* by Martin Luther King, Jr. (copyright 1963 by Martin Luther King, Jr., copyright renewed 1991 by Coretta Scott King); and *Stride toward Freedom: The Montgomery Story* by Martin Luther King, Jr. (copyright 1958 by Martin Luther King, Jr., copyright renewed 1986 by Coretta Scott King). Reprinted by arrangement with The Heirs to the Estate of Martin Luther King, Jr., c/o Writers House, Inc. as agent for the proprietor.
   A World View of Race by Ralph Bunche (copyright 1936 by Ralph Bunche, copyright renewed 1964, 1992, by the Estate of Ralph Bunche). Reprinted by permission of the Estate of Ralph Bunche.

This is a volume in Critical Perspectives, a Guilford series edited by Douglas Kellner.

LIBRARY OF CONGRESS CATALOGING-IN-PUBLICATION DATA

Moses, Greg.
    Revolution of conscience: Martin Luther King, Jr., and the philosophy of nonviolence / Greg Moses ; foreword by Leonard Harris.
        p.   cm. — (Critical perspectives)
    Includes bibliographical references and index.
    ISBN 1-57230-169-4
    1. King, Martin Luther, Jr., 1929–1968—Philosophy.   2. Nonviolence—United States.   3. Afro-Americans—Civil rights.   4. Afro-American intellectuals.
I. Title.   II. Series: Critical perspectives (New York, N.Y.)
E185.97.K5M65   1997
323′.092—dc20   96-35442
                                                              CIP

FOREWORD

We have a well-formed vision of Martin Luther King, Jr., and the civil rights movement even before we open this book. When we arrive at the end of Moses' analysis, however, our vision will be different. At the very least, we will see afresh the logic of nonviolence, and we will feel the need to ponder the overlooked consequences of believing in King's ethical position. King's ethical requirement to alleviate poverty, his demand for direct action, his insistence on challenging character virtues, and his position in an historical progression of activists provides a vision of King's principles as living agents. Moses allows us to see that nonviolence is a resource for human liberation. Reading King through reading Moses is to discover a dialectic that philosophy has been and continues to be evading: That in the here and now King's prophetic ethics and action-oriented philosophy are viable options for the pursuit of justice.

It is the logic of nonviolence in the human drama that I will, briefly, revision and reponder.

Universal human liberation, universal dignity, and the elusive search for the good are integral features of the human drama. The struggle to achieve emancipation from slavery, serfdom, and indentured servitude, however, has required monumental sacrifices in the same drama. And the various battles to end the miseries caused by the existence of disenfranchisement, anomie, alienation, and stereotypes are objectives motivated by a deep sense of outrage. Yet, in our endeavor to achieve the ideals of the good, change the structures of domination, and end the seemingly intransigent miseries befalling the human family, we face the most engrossing of all human challenges: By what method will we effect change so that universal human liberation can be a living reality?

An alluring trap in the concept of dialectics has been the notion that change requires using the very method, such as violent confrontation, that we hope to destroy. Change, in this view, is an unfolding of the already "there" of a given phenomenon; for example, if humans are inherently violent then it is through the use of violence that humans can destroy their tendency to be violent. The idea that change is an unfolding of the already "there" has been a dominant idea since the dawn of dialectics, and the belief that humans are unalterably prone to violence is a feature of humanity that has long been considered already "there." Nearly every account of revolution, whether emanating from the radical democracy of Henry David Thoreau, the justification of slave revolts by David Walker, or Karl Marx's analysis of class struggle, assumes the existence of a nearly unalterable regard by humans for the power of coercion through violence, and thereby a propensity to be violent.

Haunting these theories of change is the specter of a human nature that is not inherently prone to violence. Here, Moses provides an interpretation of King that makes King's view abundantly clear: The power of violence is not absolute; it is not "there" in human nature as unalterable and given; change is possible through the aegis of nonviolent direct action. The seeds for the destruction of violence are thus to be located not in the unfolding of the "there" of violence through its use, but in the unfolding of other features of our being. The "ancient philosophical injunction to know ourselves as we have never known ourselves before" has a crucial role to play in the process of change in King's view. Knowing ourselves includes knowing that violence is the desperate voice of the unheard, the discursive platform of despair, the frustration of the poor, and the fear of the empowered. Moses uncovers and makes clear King's psychological analysis—an analysis that is compatible with his logic of nonviolence.

Sympathy for the other when the other is the terrorizing authority of segregation, exploitation, and callous indifference is frighteningly redemptive. Sympathy, compassion, love, and justice are, as revealed by Moses, values directly connected to King's direct action—the direct confrontation and transformation of structures of domination, exclusion, and exploitation through the motivating influences of our conscience and principles. King's pluralism and pacifism do, as Moses argues, distinguish King's structural theory from classical approaches. King's explanations of domination allow him to infer solutions that use nonviolent direct action. Active creative tension, not romantic quietism, and critical optimism, not pessimism, are modus operandi for change. The civil rights movement, as a masterful moment in the progression of this unfolding, established the actuality of an alternative history, practice, theory, and way of living. The power exercised by the civil rights movement continues to stand as a monumental human achievement. Nonetheless, the power of nonviolence is in stark opposition to the power of violence.

Power is the mastery of coercion. Power is most starkly represented by the supreme authority of the threat to terminate life, cause permanent pain, cripple, and psychologically damage. These capacities form the rhapsody of violence as an omnipotent force. The allure of violence is that its owners are omnipotent over the nature of life. They are power incarnate, authority expressed, and masters of all the space and shapes before their gaze. The lords of violence have been the masters of the future because they could decide what would happen to those in their domain; they could name whether the use of terminal force is criminal, mad, defiant, heroic, good-natured, or simply obedient to the rule of law.

Tenacity, courage, and fortitude are virtues historically associated with persons willing to practice violence. Honor, dignity, and praise are nearly always reserved for members of moral communities that have used, or are willing to use, the violence believed needed to protect their community.

Moses argues persuasively against the myth that nonviolent direct action is necessarily associated with timidity and softmindedness. Tenacity, courage, and fortitude are virtues of pacifists. Honor, dignity, and praise are also bestowed on pacifists. The exercise of coercion, through the aegis of nonviolent challenges to conscience, fundamentally alters historically entrenched conceptions of human nature and the logic of change. The pursuit of such higher purposes is one that gives force to the struggle for universal human liberation and emancipation.

Moses has provided a way of thinking about King: The terms of equality, structure, nonviolent direct action, and justice provide a repositioning of King. Rather than seeing the civil rights movement as a special circumstance or historical accident, we can establish it in the flow of the history of a definite struggle.

Whether or not we agree with King's radical way of seeing change, his challenging conception of human nature and psychology, or his requirement for direct action, we can no longer evade the terrible mirror King forces us to look into, and through, to see ourselves as agents in a moral community. We are compelled to rethink reality, reread King, and understand King's contributions to the progressive history of struggle through the terrible sacrifices of women, men, and children in a desperate effort to avoid chaos and face the specters haunting our lives.

Revisiting and repondering by reading King, through reading Moses, allows us to begin again the jagged, but unbroken, march toward justice.

LEONARD HARRIS, PH.D.
Purdue University

PREFACE

In the United States of America, violence is common creed. Witness our movies, newspapers, popular literature, favorite TV shows, or the possibilities we harbor whenever we hide a gun. Yes, the Klan and its spiritual cousins thrive on a visceral attraction to violence, but there is something about violence that enthralls us all. And the glorification of violence requires an exacting myth, because any violence under-taken by ourselves—directly, by proxy, or vicariously—must be stringently justified. And since none of us has escaped the heritage or thrill of violence, we are all implicated in this art of war. Into such a context, nonviolence arrives as a curiosity and a threat. Systematic pursuit of the logic of nonviolence entails strangeness—strictures that discomfit one and all.

Martin Luther King, Jr., pursued the logic of nonviolence. With tireless persistence, he confronted myths used to justify violence and, one by one, demolished them. Of course, he did not do these things single-handedly, but his single-mindedness was a crucial feature of every movement he assisted. Each step of the way, he sought to prove that the power of violence was not absolute, that an army of love can win. If what King sought to prove is true, our usual view of history disintegrates, and with it go all myths that attempt to justify violence. For if it is possible to *empower ourselves nonviolently*, and if this possibility has been demonstrated in actuality, then a vital American creed has been challenged and refuted—the horror of our violence exposed.

Where there was once inexorable destiny, there is now a choice. And, for all our celebrations of freedom and independence, some choices are so unsettling that we would rather not acknowledge them. What everyone immediately fears about nonviolence is that it demands too much.

The demanding character of nonviolence may be easily evaded, however. "White Power" (as contrasted with Black Power) still works upon a platform of violence. The obvious terrorism of White Power is continually re-enacted, reminding us that a brutal legacy lives on. While such actions may be increasingly denounced or deplored, important assumptions of White Power are affirmed in quiet ways on a daily basis. King's philosophy of nonviolence confronts both the obvious terrorism and the quiet practice of collective domination. As a result, he provides a rigorous logic of liberation that digs much deeper than superficial denunciations of bigotry or hatred. To stop the most obvious offenses is not sufficient for the kind of diligence that King encouraged. Yet our commonplace understanding of King still fixes his contribution in a simplistic way.

It is true that King was born into a struggle where black terrorism was suicidal. Thus, to begin with, black terrorists could not ride home, take off their sheets, and resume respectable roles in their communities. Other means of power had to be found. This peculiar and well-known feature of King's environment leads us to conclusions that sell King's genius far short of its actual value. Had King worked from a position of *strength*, we reason, he would not have needed nonviolence. Thus, we conclude, nonviolence is an inevitable confession of weakness. From this point of view, nonviolence is a glorified victimology, by means of which pathetic subjects embrace an endless spiral of abuse. The process of our reasoning has required us to affirm that strength finds its true measure in violence. And this is the requirement that King's logic of nonviolence rejects. For King, nonviolence is the high road to true power, not because one refrains from violence, but because one rejects the entire outlook that assumes violence is a sign of strength. The logic of nonviolence seeks power within a disciplined framework that views violence as inevitably short-sighted.

The circumstances of Jim Crow America invite three other misconceptions that tend to encourage light treatment of King's philosophy. First, it is assumed that King simply imported nonviolence into black communities through his charismatic leadership. Second, it is argued that the circumstances of his day were so unusual as to limit the applicability of the principles of nonviolence. Third, it is taken for granted that King's ethic of nonviolence was addressed to black ears only. The combined effect of this triple misconception leaves us thinking that King's nonviolence is neither representative of, nor durable for, communities of struggle. At any rate, nonviolence is chiefly a strategic method to be employed, or not to be employed, by angry and aggrieved populations. Such is the weight of our common perception. In this book I argue, however, that King's principles of nonviolence were distilled from long experience with struggle and remain valid resources for human liberation in multiple contexts. Furthermore, King's nonviolence is addressed to each and every ear that is concerned with justice as a desirable excellence. In other words, there are crucial challenges remaining for white America, too.

Specialized scholars are now generally aware that King's values are exemplary of cultural currents developed in African America, especially in the black church (see the *Journal of Religious Ethics*, Fall 1990). What I hope to contribute in these pages is an interpretation of King that flows out of a more secular line of activism defined by such thinkers as Frederick Douglass, W. E. B. Du Bois, A. Philip Randolph, and Ralph Johnson Bunche. Of course, James Farmer, Bayard Rustin, and the late Cleveland Robinson belong here as well as others, but instead I turn to the great mystic teacher Howard Thurman, because somewhere the religious dimension of King's struggle must be explored in greater depth.

In the following pages I seek to fathom the deep reservoir of philosophical possibility that King was exploring and indicate why I think American culture resists the systematic development of nonviolence as a logical approach to human relations. Psychologically, we are challenged to examine whole constellations of assumptions and attitudes that pass for normalcy. As a nation, it appears that we thrive on antagonistic paranoia. Now that the cold war is over, numerous observers wonder where we will find our next enemy. Whatever the legitimate issues may have been that pitted the superpowers in an embrace of mutually assured destruction, we should also examine the deeply compelling appeal of conflict, aggression, and subterfuge in our shared experience. Perhaps we need a moral equivalent of war, and perhaps we owe the Puritans for this and other temperaments. Nonviolence warns us that this primal urge to destroy has a relentless appetite that will, when all else fails, settle for self-destruction.

With feminist scholarship especially, we are learning how our interpersonal norms are shot through with a tenacious, masculine voice. And feminist scholarship will continue to illuminate our understanding of the roots and consequences of nonviolence. It was Rosa Parks and the women of Birmingham, Alabama, who instigated the boycott that made King famous. Thus, another whole study should be done to explore how the male heritage presented in these pages reflects female genius. Both feminism and nonviolence have a way of provoking angry denials. Men are flustered by critiques of patriarchy in much the same way that whites are perturbed by discussions of racism. And I think this is because our ingrained attitudes are not like files in our desktop computers that can be searched, selected, and deleted with a few clicks of technology. Unlike the files in our computers, our attitudes are attached to us in passionate ways. Our myths tell us who we are. As illegitimate as racism and violence may be, King understood how they are connected to people in complex ways, and he was willing to acknowledge the pain that often accompanies the debunking of our most illegitimate tendencies. What if computers really liked some folder of data to the point that it cherished the folder *as self?* No doubt, we would hear our computers shouting about "reverse discrimination" as the racism folder got marked for deletion! On the human level where these problems really reside, any exorcism of the mythology of violence is going to be a complex matter that requires righteousness and courage, yes—but also unwavering patience and sympathy.

King continually argued that we must have sympathy for the devils that confront us. Otherwise, we become demons ourselves. This was important advice to keep in mind as King drilled deeper and deeper into the subterranean world where each of us confronts the bedeviled self. Perhaps the white Americans who peered at the television images of Birmingham or Selma could not help but see in the uniformed figures of the police and sheriffs just so many demons. In the Chicago suburbs, however, when white people stepped from their own front porches to throw stones at King, a whole new dimension of analysis was called forth. White America would now have to confront itself in new ways, which of course it refused to do.

The reformist disappointments of Chicago and afterward, the decline of King's prestige, and the rejection of nonviolence have been attributed to various internal problems of King's philosophy, but what ended King's pursuit of nonviolence came from the impulse of a trigger finger that still holds sway even decades later. The logic of nonviolence itself is bulletproof, and may be the best defense we can muster against the demons we harbor within. Thus, the importance of this logic begins in the social and political realm outlined in the following pages, but the pursuit of nonviolence cannot be stopped short of the ancient philosophical injunction to know ourselves as we have never known ourselves before.

*   *   *

Postscript from Oklahoma City: After completing my study, I had occasion to visit Oklahoma City in the aftermath of the April 1995 bombing. There I walked the bewildering perimeter of chain-link fence that marks the zone of destruction left by the bomb. I now hold in my hand a shard of glass brick exploded from God knows where in that terrible, unspeakable instant of death, and I can't help but think of the question that we sometimes find ourselves asking, namely: what if King were here? What if King had been here all along? During the final months of his life, King was struggling to reach out to the frustrated masses of white America. He was trying to show that the logic of nonviolence was applicable to a wide range of social distress. I think that his experience in Chicago shocked him into a new dimension of engagement with white America, and he set out to prove that white fears and black frustrations had common causes that could be addressed by the logic of nonviolence. In the Poor People's Campaign planned for the summer of 1968, he would link the frustrated hands of black and white together for a nonviolent show-down with the federal government in Washington, DC.

I think it is safe to say that no one has been able to pick up where

King left off. In place of the logic of nonviolence, we have a politics of denial, divisiveness, and destruction. Coretta Scott King has counseled on several occasions that violence is often the desperate voice of the unheard. It is truly the grim paradox of our so-called age of communications, peppered with each season's rave messenger, that the violence of the unheard should seek ever more destructive platforms of despair. The alternative is a vigorous program of nonviolence, persistently developed and carefully implemented. The strenuous requirements and risky nature of nonviolence will not be denied by those who know it best, but as we survey the debris-strewn blocks and exploded clutter of Oklahoma City, we see the horrific alternative that takes shape when the spirit of nonviolence has died.

ACKNOWLEDGMENTS

I have been working on this project for several years, and there are many people who have assisted me in it. I begin more than a decade ago, when John McDermott addressed the Society for the Advancement of American Philosophy (SAAP) at a meeting in College Station, Texas. That presentation drew me toward the pursuit of philosophy, thereafter always accompanied by McDermott's generous advice and support. At a subsequent meeting of SAAP in Atlanta, James Gouinlock arranged a symposium on King's philosophy, presented at Freedom Hall, on the grounds of the Martin Luther King, Jr., Center for Nonviolent Social Change. I have since called upon Professor Gouinlock's advice through various transformations of this manuscript.

As a graduate student at the University of Texas at Austin, I looked for a mentor who would favor explorations outside the philosophical mainstream. Professor Douglas Kellner encouraged me to pursue King's philosophy of nonviolence as a topic for my Ph.D. dissertation, and he provided helpful guidance. Supplementing Kellner's work on my dissertation committee were Professors Harvey Cormier, Kathleen Higgins, John McDermott, Ronnelle Paulsen, and Robert Solomon. Every graduate should be as fortunate as I was to have such a stimulating and wise committee. The main themes of this book were developed in the process of completing that dissertation. Professor

Lester Kurtz, also from the University of Texas, organizes annual conferences on nonviolence in which I have been privileged to participate. The concluding pages of this book were originally developed for one of those conferences. Finally, I would like to thank The Guilford Press editors Peter Wissoker and Anna Brackett, and copy editor Kelly Waering—as well as the anonymous reviewers—for their invaluable assistance.

Four other professors were kind enough to read versions of this manuscript. Laurence Mordekhai Thomas was generous with his time, thrilling with his inspiration, and dedicated to the truth that King was a great thinker. Leonard Harris was serious and provocative, but soothing and gracious. I am still working on questions that Thomas and Harris raised, so I know there is more to come. As for Larry Hickman, my much esteemed colleague and friend, the reader will find me groping after Hickman's logic of technology in these pages, thankful for his influence and prodigious support. Finally, Robert Calvert, who is a national treasure, graciously agreed to read the evolving text from a historian's point of view.

Back at the King Center, I had begun a decade-long acquaintance with the family of activists who make it their daily business to keep King's dream alive. Needless to say, their work is not easy, and it is rarely appreciated. Within the workings of King Week, now known as the National Holiday Celebration, I was fortunate to share the living experience of the movement. Two people in this context were especially helpful with this manuscript. First, there was Geri Allen, my "movement mother," as I sometimes call her. For Allen, a movement veteran since 1960, nonviolence is a living philosophy, rigorous and invigorating. More than any other reader, she insisted upon an African American interpretation, and (sometimes despite the misgivings of others) she prevailed. With respect to King's intellectual heritage, Allen had a persuasive ally in Broadus Butler, who served for a time as director of the King Center Archives. Butler spent several days guiding me toward many of the sources to be found in this study. What Butler suggested cost me a few years of time as I sought to re-educate myself in black philosophy, and I am still unwrapping Butler's gift.

Having mentioned Hickman and McDermott, I would like to expand upon my gratitude to the College Station community. Herman

Saatkamp was a colleague and protector for many years. As department head in philosophy at Texas A&M University, Saatkamp allowed me to develop curricula in support of my investigations into African American philosophy, and deftly managed to fight the annual budget battles in ways that kept me gainfully employed as a scholar and teacher. Those were the days! Also, Gregory Pappas and Robert Burch have each encouraged my forays into black philosophy, and their support has been gratifying. Pushing a little further back in time, I first entered graduate studies through the Department of English at Texas A&M, and would thus like to mention at least the names of Forrest Burt, Mark Busby, Richard Costa, Norman Grabo, and Robert Newman, among many friends and colleagues who have contributed something to the better parts of me.

Finally, I would like to thank Pamela Kaye Harmatiuk and Elizabeth Porter, who have provided a depth of friendship that exceeds any possible accounting.

As I commend the rest of this book to the reader, the advice of Professor Gouinlock nags me on account of my inability to fulfill it. I would be more convincing, he says, if I were less enthusiastic in my tone. Of course, he is correct. To him and others who encouraged the best possible book, I apologize for the shortcomings that remain.

CONTENTS

Introduction   THE LOGIC OF NONVIOLENCE   1
   Martin Luther King, Jr., and the American Intellectual   1
   King's Life and Thought   10
   King and Contemporary Thought   14

Chapter 1   EQUALITY   23
   Frederick Douglass and the Criteria of Intellectual
     Honesty   23
   King's American Dream   30
   The Example of Frederick Douglass   36
   Philosophy's Color Line   43

Chapter 2   STRUCTURE AND RACE   46
   W. E. B. Du Bois and the Problem of the Color Line   46
   Reviewing King's Usage   53
   Nineteenth-Century Precedents   64
   The Century of the Color Line   80
   Little Kingdom of Salt   89

Chapter 3   STRUCTURE AND CLASS   95
   A. Philip Randolph, Ralph J. Bunche, and the Context of
     Class Analysis   95
   Classical Foundations of Structural Theory   99
   Class Analysis Meets Race   107
   Randolph vs. Du Bois   113
   Imperatives of Radical Theory   121

Bunche's World View   125
King and the Race–Class Question   138

Chapter 4   NONVIOLENT DIRECT ACTION   144
Howard Thurman and the Ethics of Love   144
Jesus as Ethical Model   151
The Tactic Defended   155
Breaking the Cycle of Fear   162
Six Aspects of Nonviolent Struggle   168
An Experimental Technique   176
Thurman's View of Jesus   180

Chapter 5   JUSTICE AND LOVE   185
Of Ends and Means   185
Bringing Love to Black Power   191
Bringing Justice to Liberalism   195
King's World House of Tough-Minded Love   202
Jesus in Jail in Texas   206
A Philosophy of Liberation?   211
Epilogue for a Tough Mind   219

Appendix   227
Bibliography   229
Index   234

Introduction

---◆---

THE LOGIC
OF NONVIOLENCE

*What intellectuals can do for the extension of the
democratic way of life is to discipline our thinking
critically into some sort of realistic world-mindedness.*
— ALAIN LOCKE

MARTIN LUTHER KING, JR.,
AND THE AMERICAN INTELLECTUAL

The life of Dr. Martin Luther King, Jr., has already become a textbook
life, fated to unending paragraphs of interpretation. Forever, individuals will turn for inspiration to the mass movements of Montgomery,
Birmingham, Selma, and the 1963 March on Washington. In the
center of all this fascination is a brilliant reformer who captured the
world with his charisma, whose importance is secured because he
personified the history of his time. I, too, am compelled by the
memory of King, the great American reformer. Like millions of others,
I feel that I have been affected personally by experiences "before and
after" King.

However we evaluate the significance of the King years, whether
to minimize or maximize their features, we are pressed to agree that
something important happened. Thus, the historical questions are

1

fascinating and meaningful. More central to this book, however, is the logic of nonviolence. The question I would like to ask of King's life is thus a little different: how does King's logic of nonviolence contribute to the larger life of the mind? Apart from King's abilities as an activist—if we can set aside all those remarkable events for the time being—what is his legacy as an intellectual? Imagine, for instance, that King had bumbled through his speeches and had failed to attract any following at all. Suppose that he was no great orator, not a bit charismatic. If we disregard the historical ability of his words to move (or not move) masses or classes of people, King's words might then be called to judgment as something besides rhetoric, and we might ask if he had said anything worth remembering.

I will argue that King said a great deal worth remembering. Taken as a whole, King's published writings and speeches articulate a powerful analysis of the human condition. His propositions should rightly provoke critical thought in response. Since we have not escaped the questions that confronted King, we should think more seriously about the answers that King offered. What does it mean to value a principle such as equality? What advantage do we gain by analyzing history in terms of such concepts as racism, poverty, or violence? Experiencing such values, discerning such concepts, what kind of ethics do we choose to guide our behavior? What is justice, and how do we serve its ends? King's answers to these questions have been recognized for the beauty of his rhetoric, but are his answers reasonable? I answer that, not only are King's answers reasonable, but they deserve eminent consideration for their contribution to the history of philosophy.

To state my guiding thesis, I think that King establishes grounds for a new age of social and political philosophy, superseding both tired schools of thought that sought to legitimize cold war antagonisms, namely, Marxist-Leninism and what I dub "cowboy capitalism." In doing this, King reinvigorates the deepest spiritual motives that may be found in the human quest for justice, but he refuses to play loosely with tough material realities. Despite past denunciation of Marxist preoccupation with materialism and class analysis, today's victorious capitalism threatens to invoke a salvation that is wholly materialistic and viciously divisive. Against this threat, capitalism's trusty twin, liberalism, has very nearly lost heart. King felt the pressure of these ideological strictures and declared himself in favor of none of the above. So long as we can resist the urge to rush King into one or another corner of preconceived theory, we will learn much. There is today no single school of thought that can claim comprehension of the distinctive logic that King was trying to convey.

In order to appreciate King as an intellectual, I undertake two approaches. First, I explicate King's social and political philosophy on its own terms. For King, words such as *equality, structure, direct action, justice,* and *love* are the organic materials that constitute his intellectual perspective. It is important to see how these terms work in King's own language of thought. Second, I place King's systematic philosophy in a context of African American agitation. From Frederick Douglass to W. E. B. Du Bois, A. Philip Randolph to Ralph Johnson Bunche, and Howard Thurman to Martin King, we may construct a genealogy of intellectual development that makes distinctive contributions to truth. After we have taken King seriously for his terms and concepts, and after we have situated these thoughts in a tradition of African American philosophy—only after these preliminary investigations have been completed may we begin to appreciate King as an intellectual. Thus, I hope to demonstrate in the following pages how King provides a fascinating touchstone to the history of African American philosophy and establishes on these grounds a starting point for a philosophy of liberation distinctively relevant to our contemporary times and the future.

If King's brief career can be divided into early and late years, then this book concentrates on the later years, after Selma. Particularly in these last years of King's life do we find the value of his intellectual work, because these difficult months are more important for what King tried to tell us than for the achievements he won as a reformer. From 1966 to 1968, King was formulating his most mature criticism of contemporary civilization, exercising his considerable intellectual abilities to forge an analysis of history that would serve intelligent efforts to personalize our habits of culture. Chaos or community?— King's last great question was swallowed up by a spate of bad reviews aimed not at his logic but at his style, his momentum, his political ability to unsettle America. I would like to revive King's important question in order to show that his logic is compelling and relevant, uniquely suited to reflections on a new millennium.

Various objections, both severe and less so, are likely to be heard at this point, but they generally revolve around a common axis. Each objection in its way would deny King's originality. Perhaps one critic claims that King is merely derivative of Gandhi, another that King had ghostwriters or that he plagiarized. Certainly, some say, King was a talented activist with a Ph.D., but no philosopher. In sum, the prevailing attitude toward King recognizes many things, but never an original mind. There is no quick way to overcome prevailing attitudes, and each of the above objections has its force. However, one cannot develop a satisfactory judgment about these issues until one carefully weighs the logic of King's published writings. In the following pages I hope to show how King shaped a logic of nonviolence that was authentic and distinctive. To open the argument, I ask the reader to agree to two things. First, King was nobody's puppet—somehow he gathered up his own thought, which he articulated in distinctive form. Second, no other single source incorporates all aspects of King's contributions.

True enough, King learned from many people. The following study, in fact, introduces influences not widely acknowledged. This book even suggests a new source for King's textual borrowings. Nowhere, however, do we find that the breadth of King's thought can be stuffed into anyone's preconceived package—and this is how I begin to make the case for King's originality. When we have turned over all the leaves of King's expressions, we indeed find a groundwork of ideas distinctly his own. How else could King differ so often from those around him?

Scholars have wearied themselves a great deal about the problem of authorial intent. In general, they warn us not to attribute to authors intentions that may in fact be our own. Some scholars question whether intentions exist at all. I do not deny that King had intentions. Clearly, King's words were chosen for various momentous occasions. But I think King also chose his words to effect a better understanding of our shared predicament, and that is why it is important to read King as an intellectual. Over the years of his career, there is an integrity that disciplines King's thought and that provides a continuity of conception. I do not doubt that King has an original mind. It seems to me obvious that we would find influences in any intellectual's work. The mere fact that King was influenced in his thinking by others need not cause us to deny his originality.

In the following chapters, we will see how King's intellectual pursuit of nonviolence, informed by generations of militant struggle, was seeking deeper roots of reflection and analysis. With a careful ear to his critics, King was reformulating the logic of nonviolence to answer more and more comprehensive conceptions of the world at large. He was clearly admitting weakness in some areas, but was honestly pursuing the road of reason. And reason, for King, was the measure of humanity. For instance, King argued that affirmative action was a reasonable policy to compensate against ongoing historical discrimination. He argued that American habits were stubbornly racist, even after the victories of the civil rights campaigns. And he argued that racism was one mechanism of systematic oppression, bolstered by class conflict and violence. As his analysis of oppression became more complex, so did the problem of liberation. Thus, the great protest leader had to confront honestly the limitations of his own thinking. The concept of mass nonviolent direct action had to be recontextualized. More emphasis had to be placed on other dimensions of liberation, such as education and organization. More thought had to be directed toward a logic of coalitions. And nonviolence, pronounced for the tenth time dead, had to be resurrected for new challenges. These are only a few of the considerations that occupied King as an intellectual during the final years of his life.

Every intellectual has his or her milieu, and Andrew Young reminds us that King did not leap full-grown from the head of Zeus (or any other Greek god) (Kearns 1988). While King often wrote as if his intellectual heritage sprang solely from readings required in graduate school, this book will demonstrate that another kind of heritage informs King's philosophy. In the works of Frederick Douglass, W. E. B. Du Bois, A. Philip Randolph, Ralph J. Bunche, and Howard Thurman we find the roots of an intellectual heritage more organic to King's own experience than any sum of sources from the white tradition of Western liberalism. Although the black tradition of intellectual agitation has been marginalized in studies of King to date,

I hope to convince the reader that King's philosophy is best under-stood when it is considered in relation to the experiences and writings of key African American activist intellectuals.

These brief remarks suggest a genealogy of African American thought in which King participated. The outlines of such a school were first proposed to me by Broadus Butler in a conversation at his office at the archives of the Martin Luther King, Jr., Center for Nonviolent Social Change in Atlanta. I refer to this school as the "Heroic Age of American Philosophy," following terminology adapted from historian George Woolfolk, who, in discussing the life of Prairie View A&M College President W. R. Banks, speaks of a "heroic age of education" (Woolfolk 1981). Angela Davis has recently observed that too many narratives construct black identity in heroic opposition to white oppression, with the consequence that multitu-dinous aspects of human identity are ignored. With her cautionary words in mind, I tender the designation of a Heroic Age nevertheless. I hope to show that the kind of heroism indicated is something different from the usual Hollywood fare.

In Chapter 1, we see how Frederick Douglass establishes impor-tant parameters for intellectual heroism. What does a black man say on the occasion of the Fourth of July—"Independence Day"—to a white audience in 1852? Even when the black man has escaped the bonds that bind his race, what does he say to white folks about the state of the nation? An intellectual has choices. Douglass doesn't have to call down the judgment of heaven, but he does, and in doing so, he opens a tradition that King may later respect or reject. I argue that King respects the method of Douglass when he lifts up the high principles of the American creed and calls down the judgment of God. America, especially white America, must be called to a higher purpose than its self-serving existence.

In Chapter 2, W. E. B. Du Bois defines the problem of the twentieth century as the problem of the color line. How does this declaration help us to understand our ongoing problems of racism? Can't we just be color-blind? By dwelling upon racial prejudice, don't we contrib-ute to our own entrapment, harden lines of power, and make our predicament essential to the order of things? Du Bois makes a vocation of considering the color line as a topic for intellectual pursuit. When

King chooses the same vocation, he follows steps already taken by Du Bois, whose energies seemed endless. The facts of the color line are to be sifted, quantified, and redefined as crisis. Intolerable conditions demand study and analysis, because social transformation must happen—better that it be predicated upon informed social intelligence than ignorance. Thus, we find roots for King's logic in the legacy of Du Bois, sometime professor at Atlanta University.

In Chapter 3, A. Philip Randolph demonstrates a limit to race analysis. Some oppressions are not wholly racial, even when inflicted along racial lines. Thus, democratic liberation cannot be satisfied along racial lines alone. One must confront other interests and forces. For instance, the struggle for racial democracy entails a struggle for economic democracy. Enter now the race–class question. Is the ghetto a product of color prejudice, or of labor exploitation? Ralph J. Bunche presses class analysis to a limit of its own when he argues that one evil—oppression—is the common denominator that dissolves racial prejudice into class conflict. King himself seemed to press against this conclusion in the final year of his life, but we want to be careful here. Class analysis has dogmatisms that King will not embrace. Sometimes, intellectual achievement is distinguished by conclusions one refuses to draw, and King never reduces the terms of racism to class conflict, although he discerns vital connections between the two.

As the social analysis of Du Bois and Randolph is being presented, the reader may sometimes wonder how these materials are relevant to King. I answer that laying such groundwork is essential to developing the logic of nonviolence. Because American thought remains largely individualistic and opportunity-oriented, one is continually challenged to weigh in the evidence that racial exploitation and economic exploitation are indeed systematic realities in the land of the free. American thought also remains stubbornly embedded in habits of moral reasoning that work in terms of intentionality and character. Although these are interesting ontological categories in any traditional sense, important developments in social and political thought during the past century have encouraged moral reasoning in terms of habits and consequences. This pragmatic turn has been largely neglected, indeed suppressed, in official philosophical histories. Without attention to this pragmatic emphasis, however, concepts of collective evil remain difficult to grasp, and the logic of nonviolence loses its force. By presenting extensive samples of social analysis undertaken by Du Bois and Randolph, I hope to convey a sense of the historic authority that anchors ongoing claims about the salience of race and class as structural categories of philosophical analysis.

King saw more clearly than anyone else how racism and poverty thrive upon violence. His logic of nonviolence seeks to purge violence from social relations in order to alleviate oppressive mechanisms and conditions. Thus, Chapter 4 examines King's ethic of action as it is influenced by the masterful hand of Howard Thurman. When King was a seminary student writing about the meaning of Jesus, he quoted Thurman "hot off the presses." This borrowing has not been previously noted, perhaps because scholars have forgotten Thurman, but King obviously kept up with the gentle giant. Comparisons of King and Thurman can be illuminating (Fluker 1990). We are told by Thurman that the two men watched the world series together on television at Thurman's home in Boston, back in 1953 or thereabouts. What sorts of issues did they mull over as they enjoyed the spectacle of the powerful new medium of television? I asked Leonard Harris to speculate on this. He imagines them asking, "How can we be a baseball game?" Using the new medium of television, how could they convey the power of love, expose the evil of violence, and shake America free from its shackles of racism? While concentrating on King's role as an intellectual, we need not downplay altogether our sense of drama.

At heart, King was a process philosopher; he had no fondness for static categories. The concept of justice, in particular, was not to be subjected to a paralysis of analysis. For King, the concept of justice necessarily compelled further action, because injustice was both pervasive and intolerable. The process of nonviolence, therefore, was King's best answer to the question of justice. Yes, the process of nonviolence required patient analysis, but the goal of nonviolence could not be analyzed into existence. At some point, someone must act. Chapter 5 explores the framework provided by King's concept of justice. From this point of view, we see how King criticized white liberals, Black Power, and middle-class gradualism. Each had adopted processes that would inevitably miss the point.

Concluding remarks in Chapter 5 will indicate what King meant when he spoke of a revolution of values. His logic of nonviolence engaged high principles in order to elevate social practice; and he offered a general method of social change whereby liberation could proceed under urgent circumstances. Yet, always King's philosophical vision exceeded his reformist activities. We know that King's activism was informed by a dream. But we don't usually insist that the dream itself be but one illustration of King's comprehensive and radical theory of justice. With startling elegance, King argued that justice is literally bound to love—that is, the two are inextricably linked. And I think philosophy would be enriched were it to take King's theory seriously. Our memories of King are affected so much by the legend of his soft heart that we forget that his conception of love also demanded a tough mind.

The critical reader will have misgivings not yet dispelled by these introductory remarks. I will briefly anticipate one objection, sure to be raised by some—namely, that I have not dealt sufficiently with King's religious faith. On one side, critics will argue that I have been soft on religion. From this point of view, King's faith counts against his intellectual credibility. There is a lingering suspicion that preachers perpetuate a lie that cannot live. To the secular critics, I try to demonstrate in Chapter 4 that, whether one believes in God or not, King's philosophy of nonviolence is based upon a compelling ethic of love. On the other side, there will be complaints that I have not taken sufficient account of the positive contributions made by King's faith or the tradition of the black pulpit. To the latter critics, I would recommend the masterful studies by Lewis V. Baldwin, Richard Lischer, and Keith Miller cited in the Bibliography. Indeed, honest appraisal must grapple with King's religious dimension, but this need not diminish King's philosophical value.

I hope these introductory remarks have helped the reader to see how the logic of nonviolence defines an area of study not fully accounted for by either rhetoric or history. Defending King's intellectual contribution is not the same as defending King's activism, faith, or powers of oratory. Today, King's activism is indeed the source of our interest. Further down the road, when names like Birmingham have slipped into the dusty bowl of history, perhaps then we'll have a more compelling interest in what King said, not what he did. This is, after all, the way we know our intellectuals best.

KING'S LIFE AND THOUGHT

Although King developed his philosophy as he was questioning the reigning canons of Western civilization, we can better understand his concepts when they are explicated in relation to experiences, influences, and historical predicaments that served as the organic subject matter of his thought. At the age of five, for instance, he was impressed by the soup lines of the Great Depression. At the age of six, the father of a white playmate ordered his son never to play with King again. At the age of fifteen, King won an oratorical prize by celebrating the ideals of the United States Constitution. Riding in a bus on his way home from the speech King was ordered out of his seat. Reflecting from behind the veil that was dropped between him and the white passengers—not only on the bus, but planet Earth—King recalled, "It was the angriest I have ever been in my life" (Washington 1986: 343).

King's early years were shaped by the realities of economic depression and Jim Crow segregation, yet he was born into a family of relative power and prestige. Thus, in the midst of a turbulent American reality, King was observing life from a comparatively secure position within the African American community. "It is quite easy for me to think of a God of love mainly because I grew up in a family where love was central and where lovely relationships were ever present. It is quite easy for me to think of the universe as basically friendly mainly because of my uplifting hereditary and environmental circumstances. It is quite easy for me to lean more toward optimism than pessimism about human nature mainly because of my childhood experiences" (Carson 1992: 360). If evil could not be driven from King's larger world, it could be crowded from his personal life. When King wrote these words, he was student body president of Crozer Theological Seminary, soon-to-be valedictorian, and an emerging talent of rare promise.

In an important way, King is representative of an historical era when the Black Belt of the American South emigrated out of rural peonage into urban opportunity. As Pettigrew reported in 1964, "this massive movement leads directly to a more sophisticated people capable of effective protest, a people more cognizant of what discrimination over the years has denied them" (Pettigrew 1964:181). Optimism ran high. In 1954, 64 percent of African Americans polled felt life would soon be better; in 1963, 73 percent felt that "the racial attitudes of whites would improve during the next five years"; 63 percent thought "whites would accept racial change without violence" (Pettigrew 1964: 185). Like no other single individual, King represented this tidal wave of aspiration, produced under the very specific conditions of the United States during a "postwar" period. Consequently, these moments of history have been aptly named the King Years (Branch 1988).

Questions of philosophical importance arise out of the King Years—questions that King himself posed and considered in his public communications. "A Letter from the Birmingham City Jail" is a philosophical essay as well as a political document. King draws distinctions between justice and injustice as he provides a philosophical justification for his militant involvement in the affairs of Birmingham: "I am in Birmingham because injustice is here" (King 1964: 77). In Birmingham, King finds three reasons to judge segregation laws unjust: they degrade personality, are inflicted upon a minority while the majority is unaffected, and are enacted by a majority while the minority is prevented from participating in the deliberations. Thus, King argues that he is obliged to present his body in protest. When Thoreau was asked why he was in jail, he replied, "Why are you out there?" In the same manner, King argues his right to protest the structure of Southern segregation.

Various references to intellectual history that we find in "A Letter from the Birmingham City Jail" confirm that King did not leap into philosophical debate without sources of influence. King defers to Aquinas, Augustine, Bunyan, Buber, Jefferson, Socrates, Niebuhr, and Tillich, among others. King lived in a universe of ideas and influences. There were African American mentors, European and American sources, white educators, Christian pastors, experiences in the South, and his acquaintance with the proverbs of Ptahotep, the cult of

Isis—and, yes, even his ghostwriters—to draw upon for reflection and inspiration.

King published six books: two collections of sermons, *The Measure of a Man* (1959) and *Strength to Love* (1963); a collection of radio addresses, *The Trumpet of Conscience* (1968); and three books that I call "movement books." The first movement book, *Stride toward Freedom* (1958), is a philosophical account of the Montgomery bus boycott, including a general outline and defense of the method of direct nonviolent protest. The second movement book, *Why We Can't Wait* (1964), is a philosophical account of the 1963 Birmingham campaign for jobs and freedom. In "A Letter from the Birmingham City Jail," reprinted as a chapter in the book, King offers a philosophical defense of nonviolence addressed to moderate white clergy. The last movement book was published in 1967 in anticipation of a national campaign against poverty. Entitled *Where Do We Go from Here: Chaos or Community?*, King's last monograph is a complex interweaving of language coalesced from his previous works, along with language from his later years.

The cumulative effect of this book is prophetic and philosophical. Although *Where Do We Go from Here*, like his other movement books, was composed in the wake of a successful campaign—this time in Selma—the main focus of the book is on the crisis of the civil rights movement after Selma. King gives a philosophical account of the civil rights movement in an effort to assess the significance of an antici-pated Poor People's Campaign. The penultimate chapter ends with the book's main conclusion: "The time has come for us to civilize ourselves by the total, direct, and immediate abolition of poverty" (King 1967: 166). King's supporting arguments represent the sum of his philosophy of nonviolence at its most mature phase. As with the other movement books, King's last monograph contains a systematic defense of nonviolence, this time largely addressed to critics from the Black Power movement. My purpose here is to reconstruct King's philosophy of nonviolence systematically through careful examina-tion of this important monograph.

While King's historical actions represented a freedom movement, his philosophy of nonviolence also represented an intellectual devel-opment in social and political philosophy. As King saw it, the con-science of humanity was in need of a modern-day gadfly to sting the status quo from its listlessness—a contemporary prophet to call down righteousness like a mighty stream. Thus, King routinely defended his philosophy of nonviolence for its unique ability to meet the demands of contemporary liberation. As the tide of optimism grew in the wake of successful campaigns in Montgomery and Birmingham, confidence in nonviolence also grew. During the "revolution of 1963," nonviolence attracted legions of followers. The Nobel Peace Prize was awarded to King in 1964. Then, again in Selma, in 1965, a Bloody Sunday of oppression was transformed nonviolently into a triumphant crusade for voting rights legislation. Reflecting upon the glory days of the civil rights era, King once wrote that nonviolent resistance had become "the logical force in the greatest mass-action crusade for freedom that has ever occurred in American history" (King 1964: 25)—hence my own emphasis on the *logic* of nonviolence throughout the pages of this book.

As King and his philosophy rose upon a tide of optimism, however, the fortunes of American history did not rise accordingly, and King was left to withstand a groundswell of disappointment and despair. In the summer of 1966, advocates for Black Power doctrines, reflecting their frustration with both King himself and the omnipresence of white power, staged an extended open protest against integrationists' nonviolent theory of social change. In Chicago, King was booed by Black Power advocates. "They were now hostile because they were watching the dream that they had so readily accepted turn into a frustrating nightmare" (King 1967: 45). Even though King was at one time able to speak in behalf of a freedom movement that was achieving important victories, in his later years he was called upon to account for the fact that the movement and its philosophy seemed to be confronted by a kind of performance gap that was possibly unbridgeable. Both the logic and the practice of nonviolence had lost credibility. King determined in this last (as it turned out) movement book to show that the principles and practices of nonviolence were still relevant and effective. This general sense of predicament looms large as we approach a philosophical explication of King's logic of nonviolence as articulated in the last of his movement books.

I have identified five terms that I consider essential to a systematic explication of King's philosophy of nonviolence as found in his last book. These terms are: *equality, structure, nonviolent direct action, justice,* and *love.* This book is arranged as a critical examination of King's use of each term in order to develop the conceptual contours of King's mature thought.

KING AND CONTEMPORARY THOUGHT

In this book, I attempt to mark some new trails for King studies and to widen paths cleared by others. To be sure, I have taken a path begun by Hanes Walton, Jr., in his book on King's political philosophy (Walton 1971). Since Walton, others have helped to clear the ground. Ervin Smith has analyzed King's ethics (Smith 1981). John J. Ansbro has probed the resources of King's mind (Ansbro 1982). Kenneth L. Smith and Ira Zepp have reconstructed King's systematic conception of the beloved community (Smith & Zepp 1986). Cornel West has appreciated King as an "organic intellectual" (West 1989). Walter E. Fluker has examined King's idea of community as it relates to the work of Howard Thurman (Fluker 1990). And James H. Cone has compared the alternative perspectives on America offered by King and Malcolm X (Cone 1984, 1991).

For the most part, however, major studies of King have usually focused on other aspects of his complex life. There are a dozen biographies and several critical reviews of King's role in history (Bennett 1964, Branch 1988, Garrow 1986, Lewis 1970, Oates 1982, Reddick 1959, etc.). Some recent studies explore cultural sources drawn from "liberal theology" and the "black folk pulpit" (Miller 1992, Baldwin 1991, Lischer 1995). Efforts are under way to connect King to the emerging genealogies of Prophetic Pragmatism (West 1989, Harris 1983), Afrocentric Rhetoric (Asante 1987), and Liberation Theology (Cardenal, in Randall 1983). And the first volumes of *The King Papers* have been released (Carson 1992, 1994).

In short, there is abundant literature about King and his philosophy of nonviolence, but such literature gets little attention from the profession of philosophy. At last check, the *Philosopher's Index* posted but few listings about King. Yet, philosophical interest in King persists, and "A Letter from the Birmingham City Jail" may be seen lately to have entered the pages of a few introductory textbooks in philosophy (Castell, Borchert, & Zucker 1994, Hallman 1995, Kessler 1995, Soccio 1995). This book seeks to encourage further interest in, and study of, King as philosopher.

Before turning to more detailed consideration of the literature to date, it is important to recall a sort of academic rule of thumb, passed along in seminar rooms, to the effect that thirty years may pass before events and ideas begin to receive adequate scholarly treatment. According to this rule of thumb, the King Years are still too close for the kind of dispassionate consideration necessary for scholarly analysis. All studies to date, including this one, may still be considered "too early." Certainly, there is some merit in applying the thirty-year rule to the King Years. Scholars are only now beginning to collect a definitive edition of King's works, and it will be decades yet before the basic documentary evidence relating to King's life will be available in anything approaching complete form. It will also take another generation of scholars to be able to look at King through truly dispassionate eyes. We are still too much participants in the King Years. We remember with intense feeling how we responded to the turbulence of the King Years, and our scholarship to date reflects the intimate way in which our attitudes toward King were formed by the heat of battle. One hopes, however, that these early works will be of service to future scholars for their own unique perspectives.

In *The Political Philosophy of Martin Luther King, Jr.*, Hanes Walton, Jr., offers an important outline of King's political philosophy and an eloquent preface to the study of King's philosophy. "The impact of his personality, leadership, and ideas are of a magnitude and a kind that warrant special consideration of his thought, particularly in relation to what he considered to be the good life and what was implied in the achievement of that dream by nonviolent means" (Walton 1971: x). To achieve an understanding of King, Walton stipulates the important need to treat "the broad historical background of the movement toward freedom which King inherited" (Walton 1971: 9). Thus, Walton's book opens the study of King's philosophy in helpful ways.

Because King does not offer an alternative form of government, however, Walton declares that King's political philosophy is incomplete

(Walton 1971: 39). But on this point of philosophical completeness, I think Walton is too formalistic. King's political philosophy is simply not challenged to provide an alternative form of government. The chief problem confronting King is how to advance social change under conditions of modern "industrial democracy." King's leading principles seek to awaken latent cultural values in order to transform "from within" the energies and priorities of America's "racist imperialism." Within such a social structure, an "Economic Bill of Rights" is sought. If some subsequent situation places America in a position to move beyond the Constitution, then King is prepared with a few guiding principles and a healthy respect for experience and reason, but he does not "complete" his philosophy by anticipating what form of government we might construct under such circumstances. Rather than see King as failing to meet a checklist of preestablished criteria for completeness, I would argue that King offers us a new paradigm of completeness. And this new model poses interesting and important challenges to the pursuit of wisdom undertaken by social and political philosophers. We shall see, for instance, how King provides outlines for a research program in nonviolence studies.

Secondly, Walton joins with many scholars in observing that King's mind was primarily "deductive" (Walton 1971:40). No doubt, King's approach was principled, but I will argue that we must try to appreciate King's organic development of principle if we are to keep the philosophy of nonviolence alive for further experimentation. Walton senses a need to temper the absolutist declarations of a political theology, but I think Walton insufficiently appreciates the ways in which King's philosophy of nonviolence is genuinely engaged with a flux of facts and situations. It is a healthy caution in political philosophy to be wary of neat architectures, so this feature of King's thought demands scrutiny. In the following pages, I hope to show that King's elegant system of thought engages complex questions of fact in ways more rigorous than are immediately apparent.

In another passage, Walton says that King nowhere presents arguments as to why a "love ethic" should be necessary to liberation:

> In the face of hard economic facts, does one need the addition of
> a love ethic to the message spelled out by boycotts and demon-

strations? For King the answer in an unqualified yes, but nowhere in his speeches or writings does he cite reasons why this might be so. Nor does he allow for alternative attitudes to that of a highly idealized, for most mortals impossible goal of love. (Walton 1971: 81–82)

All King can do, it seems, is appeal to preexisting religious fundamentals. In response to Walton's challenge, I will outline a coherent psychological analysis of hate and fear that serves to discipline King's logic of nonviolence. Since racism feeds upon fear, it can only be conquered when fears are deconstructed, so to speak. Nonviolence seeks, in psychological terms, to liberate conscience from fear, hate, and anger. This is a direct benefit to the struggling classes. Moreover, nonviolence seeks to reassure oppressors that justice, not domination, is the goal of confrontation. And this, too, King argues, is a benefit for the struggling classes. If King does not argue these points at length, it is because he has implicitly incorporated the analysis already presented in Thurman's 1949 treatment of *Jesus and the Disinherited*. Although it is already traditional to view King in the ways that Walton suggests, I hope that my lengthy treatment of the concept of structure will render the traditional view more problematic and qualified.

Ervin Smith (1981) more recently, offers a helpful sketch of King's ethics, but again the treatment could be usefully augmented. For instance, Smith concentrates on King's earlier works and the notion of "freedom." The present study complements these considerations by focusing on King's last book and the notion of "equality." Certainly, equality entails some considerations of freedom, but I will argue that the shift in emphasis marks a period of maturity in King's thought as he grapples with the predicament of the movement after Selma.

Smith and Zepp (1986) offer incisive appraisals of the theological currents that King encountered during his formal education at Crozer Theological Seminary and Boston University. They speak with special authority (Smith was one of King's instructors at Crozer) when they declare that King "could no longer be a fundamentalist" subsequent to his seminary classes (Smith & Zepp 1986: 19). And they recognize that King's formal education presented an opportunity for him to explore new grounds for "beliefs about ethics and society already growing from his own experience as a Black man in the South" (Smith & Zepp 1986: 19). These are valuable premises for our understanding of King. But I think it is also worthwhile to explore the *secular* logic of nonviolence, and the ways in which King's philosophy builds upon premises that grow out of the struggle for African American liberation. Furthermore, I think more work could be done on the African roots of King's philosophy. At Crozer, King encountered the ancient teachings of the Egyptian vizier Ptahotep via the scholarship of James B. Pritchard (1958: 234–237). And I think the impact of such sources (neither theological nor Western) may be fruitfully explored.

Ansbro extends the treatment of King's liberal education and comes closest of all to a detailed exposition of King's systematic concern. In turn, Baldwin, Lischer, and Miller offer energetic scholarship that identifies disparate sources not necessarily acknowledged by King nor so easy to identify as college texts and teachers. Neither Ansbro, Baldwin, nor Miller, however, is eager to show that the mind of King is philosophical. As with Walton's "deductive" exposition, Ansbro's method of presentation, and Miller's interest in homiletic form, King comes across as a kind of Neoplatonist who deduces his whole system from first principles. What this study hopes to offer is a rougher texture for King's thought—more engagement with contemporary conditions and their melioration, more of a sense of philosophy as a lived human experience rather than a saintly faith or mere intellectual assent.

The most helpful biography for the purpose of this study is Bennett's (1964), which begins with the legacy of Thurman. It is Thurman who personally meets with Gandhi and brings back influential impressions in search of systematic liberation. Heavily documented treatments of King's life by Branch, Garrow, and Oates are always handy for reference, and the first volumes of The Papers (Carson 1992 and 1994) offer invaluable thoroughness in textual presentation and commentary. Scholarly presentation of King's early work helps us to understand his persistent reconstruction of fundamentalist literalism in search of deeper truths of spirit. King's method of reading the spirit of communication between the lines of text is an art that he used with great skill from an early age.

Three separate attempts to establish genealogies along nationalistic lines are of interest here. Cone's "Black Theology," Asante's "Afrocentrism," and West's "Prophetic Pragmatism" each entertains filiation with King as an inspirational, if implicit, mentor. In the case of Cone, there was early support for Black Theology from King's associates, if not from King himself. This instance suggests a pattern wherein all the Black Consciousness movements stemming out of the King Years owe something to King, even in their explicit efforts to break with his tenets. The resulting ambivalence is exemplified by Asante, who on the one hand declares that King's philosophy could never lay claim to being an Afrocentric statement (Asante 1980), while on the other hand he cites King's rhetoric as exemplary of the development of the Afrocentric rhetorical form, nommo (Asante 1987). As explicated by Asante, nommo is the rhetorical challenge of transforming audience into community. It is no wonder that he finds King to be a superlative practitioner of this Afrocentric mode of expression. In fact, King's philosophy may be fruitfully pursued from an African perspective as well. This study places emphasis on the American branch of the diaspora. If, as Senghor suggested, African thought is participatory rather than analytic, then King's mode of philosophy indicates how consciousness may be developed in a participatory way without losing any of its critical force (Senghor 1965: 29).

This leaves us to consider the prophetic pragmatism and critical nationalism of Cornel West as it is anticipated and supported by the scholarship of Leonard Harris. The anthology of African American philosophy collected by Harris (1983) emphasizes a theme of social transformation, exemplified by Douglass, Du Bois, Locke, or Davis. West takes up the suggestion, championed by Butler's (1983) essay on Douglass, that traditionally white American Philosophy might properly be integrated with such a lineage and thus be enriched. Whereas Butler offers up the example of Douglass, West offers Du Bois. Why not, in our pursuit of an American Philosophy, wed the African American tradition of prophetic challenge to the pragmatist's process-oriented search for amelioristic truth? West's exploration of prophetic pragmatism suggests the importance of King, and his recent dialogue with Michael Lerner confirms the influence (Lerner & West 1995: 18). It seems that further consideration of King cannot be avoided, nor can more extensive speculations be delayed, that might integrate the humanistic endeavors of our "separate but equal" habits of philosophy, black and white.

Anthony E. Cook (1990) has lately demonstrated in outline how King may be invoked as an alternative to deconstructive critical theorists. Although Cook is especially concerned with legal theory, and although he works within the limits of deconstructionist terminology, he offers an important example of how contemporary modes of academic thought perpetuate racial tensions and how, finally, King may be used to advance academic thought beyond its steadfast, racist limitations.

Together, West and Cook demonstrate how King's philosophy may be brought to bear on living philosophical issues. The list of creative issues available in this regard is as long as one would have it, once the outline of King's distinctive contribution is appreciated. What, for instance, might feminist philosophy learn from King's construction of the love ethic? What might postmodern theorists make of King's pluralistic approach to structure? These questions are fascinating, but they divert us from our main purpose in this book. What we are trying to do here is establish the groundwork of King's thought in a context that encourages us to see the many issues that remain untouched by mainstream philosophical developments. My fondest hope is that the reader will put this book down with a sense that much more is yet to be said.

Most sympathetically related to this study are articles by Manning Marable and Kenneth L. Smith. In his 1988 article on King's last years, Marable reminds us that King became "one of the three or four most influential figures in the world" (Marable 1987: 19). At this apex, King took risks. He denounced the war in Vietnam, took his movement north to Chicago, and, finally, undertook to abolish poverty from the United States: "Class, not race, would be the tie which would bind the new coalition" (Marable 1987: 25). In the end, "unlike nearly all of his contemporaries, King consistently challenged himself to draw new correlations between poverty, racism, and war" (Marable 1987: 27).

Smith's 1989 article on King's last three years seeks (with Marable) to cut short any trend, begun by scholars and continued by commercial media, toward viewing King as just a dreamer in search of abstract oneness with God's love: "the fact has been overlooked that during the last three years of Dr. King's life he linked the militarism of the Vietnam War with the domestic issues of racism and economic exploitation" (Smith 1989: 271–272). Contrary to Smith, however, this present essay does not take seriously the suggestion that King became a Marxist. Rather, this essay attempts to show how King's philosophy of nonviolence signals a viable supersession of Marxist philosophy.

Nowhere does the tension between academic and lay audiences assert itself with more force than upon the question of Marxist theory. Indeed, it is tempting to suppress the whole question from a book that seeks engagement with general readers. American popular culture eschews the slightest insinuations of Marxism, and this poses grave challenges to academic freedom of thought. At one time, however, the risks were greater than today. Therefore, I am going to broach the topic of Marxism even though I am attempting to attract as wide an audience as possible. I hope doing so does not create a sideshow that detracts from the main contribution here attempted. To the general reader who may be confused about this language, let me confess that I believe many of the issues that still confront capitalist society receive classic formulation in the works of Marx. For instance, Marx confronted the revolutionary nature of the capitalist business cycle. Whenever we read of scheduled layoffs numbering in the thousands, the massive exportation of jobs, rising profits amid stagnant wages, or falling stock prices in response to rising employment levels, we glimpse contemporary manifestations of phenomena that Marx worked hard to understand. And Marx attempted to understand such dynamics from the point of view of the blue-collar worker. These achievements of thought are not made irrelevant by the devolution of the Soviet bloc nor by the transformation of U.S. labor markets into service economies.

As we shall see, King was not afraid to discuss Marx. Written in the shadow of early-fifties McCarthyism and Red paranoia, King's first book, Stride toward Freedom (1958), directly confronts the value of Marx. For King, there was something compelling about Marx's attention to workers and their struggles. At the same time, he expressed concern with Marxism's tendency toward materialism, atheism, and totalitarianism. As with all great intellectuals, King was not afraid of anyone's opinions and was able to see in every serious work some indications of abiding truth. Yes, in King's philosophy, the important element of class struggle is lifted up from Marxism, as is the general criticism of individualistic capitalism. But King's analysis of the "triple evils" contributes a systematic approach to racism and violence that advances beyond Marxist achievements. Furthermore, King's prescription of nonviolent mass action presents us with something quite different from the kind of proletarian revolution envisioned in Marxist thought. When the young people of Eastern Europe, schooled since birth in the refinements of Marxist theory, brought down walls and dictators to the tune of songs made famous in the American South, it became obvious that Marxism had been superseded. This essay suggests that the most appropriate herald of the new age is King. In the wake of the nonviolent lifting of the "Iron Curtain," the worldwide challenge becomes the task envisioned by King—to transform the structure of racist imperialism from within.

In sum, the power of King's personality has been a mixed blessing to our understanding of his intellectual force. On one hand, King's historical achievements seem to guarantee that his writings will not be forgotten. On the other hand, the charisma of his authority tends to render his writings most interesting as "rhetoric" rather than philosophy. This study argues that there is a philosophy of nonviolence worthy of serious intellectual pursuit to which King's logic of nonviolence offers important contributions. In succeeding chapters we shall see how King develops his concepts of nonviolence in order to show how justice may be understood as a process that asserts the primacy of establishing a sense of community amidst a milieu of chaos. To begin the explication, we next turn to the concept of equality.

Chapter 1

———•———

EQUALITY

The history of philosophy is the only philosophy that
should be taught in a university.
— SANTAYANA

FREDERICK DOUGLASS AND THE CRITERIA
OF INTELLECTUAL HONESTY

Although Martin Luther King, Jr., lived a century after Frederick Douglass, the two reasoned in similar ways about the problem of America. Both confronted large white audiences with truths that were not platitudes. Both said the Constitution challenged America to a higher destiny. Key clauses of the American creed affirmed self-evident truths such as equal rights, freedom, and justice for all; yet these pronouncements in practice were applied with systematic double standards. In confronting this two-faced character of American popular culture, Douglass and King argued that lofty principles deserved deeper understanding and wider application. Both asserted that human affairs should be guided by universal moral principles. The difference between right and wrong could not be evaded, because each bore different consequences. As America sowed, it would reap. Should white America ever desire unity with black America, it might be a great day. In the meantime, Douglass and King wrestled with a nation in conflict with its own moral pronouncements. In this chapter we will explore ways in which Douglass and King established common methods of approach to public philosophy in the United States of America. Both thinkers unwrapped gifted meanings hidden within American discourse and urged attention to the honest pursuit of principles.

In 1852, Douglass, then in his mid-thirties, stepped up to a podium on the occasion of the Fourth of July. On that day, in Rochester, New York, with slavery still the established way of life in the South, Douglass delivered a classic speech. "What have I to do with your high independence?" challenged Douglass. How dare you celebrate your freedoms in front of me! This intellectual had escaped the worst, but he refused to join in celebrating freedoms his people could not share. It would be his chosen duty to mark the American distance between creeds and deeds. King's classic "Letter from Birmingham Jail" also spoke to a white audience. The 1963 letter was addressed to white clerics who wanted King out of town. In the letter, King told his dear fellow clergymen that, frankly, they were worse enemies than the Ku Klux Klan. At least the Klan was forthright about its intentions, while white moderates, on the other hand, cloaked their racism with the delusion that things were okay the way they were. Like the Independence Day speech delivered by Douglass, King's letter contrasted white perceptions with black realities. If King had his dreams, he well knew the distance between dreams and delusions. His own dreams were meant to overcome present conditions, not to perpetuate them.

After slavery was abolished, Douglass watched the rise and fall of Reconstruction. White America had indeed warred with itself over the civil future of African Americans, but by 1877 both political parties had regrouped around a race policy that would come to bear the name Jim Crow. As an aging statesman, Douglass was made to feel the weight of a ponderous struggle ahead. In 1883, he addressed an audience at Lincoln Hall in Washington, DC. The Supreme Court had just declared the Civil Rights Act of 1875 unconstitutional. It was an earthquake of a ruling, and time itself seemed to lash backward. At that time, Douglass spoke about moral principles that could not be flaunted. Striking down civil rights would loose a moral cyclone, he warned. Like Douglass, King also spent his last years under the weight of things to come. Although King saw passage of the 1964 Civil Rights Act, he also witnessed subsequent backlash against civil rights. In Chicago, he saw firsthand how segregation still ruled the neighborhoods of white America. By 1967, black optimism was at a low point. As King tried to resurrect hope for a nation, he was also working to overcome his own dismay. Everyone agreed there had been a recent backlash in public opinion. King's dream appeared to be threatened by events that could quickly become a nightmare (Cone 1991). Like Douglass, King warned of moral shipwreck. As we approach King's concept of equality, we shall find methods tested and inscribed by the logic of Douglass. King's nonviolence thus presents itself as a type of philosophy that was forged upon the anvil of American popular culture.

By 1967, white America had grown weary of the civil rights struggle, and black America had suffered false hopes. Under such circumstances, King was challenged to gather his thoughts in a manner that would heave America to a new plateau of racial reconciliation. To meet that strenuous objective, King gathered his analysis around the principle of *equality*. The term appears early and often in King's later discussions, especially in his last monograph, *Where Do We Go from Here: Chaos or Community?* More than any other principle, equality would establish the standard for judgment during King's last years. Like Douglass, King argued that high principles of the American creed provided worthy guides for social progress. Within the realm of popular discourse in America, *equality* is one term that enjoys near-unanimous approbation. Thus, the philosopher who goes to market in America finds much raw material already in circulation. In King's last monograph, the concept of equality is lifted out of the American marketplace and weighed for its worth. When King finds that the concept is not being traded at its proper weight, he encourages wholesale upward revaluation. So long as equality is handled like a wooden nickel, as it were, the moral economy of America verges upon bankruptcy.

King was not only confronting stubborn white racism, but he was also defending the logic of nonviolence to skeptical or complacent African Americans. The year 1966 marked the first time that King was booed off a podium. Reeling from the ugly local reception accorded King's marches through Chicago's white neighborhoods, a black audience in Chicago turned against the great reformer and jeered at his philosophy of nonviolence (Ralph 1993). Black Power would now lead the vanguard of the civil rights struggle. King was "too patient," he "compromised too much," and he "liked white people." In effect, they were all—King, nonviolence, and white people—expelled from the black vanguard for lack of performance. Such was the situation that confronted King when he took a retreat to Ocho Rios, Jamaica, in January 1967. "The days in Jamaica were the first time in his adult life that Martin King was free of the telephone and its demands for any stretch of time" (Garrow 1986: 543). Yes, it was nearly "Negro History Week" in America as King began his month-long retreat. Where would he go from here?

When King emerged from Jamaica, he was ready to address America again. Taking first things first, King noted that white America had fled the cause. Having supported black efforts to vote in Alabama, white America decided it had done enough. After Selma, white America resumed its traditional posture, and black America was again battered by a spirit of segregation. Who in the white neighborhoods of America would be willing to step forward and continue the struggle? Who would feel that more effort was urgently needed? Who was able? For the vast majority of whites, civil rights was a painful crusade that had ended judiciously if not soon enough. White people were happy to believe that the whole thing was finally over. What principle might rouse whites from resuming their latter-day Rip Van Winkle snooze?

Equality, answered King. That's what Americans might want. And why not? Who would refuse to press the case for equality among all fellow Americans? If white Americans would not accept equality for black Americans, then what might be their excuse? King's answer was direct—white America had calculated the cost of equality and had decided it would not pay. Even though the country had been founded upon the principle that "all men are created equal," white America still reserved the right to interpret that principle in its own interest. Even Thomas Jefferson, who wrote those words into the Declaration of Independence, was himself a slave owner. Thus, defining American principles was largely a matter of convenience for white America. When used as a handy slogan of struggle against colonialism, equality was honored, but when it posed a philosophical dilemma with respect to slavery, equality got short shrift under the guise that blacks were not really "men."

By raising the issue of equality, we see how King's logic of nonviolence tugged at cultural connections embedded within the American experience. The terms used by white America were important to King, even as he sought to reform and redefine them. This aspect of King's approach drew harsh criticism from some quarters. Malcolm X, for instance, argued that King's terms were not up to the task of liberating African Americans. The struggle for civil rights, and its engagement with American contexts, he argued, should be replaced by a fight for human rights. Whereas the former was doomed to failure within American limits, the latter might succeed in alliance with a global movement for black liberation. A human rights campaign could seek intervention from the United Nations, for example. In response, King argued that black Americans would have to organize their own struggles at home. Surveying the globe, King did not see another nation that was prepared to intercede in America's domestic conflicts. Thus, like it or not, the debate would have to be undertaken on American terms.

When King introduces the term *equality*, he never provides the obligatory formal definition. Here is a term so widely celebrated in American culture that King claims his right to use it just like anyone else. By refusing to define this term in a formal way, King invites us to reflect on the double standard that is revealed when it suddenly becomes necessary for an American to provide a rigorous definition of equality. The meaning of the word had been "clear enough" to certain revolutionaries who deployed it in a war for independence. Since that time it had been "clear enough" to countless orators on the Fourth of July. King is not being anti-intellectual in his refusal to pause for definition's sake; he is simply claiming his birthright to certain conventions of American discourse. Yet, time and again, debates about equality would reveal a peculiar double standard. Whereas equality might be celebrated as an idea that once rightfully fueled a revolution, it often becomes an analytic curiosity when deployed in debates concerning black Americans. In short, the American meaning of equality has often been left deliberately vague for reasons of self-interest, while demands for definitional preciseness have obstructed its use in service to the disadvantaged. In some instances, demand to provide a formal definition may be just another method of postponing engagement with real issues.

King throws the term *equality* into play with a calculated innocence. It is a plain word with plain meaning and a fit principle to measure American reality by the plain light of day. Thus, King begins his dialogue with white America in 1967 by assuming a principle already acknowledged as a cultural value (albeit one harboring elements of duplicity, as we have seen). Let those who do not feel the force of King's approach scurry for definitions. Let those who feel the force, but want to deflect King's challenge from its intended target, demand elaborations. Honest white Americans might well admit that their perplexity over King's usage was not the result of a cognitive puzzle, but a moral one.

Surveying the nation in 1967, King observed that white America had responded in two ways to the challenge of equality. First, having calculated the cost of equality, white America concluded that black America had come far enough. Second, in order to cling to equality as a cultural value, white America redefined the term to meet new needs. While black Americans insisted that equality meant just what it said, white Americans were equivocal. Equality was taken to mean improvement. Things were less unequal than they used to be—look at the new laws on the books!—and thus the principle of equality had been sufficiently honored for the time being. In short, equality had long ceased to be a rallying cry for white America, and from King's point of view this change in attitude was cause for shame.

Even if King managed to revive equality as a theme for black liberation (difficulties with white America aside) he would have to confront another kind of challenge. "Black Power" does not sound like equality. King argues that, if terms of liberation must be carefully chosen, then Black Power is truly an ill-conceived slogan. Thinking back to the Chicago crowd of black militants, that booed him into retreat, King tries to frame an argument that would convince them that equality is the better slogan. But how could he win back an audience that was already tired of listening to him? How dare he argue the positive value of a traditional American framework to people who had become so repulsed by such terms of debate that they had begun spelling "America" with the Klan's own "k" in place of the "c"? In the emerging war of judgments over King and Black Power, the worth of America's core values was itself called into question. In this brave new world of black revolution, America's great reformer had suddenly become quaint and ludicrous.

King's quest for equality was neither winning friends nor influencing enemies. Both sides found King dismaying. Everyone agreed that the nation was in crisis, but white America could blame trouble on the "troublemakers" who led protest marches. White neighborhoods of Chicago flung their hatred directly at King. Meanwhile, black voices questioned whether nonviolence alone could be expected to achieve their goals. After Chicago, it seemed that nonviolence had reached its limits—whites were no longer responding with moderate compromises, and blacks were no longer volunteering to be punched. At the same time, black aspirations for change remained undiminished, and so the impulse to confront white America at this particular juncture jumped the track of nonviolence, literally took up arms, and openly called for revolution as a kind of colonial liberation.

In retrospect, we may observe that the concept of equality outlined by King was foundational to his mature logic of nonviolence. When compared to other philosophies of power—white or black— nonviolence alone insisted upon a single meaning for equality. Under the terms of the logic of nonviolence, opponents also were considered equal. Nonviolent protesters suffered a great deal for this conviction. Fellow citizens were just that, even when they oppressed—and whatever dignity they had was not to be impaired, nor were their bodies to be abused in the pursuit of justice. Thus, nonviolence required an ethic of equality that was easily discarded by other theories of justice or liberation. For King's logic of nonviolence, equality could have this sort of meaning without being formally explicated.

In sum, the concept of equality stands at the center of value for King's logic of nonviolence. Within that logic, he tried to define America's crisis as a crisis of principle. When King was assassinated, the concept of equality lost its most incisive defender. We now turn to King's last monograph for a closer look at what he said about equality in 1967.

KING'S AMERICAN DREAM

The philosophy of nonviolence, as King saw it, was an effort to establish a dream of equality free from the past history of racist double standards. As he explained in his 1967 book *Where Do We Go From Here: Chaos or Community?*: "Jefferson's majestic words, 'all men are created equal,' meant for him, as for many others, that all *white* men are created equal." Neither Thomas Jefferson, George Washington, Patrick Henry, John Quincy Adams, John Calhoun, nor Abraham Lincoln "had a strong, unequivocal belief in the equality of the black man." George Washington might have wished in his soul that slavery would be gradually abolished, but he never made this wish public. "Here, in the life of the father of our nation, we can see the developing dilemma of white America: the haunting ambivalence, the intellectual and moral recognition that slavery is wrong, but the emotional tie to the system so deep and pervasive that it imposes an inflexible unwillingness to root it out" (King 1967: 76–77).

With sober acknowledgment of white America's racist habits of heart, King appealed to the high principle of equality as a beacon that might illuminate a better day. "A people who began a national life inspired by a vision of a society of brotherhood can redeem itself. But redemption can only come through a humble acknowledgment of guilt and an honest knowledge of self." In the fashion of Baptist preachers, King moralized the predicament of America in the form of a parable. Like a prodigal son, America had strayed into a life of debauchery—in this case, "the far country of racism"—leaving behind an honorable home of righteous ideals. "Its pillars were soundly grounded in the insights of our Judeo-Christian heritage: all men are made in the image of God; all men are brothers; all men are created equal; every man is heir to a legacy of dignity and worth; every man has rights that are neither conferred nor derived from the state, they are God-given" (King 1967: 83–84). The parable illustrated the central thesis of King's logic of nonviolence, indicating a judgment that was not elusive. The principle of equality would make a worthy foundation for social order—and would provide an illuminating test for social disorder.

As revolutionary America once declared these truths to be *self-*

evident, "that all men are endowed by their Creator with certain inalienable rights," so, says King, may America return home to her revolutionary truths. "As a first step on the journey home, the journey to full equality," says King, "we will have to engage in a radical reordering of national priorities." Another American revolution, founded upon some insights from the first one, might return prodigal America to a home not so much past as principled—not exactly a return to where we were, but a journey toward where we ought to have been headed all along. King does not shy away from terms that are radical or revolutionary. He insists upon the urgency of the crisis at hand. According to the timetable set by President Lyndon B. Johnson, for instance, where "the hopes of the twentieth century will become the realities of the twenty-first," King complains that "many Negroes not yet born and virtually all now alive will not experience equality. The virtue of patience will become a vice if it accepts so leisurely an approach to social change" (King 1967: 85, 88).

Having exposed the American predicament over equality, and having asserted an urgent need for ameliorating the situation, King takes stock of groups most likely to lend reliable help in the struggle for equality. For King, the realistic plan is part and parcel of any complete philosophy of liberation. He begins his assessment of the future with a confession of disappointment. "Over the last few years many Negroes have felt that their most troublesome adversary was not the obvious bigot of the Ku Klux Klan or the John Birch Society, but the white liberal who is more devoted to 'order' than to justice, who prefers tranquillity to equality" (King 1967: 88). This judgment is consonant with King's views in "A Letter from the Birmingham City Jail," which details the persistent foibles of white moderates and their clergy.

Because white moderates and white liberals share the material benefits of white power, and because they must answer to the public opinion of white publics, presses, pulpits, and broadcast pundits—even to the terrorism of white supremacists—they often find themselves in difficulties with which they are unprepared to cope. Even when these pressures are not applied, white liberals must confront the eventuality that equality may require extensive adjustments to their own way of life. Thus, "many of our former supporters will fall by the wayside as the movement presses against financial privilege. Others will withdraw as long-established cultural privileges are threatened. During this period we will have to depend on that creative minority of true believers" (King 1967: 95). This passage might be said to foreshadow white liberals' subsequent unreliability in conflicts arising over affirmative action or multicultural studies.

If few white moderates and liberals will remain as reliable allies in the effort to bring America home to equality, King turns to groups that shoulder the economic burdens of inequality: "an energized section of labor, Negroes, unemployed and welfare recipients. The total elimination of poverty, now a practical possibility, the reality of equality in race relations and other profound structural changes in society may well begin here" (King 1967: 142).

By reviewing King's use of the term *equality* in his last monograph, we see how the concept comes to play a central role in his philosophy of nonviolence. Indeed, in King's quest for allies, equality becomes the ultimate criterion, whether one is assessing labor unions or churches:

> Most unions have mutual interests with us; both can profit in the relationship. Yet with some unions that persist in discrimination to retain their monopoly of jobs we have no common ground. To talk of alliances with them is to talk of mutual deception and mutual hypocrisy. The same test must be applied to churches and church bodies. Some churches recognize that to be relevant in moral life they must make equality an imperative. With them the basis for alliance is strong and enduring. But toward those churches that shun and evade the issue, that are mute or timorous on social and economic questions, we are no better than strangers even though we sing the same hymns in worship of the same God. (King 1967: 151)

King's meaning is clear and distinct. Agreement upon the pursuit of equality will supersede even agreement upon the name of God as the movement seeks to distinguish friend from stranger. The value of equality alone meets King's demand "to be relevant in moral life." Where there is no turning toward equality, there can be no turning toward truth. Whether one applies the secular categories of the social democrat or the religious categories of the Christian democrat, King suggests that there is a common faith in equality by which all parties may be judged. Indeed, this is a remarkable claim—to which we shall soon return.

As King concludes his analysis of where we are in 1967, and as he suggests where we are going, he makes it clear that white America has not produced within its own ranks an acceptable model of development. "Equality with whites will not solve the problem of either whites or Negroes if it means equality in a world stricken by poverty and in a universe doomed to extinction by war" (King 1967: 167). Elimination of racism alone would not conclude black America's confrontation with inequality, because any collective parity with white America would reveal lingering problems of poverty and violence within white America itself. To white America, King is addressing two critical challenges—not only equality for black America but equality among whites as well. And this is how King begins to articulate a position that places him out of bounds as a civil rights leader. He begins to assert his privilege to speak about relations among whites.

"These are revolutionary times," concludes King. "All over the globe men are revolting against old systems of exploitation and oppression, and out of the wombs of a frail world new systems of justice and equality are being born." America may choose to continue along the path of hypocrisy and chaos, or it may return home to the abandoned values of equality and community. "We still have a choice today: nonviolent coexistence or violent coannihilation. This may well be mankind's last chance to choose between chaos and community" (King 1967: 189, 191). In sum, King establishes the concept of equality as fundamental to his mature philosophy of nonviolence. Yes, the term is lifted from traditional uses on the American scene, but King would also strip the term of its history as a double standard. King is not inviting any lengthy discourses that would divert attention from the force of his argument. And this refusal to be drawn into analytical diversions can be justified. Intellectual honesty sometimes requires a frank acknowledgment that some herrings are red ones.

In King's last monograph to America, the concept of equality assumes the privileged position once reserved for the concept of freedom. By choosing equality over freedom, King has relinquished an individualistic term in favor of a more relational concept. Certain theoretical advantages ensue. In theory it is possible for one to conceive of one's freedom or liberty as an individualistic trait, separable from the relative freedom or unfreedom of others. In turn, one may conceive of liberation in equally individualistic terms—one lives in a land of the free so long as one is herself free. And one may project the possibility of freedom as something that depends mostly upon individual effort. These possibilities of thought very soon become ideological traps that prevent further thought about freedom, even in the face of pervasive unfreedom. Moreover, it is possible for an individual to posit one's freedom in opposition to another's. Our freedoms may be said to conflict. Each of us has a separable right to our freedom—thus, the freedom of the property owner is violated by the freedom of the slave. Similarly, the freedom of the entrepreneur is endangered by the freedom of the laborer. Am I not free to pay wages as I see fit? Am I not free to demand higher wages? And so on. The logic of freedom becomes antagonistic.

With the conceptual move to equality, we are prevented from conceiving liberation in individualistic terms. My equality depends upon your equality. Our equality becomes a collective problem that no longer admits of individual or unilateral solutions. There is no immediate theoretical conflict between my equality and yours. It is important, then, to note that King has made this conceptual move from freedom to equality as he frames a choice between a chaos of conflicting individuals and a community of harmonizing equals. The shift is subtle in that it is not made explicit, and it is provisional in that it is adopted to meet the needs of a specific situation, but it is nevertheless profound in its implications.

For all the credit King receives in his role as a Baptist preacher, he could not be more clear about the values he seeks in his allies. It is more important to King that one be committed to equality than that one profess to be a Christian. This is why King could embrace the teachings of Gandhi. As Miller reports, King was once asked by fellow Christians to temper his public affirmations of the non-Christian (Hindu) Gandhi. "It is ironic, yet inescapably true," replied King, "that the greatest Christian of the modern world was a man who never embraced Christianity" (Miller 1992).

Once again, it may well be objected that King's use of *equality* is problematic. For instance, in earlier passages, King seems to treat the term as if it were self-defining. For black America, the term "means what it says." Nowhere does King treat any of the well-known philosophical difficulties that may attend the concept. For instance, which sort of equality does King have in mind—political equality, social equality, procedural equality, or equality of outcome? Doesn't the shift from freedom to equality nevertheless raise the question of equal freedom? Yet, without formally defining the term, King says several things about the meaning of equality. (1) Equality is already a shared value of sorts, legitimized by America's cultural heritage and worthy of honor. (2) Equality nevertheless is not honored in practice; in fact, it is evaded by America's civil society. (3) Equality does not mean domination. (4) Equality does not mean tranquillity. (5) Liberal ideals of "equal opportunity and equal treatment of people according to their individual merits" are "old concepts" in need of "re-evaluation." (6) Equality serves as a term of more rigorous moral worth than some forms of Christianity. (7) Equality involves variables that are not confined to relations between races, but rather involve relations among people otherwise classed as members of a dominant race. All these considerations hardly leave the concept meaningless.

King's use of *equality* also raises the question of philosophical foundationalism or fundamentalism. Even King's admirers suspect that his philosophical project is primarily deductive and absolutist rather than experimental or critical. Doesn't his concept of equality confirm these suspicions? I answer that King has chosen this leading principle for the work it will do, and he has reflectively calculated the worth of core values and principles. When King speaks of true believers who are guided by universal principles, he indicates an ability to maintain a reflective engagement with certain values, even against selfish interests or discomforting consequences. Nowhere does King claim that the value of equality has been divinely handed down to him, nor that all terms of American popular approbation should be elevated to the status of self-evident truth. Quite the contrary, King argues that equality is a value by which may be judged the worth of divine inspiration and which must be weaned from other persistent popular values of American civil religion. As we shall shortly see with Douglass, the value of guiding principles and their rigorous pursuit can be argued from experience.

THE EXAMPLE OF FREDERICK DOUGLASS

King refers to Douglass twice in his last monograph, both times in the opening section of the chapter on "Racism and the White Backlash." In this section King sketches the pervasive nature of racism within the history of the United States. Such a sketch could not proceed without Douglass, who for half a century served as advocate and symbol of black liberation. Douglass marked the distance between white and black reality in 1852 when he was invited to deliver a keynote address in his adopted hometown of Rochester, New York, on the occasion of Independence Day: "Fellow citizens, pardon me, allow me to ask, why am I called upon to speak here to-day? What have I, or those I represent, to do with your national independence? Are the great principles of political freedom and of natural justice, embodied in that Declaration of Independence, extended to us?" (Douglass 1852).

Declaring that "your high independence only reveals the immeasurable distance between us," Douglass searches for a subject to fit the occasion. While his audience has come to celebrate a shared prosperity, Douglass must yet listen to "the mournful wail of millions" who are kept in bondage: "To forget them, to pass lightly over their wrongs, and to chime with the popular theme, would be a treason most scandalous and shocking, and would make me a reproach before God and the world. My subject, then fellow-citizens, is AMERICAN SLAVERY. I shall see, this day, and its popular characteristics, from the slave's point of view." By such lights, Douglass casts plain judgment upon the day. "America is false to the past, false to the present, and solemnly binds herself to be false to the future." The rhetoric of the day will be blunt: "I will use the severest language I can command" (Douglass 1852).

Before Douglass proceeds with his most severe thoughts, however, he anticipates a kind of objection: "I fancy I hear some one of my audience say, it is just in this circumstance that you and your brother abolitionists fail to make a favorable impression on the public mind. Would you argue more and denounce less, would you persuade more, and rebuke less, your cause would be much more likely to succeed. But, I submit, where all is plain there is nothing to be argued." Douglass is not the flip anti-intellectual. He will defend his privilege not to persuade. "What point in the anti-slavery creed would you have me argue? On what branch of the subject do the people of this country need light? Must I undertake to prove that the slave is a man?" (Douglass 1852).

If there is a form of persuasion demanded by some, Douglass reserves his right to choose his own ground of logic. "When the dogs in your streets, when the fowls in the air, when the cattle on your hills, when the fish of the sea, and the reptiles that crawl, shall be unable to distinguish the slave from a brute, then will I argue with you that the slave is a man!"

> For the present, it is enough to affirm the equal manhood of the negro race. Is it not astonishing that, while we are ploughing, planting and reaping, using all kinds of mechanical tools, erecting houses, constructing bridges, building ships, working in metals of brass, iron, copper, silver and gold; that, while we are reading, writing and ciphering, acting as clerks, merchants and secretaries, having among us lawyers, doctors, ministers, poets, authors, editors, orators and teachers; that, while we are engaged in all manner of enterprises common to other men, digging gold in California, capturing the whale in the Pacific, feeding sheep and cattle on the hill-side, living, moving, acting, thinking, planning, living in families as husbands, wives and children, and, above all, confessing and worshipping the Christian's God, and looking for life and immortality beyond the grave, we are called upon to prove that we are men! (Douglass 1852)

Extraordinary argument is wasted when ordinary practice affirms the truth of universal humanity. Any descent into formal, terminological disputation would admit emptiness where life abounds. Douglass seizes upon concepts as they are lived in order to expose the brittle logic of more contentious spaces.

Likewise, Douglass need not indulge, on the occasion of Independence Day, any skeptical requests to prove that humans have inalienable rights.

> Would you have me argue that man is entitled to liberty? that he is the rightful owner of his body? You have already declared it. Must I argue the wrongfulness of slavery? Is that a question for Republicans? Is it to be settled by the rules of logic and argumentation, as a matter beset with great difficulty, involving a doubtful application of the principle of justice, hard to be understood? How should I look to-day, in the presence of Americans, dividing and subdividing a discourse, to show that men have a natural right to freedom? speaking of it relatively, and positively, negatively, and affirmatively. To do so, would be to make myself ridiculous, and to offer an insult to your understanding. There is not a man beneath the canopy of heaven, that does not know that slavery is wrong for him. (Douglass 1852)

Douglass warms to the challenge he anticipates from "some one of the audience"—*whose* rights would you have me argue? the rights of humans? are they not the same rights you assume for yourself? when did you last insist upon arguing your own rights?

In other words, Douglass points at last to the inherent hypocrisy of any human who would demand argumentation in favor of human rights, especially any American on Independence Day. Instead of encouraging patience with such cases, Douglass prescribes shame: "Go where you may, search where you will, roam through all the monarchies and despotisms of the old world, travel through South America, search out every abuse, and when you have found the last, lay your facts by the side of the everyday practices of this nation, and you will say with me, that, for revolting barbarity and shameless hypocrisy, America reigns without a rival." That "some one" in our audience turns out to be no rare individual, but the common citizen who would celebrate independence for himself and enforce slavery upon others.

Not only is America indicted for its civic hypocrisy, but American Christianity is condemned for religious blasphemy. Taking shelter within religious freedom, American Christians esteem their right to church more fundamental than a black person's right to freedom. This implies, reasons Douglass,

> that church regards religion simply as a form of worship, an empty ceremony, and not a vital principle, requiring active benevolence, justice, love and good will towards man. It esteems sacrifice above mercy; psalm-singing above right doing; solemn meetings above practical righteousness. A worship that can be conducted by persons who refuse to give shelter to the houseless, to give bread to the hungry, clothing to the naked, and who enjoin obedience to a law forbidding these acts of mercy, is a curse, not a blessing to mankind. (Douglass 1852)

As the secular community was judged, so will the religious community be tested by the principle of human rights. By the measure of such a test, "the popular church, and the popular worship of our land and nation . . . we pronounce to be an abomination in the sight of God."

A mode of philosophy is illustrated when we relate the story of Douglass and Independence Day. King's approach gains a precedent. Why does King not define equality in a formal way? We might hear him answer, with Douglass: "but you have already proclaimed equality as your own." Why does King not argue that equality is preferable to inequality? Again, we hear him retort that there is not a citizen of the nation who doubts that equality is right for her. Like Douglass, we might hear King ask, "Is this a question for Republicans?" Why doesn't King, if he wants recognition as a philosopher, detach himself from the urgent questions of the day? Like Douglass, he cannot ignore the voices of those who are still oppressed. It is not an evasion, but a choice of philosophical grounds, when one assumes the perspective of the rising classes. The logic of King's treatment of equality has much in common with the logic of Douglass's address. Together, they challenge the practitioners of America's civil religion to be rigorous and consistent in the application of their concepts.

Not only does King follow Douglass in the method of treating certain popular terms of debate, but King also affirms with Douglass that human affairs should be guided by universal moral principles. When Douglass was called to respond to the Supreme Court's over-turning of the Civil Rights Act of 1875, he declared that a moral cyclone had been stirred into existence that would not fail to wreak its inevitable destruction. The rights of fellow citizens may not be violated with impunity; therefore, any state that seeks to evade responsibility for any of its citizens must ultimately reap a grim reward. Likewise, King argued that America could choose between foundations of evil or good—weak foundations or strong. In our contemporary age, when philosophical viewpoints are increasingly relativistic, King's affirmation of nineteenth-century precedent is a feature sure to raise objections. Here, for instance, it will be assumed that King reveals his fundamentalist weakness, in that only religious dogma could today cling to quaint claims about universal principles. In following Douglass, however, King is not bowing to fundamentalist dogma but rather affirming something quite open to experimental verification.

When King affirms with Douglass that human affairs should be regulated by universal principles, he is claiming that there is a real difference between oppression and liberation—each has distinctive consequences that can neither be avoided nor misconstrued. And this is why King eschews ethical relativism. At the theological level, this truth may indeed reveal something about the reality of God, but for philosophical purposes one need judge only the claim that liberation is *always* preferable to oppression. If this plain truth may be affirmed, then some kind of universal moral principle is at work in human logic that helps us to distinguish between what should or should not happen. When we do what we should not do, we can eventually expect negative consequences. Since civil rights in general honor and cele-brate principles of liberation, they are something we should generally favor.

The two features of King's logic that are revealed in his concept of equality indeed announce that King operates at the margins of contemporary philosophical conversation. He picks up popular values where he finds them, and he refuses to relativize his ethics. It may not help center King's logic by claiming that he affirms nineteenth-century precedents, but the value of such precedents may be read in two ways. On the one hand, it may be said that Douglass is obviously outdated, since times and philosophies have obviously progressed. But, on the other hand, it may be argued that, from the standpoint of implementing true civil rights, certain truths have persisted and have changed hardly at all. If this second argument can gain a hearing, we may see how Douglass and King represent a mode of philosophy that still provides timely contributions. America still uses words like *equality*, but the entrenched political establishment does not readily identify with the perspective of rising classes. And the continuing neglect of basic civil rights still contributes to a crisis in the making. Something fundamental is wrong with this picture that both King and Douglass were able to discern but that others continue not to see. What is revealed in the philosophy of King, when appreciated in the fuller historical context of Douglass, is not antiquated irrelevance but heightened sensitivity to the key issues of the day.

If there is no single thing that we can call African American philosophy, nevertheless a mode of philosophy is revealed by King and Douglass that accentuates the contributions of numerous African Americans. Broadus Butler (1983) is one scholar who makes provocative claims about the role of black thinkers in America, and who thus helps to situate the philosophical importance of King's concept of equality. From Butler's point of view, black thinkers have more often proceeded from a premise of human peership, whereas, mainstream white thinkers have usually insisted that the value of peership, or equality, be rigorously demonstrated. Those whose school of thought assumes peership as foundational, Butler terms "humanicentric," whereas those who must reason toward equality—or away from it—he terms "systems-centric."

Butler asserts that African American thought is, by and large, humanicentric, with reasoning proceeding from "a perspective that presupposes that all human beings are equal qua humans and does not base human equality upon political and economic premises." European American thought, on the other hand, tends to be systems-centric, addressing metaphysical and social reality

from a systems-centric and an institutional analysis based upon European political, philosophical, and economic theories and systems rather than the broader human universalities. Thus, whether consciously engaged in formal philosophy or making philosophical expression through poetry, speech, or literature, Black American cosmological, metaphysical, epistemological, ethical conceptions, and modalities tend in the final analysis to be humanicentric as distinguished from system-centric thought. (Butler 1983: 5–6)

As humanicentric philosophers, who grant equality the authority of moral law, black philosophers have established a perspective that deserves serious attention. "Black American thinkers have contributed profound insights into what America ought to be and, by extension, what the universal condition and quality of existence of humankind ought to be," writes Butler.

As Butler employs his criteria to sort between types of philosophy, Douglass becomes exemplary of the humanicentric mode. "Frederick Douglass as distinguished from Thomas Jefferson in the realm of political thought or William James, John Dewey, Alfred North Whitehead, George Mead, or George Santayana in the philosophical arena addressed conceptual and analytical questions from a humanicentric perspective." Among the Founding Fathers, only James Madison, "like Douglass, saw mankind as *peers*, not property" (Butler 1983: 2–5, emphasis added). Thus, peership marks for Butler a principle of rare ultimacy in American thought, upheld by certain classic documents of the American civil religion. Butler reserves for African American thought the highest praise on this point, and uses the test of equality to make general claims about philosophy in the United States.

Although Butler's typology is jarring to some in the profession, his conclusions may survive the jolt. First of all, "humanicentric" is not a loose substitute for "humanistic." Butler has in mind a specific definition. The "humanicentric" thinker chooses "peership" as a normative imperative. The "systems-centric" thinker, conversely, chooses to interrogate the imperative of peership—that is, doesn't assign peership much importance. Given this technical distinction, Butler finds very few American philosophers who pass the "humanicentric" test. Furthermore, it is his thesis that African American thinkers are much more reliably humanicentric than are white philosophers or Founding Fathers generally. Even with respect to the American Pragmatists, Butler finds their approach systems-centric.

PHILOSOPHY'S COLOR LINE

If, as Leonard Harris suggests, the distinction between African American and European American traditions is "not hard and fast," there is nevertheless a need to recognize "at least two cultural foundations of American philosophy":

> Each has a different association with its heritage and each has concretized its views on an international level in different arenas. The principle, though not exclusive, thrust of Afro-American theories involve confrontation with unfulfilled democracy, human ravages of capitalism, colonial domination, and ontological designation by race. Liberation from such social consequences are the distinguishing marks of the Afro-American heritage. (Harris 1983: xv)

The observations of Butler or Harris do not assert that a claim or thought process is to be considered true or valuable "simply by virtue of its origin." It is important, however, to recognize how cultural approaches reveal logical choices. As Kwame Anthony Appiah might say, each group is working on a different set of problems (Appiah 1992). Out of the ground of culturally relevant or "racial" differences one may trace intellectually relevant or philosophical differences that may be more or less generalized after the manner of Butler or Harris in terms of various approaches to liberation, peership, or equality.

As for the approach of African American philosophers, Butler suggests that the "humanicentric" approach has "a metalogical more than a propositional function": "Thus no matter what logical system is used, he [the African American philosopher] characteristically infuses into the context a transcendent requirement that is not easily reducible to a common logical syntax. That is, that the logic gives as much attention to the value and consequences of the truth or falsity of premises as to the validity of conclusions drawn from the premises"

(Butler 1983: 6). One may write a lengthy treatise on justice or equality, for example, and take great care to draw valid conclusions from a set of premises. And yet, warns Butler, one may miss the point. Perhaps the premises themselves are ill-chosen to meet the transcendent requirements of these concepts. Perhaps consequences of the truth of a premise have been scarcely addressed.

Clearly, for Douglass and King, the "humanicentric" premise that all humans are created equal carries an importance that transcends the usual calculations and apologies that one finds pervasive in American philosophy. Whether Butler's typology accurately characterizes the thinkers he claims to sort, the important lesson for this chapter is the way in which equality, or peership, may be used as an organizing principle of philosophical import. The concept of equality developed in this chapter is a stinging rebuke to traditional American philosophy itself. The question remains, will the rebuke drive us down paths of apology and guilt, or will it spur us into philosophical transcendence of our culture-bound lethargy? The question is distinctly suited to American philosophy as it participates in a civil religiosity wherein the value of peership may be used to test the legitimacy of a national endeavor. If America does not pursue the dream of peership, then what will it pursue?

Butler's analysis suggests the question recently popularized by Cornel West and Leonard Harris: Is American philosophy itself racist? (West 1989, Harris 1995). As we formulate answers, it will be important to recall that character and intentionality cannot be the sole criteria of our moral judgments. The history of thought, including the history of American pragmatism, has begun to call attention to the moral importance of habits and consequences. If American philosophy is not a harbor for bigots, it nevertheless reproduces a predominately white profession. Books entitled "American Philosophy" habitually treat white subject matters and are consequently exclusive along the color line. The pragmatic answer to this situation is not to moralize about character or intent—either offensively or defensively—but to reconstruct habits so that subsequent consequences are nonracist in their impact. This study endeavors to assist in such reconstructions.

King's choice of equality as a universal principle clearly implies that he knows he is not addressing himself to a land of equal opportunity. Well-established proclivities in the social order appear to confirm that King was correct, and yet his judgment remains controversial in any American conversation about race. As we enter the twenty-first century, some commentators and intellectuals insist that equal opportunity now prevails. No doubt there are great opportunities in America—that much is clear. But to say that opportunities are equal would require an intellectual license exempt from historical credibility. Even the most blindered pundit would have to admit that historical inequalities have prevailed at some point in American history. Then perhaps that same pundit could tell us when such historical practices stopped! Against the fairy-tale thinking that prevails today, it is necessary to recount, once again, the most elementary truths about social structure in America. Without this foundation of education, King's philosophy of nonviolence hangs in the air and blows with the wind.

Chapter 2

———•✦•———

STRUCTURE AND RACE

There is no royal road to logic.
—C. S. PEIRCE

W. E. B. DU BOIS AND THE PROBLEM OF THE COLOR LINE

Is there a color line? It is sometimes fashionable to think not. Especially since the civil rights movement, white Americans have wanted to deny it. We used to have trouble, whites agree, but King came along and fixed all that. We now have a new, improved America. In spite of all the things white America believes, however, the problem of the century is still the problem of the color line, just as W. E. B. Du Bois said it would be in 1903. Yet, to reason about the color line is to undertake a most difficult task. In this chapter we begin exploring some of the groundwork that makes the color line intelligible. First we shall examine King's concept of structure, then we will see how Du Bois helps to orient the structure of racism within a context of color prejudice. In the next chapter, we shall turn to more explicit engagement with the ideas of capitalism and imperialism.

Paradoxically, requests to dispense with this discussion of structural racism might come from racists and antiracists alike. From the racist's point of view, the color line is nothing more than one of life's inevitable outcomes. There is nothing special to be done here, because any attempt to locate or move the color line is an unwarranted intervention in the natural laws of survival, which should not be stacked for or against anyone in particular. Attention to the color line only results in *reverse* discrimination. From an antiracist point of view, the color line can be alleviated, or ultimately erased, only if we first stop fixing it in our minds. If racism is predicated upon assumptions about race, then such assumptions may lead to racism. Taken together, these objections would have us avoid discussing the color line. Building a strong case for the logic of nonviolence, however, requires that we appropriate the concept of the color line in a rigorous way.

Although King borrows the concept of the color line from Du Bois, a new vocabulary emerges in King's use of it, indicating that the conception has been revised. For King, the color line is to be understood in terms of structure. Thus, for King, the color line will more properly be called the *structural evil* of racism, because the concept indicates a collection of habits—no matter how intentional or unintentional they may be—that perpetuates an imbalance of power between black and white collective realities. In logical terms, right away, nonviolence eschews fallacies of accident or division. True, exceptions to the rule shall be admitted. True, it is not possible logically to infer anyone's individual culpability. Nevertheless, the rule of racist structure maintains its logical force. Without blaming any particular white person, and without denying that there are powerful black influences upon American life, the logic of nonviolence nevertheless asserts that a structure of racism applies to collective relationships among groups. Furthermore, the structure of racism is a moral problem, because it perpetuates systematic injustice.

Unlike the term *equality* examined in the last chapter, *structure* is not a word that enjoys widespread currency in American popular culture. The more King talked about structure, the more dangerous he was said to be. But what is structure, and why is it so dangerous to speak about? To put it most briefly for the sake of introduction, *structure is collective injustice.* And it is dangerous to speak about collective injustice because its remedies are, by definition, revolutionary. Nevertheless, King insisted that three structural evils dominate American society: racism, poverty, and war. Taken together, these triple evils add up to something that King called, "the structure of racist imperialism." Repeating his own sentence from a 1966 article for *Ebony*, King appealed to Black Power activists by arguing that the logic of nonviolence was the best framework available for understanding and reforming structural evil in the United States: "The hard cold facts today indicate that the hope of the people of color in the world may well rest on the American Negro and his ability to reform the structure of racist imperialism from within and thereby turn the technology and wealth of the West to the task of liberating the world from want" (King 1967: 57). In this lone reference to structure as racist imperialism, King connected his own technical vocabulary to the wider world of structural analysis, and explained why the logic of nonviolence applied to America first.

In speaking of the triple evils of poverty, racism, and war, King demonstrates a manifold or pluralistic concept of structure. The struggle against racism may be more or less singled out, but it cannot be isolated from struggles against poverty or war. Within such a concept of structure, a plurality of evils may be discerned, and there is no presumption that argues for any absolute hierarchy of approach. Sexism, homophobia, or anti-Semitism, for instance, may constitute structural evils, too. Yet, none of the evils would enjoy exclusive nor dominant status in theoretical terms alone. What this means to the logic of nonviolence is that various areas of struggle are always in principle interrelated. A flexible logic of coalitions is encouraged to emerge. Is the labor question the most fundamental question of the day? Racism, sexism, or militarism? The logic of nonviolence recognizes a plurality of evils, thus opportunities to link struggles. Having said this, I do agree with Du Bois that the problem of the century is still the problem of the color line, its primacy deriving from an insistence that it not be denied, deferred, or theorized to the sidelines for the umpteenth time. Rather, it should be recognized and confronted at last.

Generally speaking, structural analysis is a double-ended project, with two concerns. In the first instance, structural analysis proceeds from a thick empirical catalog of systematic injustice that is reduced to a collective term. In the second instance, one seeks a hypothesis of struggle. Such analysis is philosophical because it pursues a normative reconstruction of value, seeking to center on the perspectives of the rising classes. With classical analysis, as developed by Marx, the chronicle of abuse is reduced to class conflict, and the hypothesis of struggle is the communist revolution. In King's logic of nonviolence, however, the litany of abuse reduces to the triple evils of poverty, racism, and war. The method of struggle is nonviolent mass action. As with Marx, King seeks to serve the aspirations of rising classes, but, unlike Marx, King is careful to preserve the peaceful options that apply when opponents strive to achieve parity as fellow humans. In other words, revolutionary vanguards are discouraged from plotting short-term violence in the name of long-term good.

King's pluralism and pacifism help to distinguish his structural theory from the classical model. Whereas classical models focus on economic structure, King also speaks about racism and war. Although classical models recognize the role of violence as a tool of oppression, only King insists that violence must be purged from one's armamentarium of struggle. And this is how the vision of communist revolution is superseded by the dream of nonviolent mass action. Thus, in response to racism and violence alike, King's philosophy of nonviolence refuses to take up tools of oppression as means of liberation. As philosophy turns from categories of analysis to categories of struggle, oppression will be confronted by mass actions that are regulated by a prophetic ethic of justice and love.

If we view King's analysis of the triple evils in the context of African American philosophy, then we find similarities and joint concerns with several of King's predecessors. With Du Bois, for instance, King declares that the problem of the century is the color line (racism), with A. Philip Randolph that the color line is also a category of capitalist economics (poverty), and with Ralph J. Bunche that the color line is international and indicates a global crisis (war). Du Bois, Randolph, and Bunche were all well known to King. Through Atlanta University, King shared institutional ties with Du Bois. In the civil rights movement, King shared organizational ties with Randolph. And King was the *second* black American to win the Nobel Peace Prize, after Bunche. King mentions all three influences in his last monograph. In a chapter on "The Dilemma of Negro Americans," for instance, King chastises the people of Cicero, Illinois, because they welcome a notorious gangster like Al Capone into their neighborhood while refusing entry to a Nobel laureate like Ralph Bunche: "His individual culture, brilliance and character are not considered. To the racist, he, like every Negro, lacks individuality. He is part of a defective group" (King 1967: 118). If Bunche is not, in fact, part of a defective group, his exclusion from Cicero illuminates how the structure of racist imperialism works.

The color line is thus one theme that connects King to Du Bois. Both worked as public intellectuals, were Ph.D. graduates of elite white institutions, and took great care to mean what they said about the color line in America. Neither one died happy about the color line. After a lifetime of heroic agitation, Du Bois expatriated to Ghana, where he initiated work on an *Encyclopedia Africana*. His passing was announced at the 1963 March on Washington. As Du Bois came of age during the waning years of Douglass, King was born in the shadow of Du Bois. This chapter shows how King's logic of nonviolence thrives upon precedents established by Du Bois, particularly the conception of the color line and the vocation it implies for intellectuals. Du Bois continually developed new approaches to the color line—he wrote books, organized studies, edited a magazine, published a journal, spoke to countless audiences, and always contributed some new thing to think about regarding the problem of the century. In this chapter we focus on the early works of Du Bois, up through the founding of *The Crisis*, the official magazine of the National Association for the Advancement of Colored People (NAACP).

By recuperating the early work of Du Bois, we see how the logic of structure is built upon years of painstaking analysis. Since it is a dynamic process that we seek to conceptualize, and since the problem never does hold still, we shall follow a historical genealogy that helps to illustrate some of the logical axioms and some of the fallacies that have attended the development of this conception. With specific reference to Du Bois, we shall see how the problem of the color line is conceptualized in terms of color prejudice. This is an important place to begin, but it is not where the concept leaves off. Randolph will place color prejudice within the context of economic interest. This placement begins to remove the dynamic of the color line from strict adherence to intentional states of mind and places it within an economic analysis of interests. In order to entertain a logic of interests, one need not assume deliberative intentions nor explicit conspiracy. The most rigorous requirement is to show how habits serve to perpetuate an unjust status quo. Some interests are served, while others are not. While no one is precisely to blame, everyone is held responsible, thus reversing the ordinary logic of the day (where everyone is blamed but nobody is held responsible).

The logic of nonviolence does not dismiss the importance of explicit intentions, but King also understands that many habits of racism have become so embedded in cultural practice that it is difficult to talk of individual choice. It is less important to blame white prejudice on whites as individuals, but more important to find social means to separate white collectives from their systematic methods of oppression. For this kind of work, struggles upon the structural field must be rigorously conceived for revolutionary results. It is the collective habit that must be confronted, not the individual personality. As we shall see, this logic provides vital links to King's over-arching appeal to love. Love without structural awareness is called "sentimental liberalism," while structural awareness without love is called "Black Power." The strenuous character of the logic of nonviolence is exemplified in its refusal to give in to moral exasperation with respect to persons while at the same time having incessantly to confront the exasperating conditions created by vicious collective habits. The Chicago experience, for instance, proved that despair could overcome reason—it sure looked like white people were inseparable from collective viciousness in that particular instance.

Before this chapter gets any longer, I would like to apologize for its "thick" style of explication. The concept of structure is best treated in its experiential details, because portraits of reality are still the best method for demonstrating that structures of evil imply questions of ethical urgency. Whether one wishes to speak of racism, poverty, or violence, it is simply not possible to get very far into the concept without using a rather wide net for gathering facts. Another important task is accomplished if we patiently recuperate a conceptual history of structure as developed by Du Bois, Randolph, and Bunche. Along the way, we are able to see how these structural concerns begin to anticipate characteristic ethical features of nonviolence. Without the use of theological deductions, we see how a logic of nonviolence begins to emerge from the dialectic of structural analysis, more or less confined to categories traditionally accepted within the discipline of social and political philosophy. This demonstration serves as a healthy corrective to any number of philosophical fallacies that would view King's concepts as so many divine revelations from which the whole system of nonviolence may be neatly deduced.

Unless King's genius is clearly appreciated on the structural battlefield, we shall miss the revolutionary vitality of his logic of nonviolence. As the following discussion reveals, the coherence of the nonviolence philosophy need not be reduced to a tidy deductive system of revealed axioms but rather may be seen as a systematic accumulation of propositions distilled from the urgent, and temporal, process of struggle. If the systematic nature of King's philosophy of nonviolence can be restored to its contingent, organic engagement with an historical process of liberation, then it will more easily avail itself of ongoing philosophical development. In short, we will better understand why activists such as James Bevel and Bernard Lafayette were fond of calling nonviolence a science (Ralph 1993: 41). King's concept of love, for instance, is too often mistaken for a revealed fixed value from which all further propositions follow in tidy, holy order. We learn more about King's philosophy of nonviolence if we consider how the concept of love emerges into an already complex field of problematic analysis. In other words, I am defending a pragmatic view of logic. I am arguing that King's logic works to resolve complex reality into manageable concepts, not by some formalistic imperative of artificially deduced ideas but by organic ethical engagement with the obdurate facts of the historical situation (see Hickman 1990). This is not to deny King's faith; rather, I am trying to explicate the kind of logic that made King remarkable, even among the faithful.

Furthermore, once we have deployed the pluralistic model of structure outlined by King's triple evils, it becomes possible to elaborate a wide range of structural issues. In addition to racism, for example, we may add sexism, homophobia, and anti-Semitism. In addition to war, we may add pollution. This genealogy of thought prepares a way for us to augment King's historical achievement with ensuing developments in liberation philosophy. Of special note in this regard are Angela Davis's investigations into sexism and homophobia, but also her patient and balanced approach to a pluralistic logic of coalitions (Davis 1985). Under the influence of Davis, monolithic models of struggle give way to pluralistic initiatives variously sensitized to the myriad ways in which struggle emerges to confront structural evil. More recently, the conversation between Cornel West and Michael Lerner begins the delicate work of reforging a black–Jewish coalition from the remnants of the civil rights movement. It is noteworthy that both parties recognize how the logic of their common ground has been surveyed and delineated by King (Lerner & West, 1995).

REVIEWING KING'S USAGE

To begin investigating King's concept of structure, we turn to the longest sentence ever written by King that we know of, found in "A Letter from the Birmingham City Jail":

> I guess it is easy for those who have never felt the stinging darts of segregation to say, "Wait." But when you have seen vicious mobs lynch your mothers and fathers at will and drown your sisters and brothers at whim; when you have seen hate-filled policemen curse, kick, brutalize and even kill your black brothers and sisters with impunity; when you see the vast majority of your twenty million Negro brothers smothering in an airtight cage of poverty in the midst of an affluent society; when you suddenly find your tongue twisted and your speech stammering as you seek to explain to your six-year-old daughter why she can't go to the public amusement park that has just been advertised on television, and see tears welling up in her little eyes when she is told that Funtown is closed to colored children, and see the depressing clouds of inferiority begin to form in her little mental sky, and see her begin to distort her little personality by unconsciously developing a bitterness toward white people; when you have to concoct an answer for a five-year-old son asking in agonizing pathos: "Daddy, why do white people treat colored people so mean?"; when you take a cross-country drive and find it necessary to sleep night after night in the uncomfortable corners of your

automobile because no motel will accept you; when you are humiliated day in and day out by nagging signs reading "white" and "colored"; when your first name becomes "nigger" and your middle name becomes "boy" (however old you are) and your last name becomes "John," and when your wife and mother are never given the respected title "Mrs."; when you are harried by day and haunted by night by the fact that you are a Negro, living constantly at tiptoe stance never quite knowing what to expect next, and plagued with inner fears and outer resentments; when you are forever fighting a degenerating sense of "nobodiness"; then you will understand why we find it difficult to wait.

King's lengthy sentence paints a picture of experience lived within the structure of racial prejudice. An immoral situation is exposed in the description of such facts. All reasoning about structure proceeds from such images. As one clergyman addressing others, King appeals to experience in this lengthy sentence of his.

King's exasperation in this passage is measured in semicolons and clauses that express the time-after-time experience of what it means to live on the wrong side of the color line. This generous heap of thoughts and recounted experiences is needed in order to fill the kind of gap that persists between those who live on the receiving end of a structure and those who don't. If there were no such gap, King would not have needed the longest sentence of his life (and this book would not need the following two chapters). Part of the logic of nonviolence requires, however, that the gap of experience be filled. As tiresome as it may sometimes seem, the exercise of drawing upon experience serves to explain, once again, how the problem feels when it is as thick as a paragraph, not as thin as a proposition. Structure is a concept that expresses a problem of experiential thickness all around. Thus, the philosophical importance of structure resides in the plenitude of historical examples.

Early in his last monograph, King argues that a "curious formula" is at work, which metes out to the black population of the United States one-half of the normal good things in life but twice the bad (King 1967: 6). Black citizens are held captive—that is, they are permanently suspended—within the lowest echelons of the labor force. "Of employed Negroes, 75 percent hold menial jobs" (King 1967: 7). How does one account for the persistence of this "curious formula"? King argues for a "structural" account:

> Depressed living standards for Negroes are not simply the consequence of neglect. Nor can they be explained by the myth of the Negro's innate capacities, or by the more sophisticated rationalization of his acquired infirmities (family disorganization, poor education, etc.). They are a structural part of the economic system in the United States. Certain industries and enterprises are based upon a supply of low-paid, underskilled and immobile nonwhite labor. Hand assembly factories, hospitals, service industries, housework, agricultural operations using itinerant labor would suffer economic trauma, if not disaster, with a rise in wage scales. (King 1967: 7)

Here King discloses the kind of structural analysis that confronts ideology with truths it squirms to avoid. The economic foundation of America demands that some workers never rise from servitude. Without menial labor, wealth has no platform to stand upon. However, in popular debates that would seek "incentives" to encourage the self-development of impoverished populations, nobody wants to talk about the "incentives" that depress wages, opportunity, or education. An unequal distribution of income is foundational to the economic system of the United States, and the burdens incumbent on the lowest positions have been forced upon black laborers. Hence, the contour of the color line.

Moreover, argues King, the menial position reserved for black Americans produces psychological consequences that aggravate the material gulf created between aspiring citizens in a democracy. The result is a "personal torment" that is organic to the experience of structure: "The personal torment of discrimination cannot be measured on a numerical scale, but the grim evidence of its hold on white America is revealed in polls that indicate that 88 percent of them would object if their teen-age child dated a Negro. Almost 80 percent would mind it if a close friend or relative married a Negro, and 50 percent would not want a Negro as a neighbor" (King 1968: 8). Thus, while inequality of incomes is a systematic requirement for enterprise and industry, quantitative discrimination harbors a *qualitative* corollary. The black citizen lives not only at minimum wage but with minimal esteem. And these are facts that persist years after enactment of the Civil Rights Act of 1964.

In addition to inequalities of economic structure and public opinion, black America is confronted with court rulings and legislative enactments that reinforce, rather than ameliorate, ongoing exploitation. Even after such promising instances as the Supreme Court's ruling on school desegregation, or congressional passage of a Civil Rights Act, subsequent history quickly corrects any undue optimism. The black citizen is too soon reminded that fundamental assumptions have not changed. Hard-won markers of progress are proven to be, "in a sense, historical errors from the point of view of white America." They have "in practice proved to be neither structures nor laws" but "barely a naked framework" for change. King recalls how the Supreme Court in one year ruled school segregation unconstitutional, then in the next year surrendered the timetable of desegregation to the local school boards. The latter "pupil placement decision" then served as a "keystone in the *structure*" to "slow school desegregation to a halt" (King 1967: 10–11, emphasis added).

Pressed into service at the lowest rungs of America's economy, disparaged as people unworthy to be considered fit for kinship or neighborhood, subject to discrimination under the law, and abandoned by white allies, black Americans after Selma are nonetheless hardly willing to retreat from their confrontation with America's obstinate inequalities. One measure of the new resolve is the cry for Black Power: "The persistence of racism in depth and the dawning awareness that Negro demands will necessitate structural changes in society have generated a new phase of white resistance in North and South. . . . Cries of Black Power and riots are not the causes of white resistance, they are the consequences of it" (King 1967: 12). When this context of negative and hostile white attitudes is joined with an economic mandate for menial labor, the twin evils of poverty and racism assert their combined force as a tyranny that is sure to provoke unrest.

Historically, King argues, the African American's struggle for justice has been frustrated by "the alliance of Southern racism and Northern reaction," which since "before the Civil War" has been "the major roadblock to all social advancement" in America. "The cohesive political structure of the South, working through this alliance enabled a minority of the population to imprint its ideology on the nation's laws." In response to the civil rights movement, the white alliance has simply "restructured old parties to cope with the emerging challenge" (King 1967: 14). Such restructuring is not to be confused with revolutionary change but rather is to be seen more as an ongoing effort to keep the fundamental form of structure in place.

King's repeated references to the term *structure* reveal his engagement with categories of collective injustice. By participating in the tradition of dialogue that surrounds the race–class question, King employs a concept of structure that is connected to economic analysis, that integrates political and ideological consequences, and that develops a moral critique for the purpose of revolutionizing the status quo. In keeping with assumptions that underlie race–class analysis, King affirms that a complex system is at work that reproduces menial employment for some, the better to provide greater enrichment for others. Then King pursues ethical relationships that bind us to moral responsibility for such inequality. In this way, King is able to isolate collective injustice in the past for moral confrontation in the present and ethical control in the future.

King's writings imply a phenomenology of structure that encompasses two moments of development. In the first moment, a privileged version of reality obstructs the value of marginalized persons. A "peculiar formula" is at work. In the second moment, individuals assert their value. In this moment of resistance, King insists that our concept of structure must be reconstructed in such a way that ethical, nonviolent imperatives are called to the service of freedom, liberation, or equality. In the initial moment of "interposition and nullification," their structure—as if it had a life of its own—imposes itself upon us, as if there were no ethical considerations that it were bound to respect. In the subsequent moment of resistance or "affirmative action," however, King will insist that we address our *common* structure, in order to reassert the regulatory value of ethical imperatives that favor the development of each and every personality.

These persistent features of King's concept of structure serve to mark his distinctive approach to race–class analysis. Along with class analysts of various kinds, including the broad tradition of scientific socialism, King will employ a model of structure, or systematic injustice. This distinguishes him from the so-called "rational choice" theorists or classical liberals with their *laissez-faire* doctrines. Among class analysts, moreover, King is a rigorous student of moral logic, adhering always to a distinction between "systems" and "personalities." Whereas systems represent our analysis of evil, personalities represent possibilities for liberation. In contrast to some doctrinaire class analysts, King insists that the value of class analysis is measured in its service to the liberation of personality. Thus, King's concept of structure, regulated by the value of personality, provides a middle way between theoretical extremes.

Certain protocols of logic become axiomatic for the nonviolent transformation of object into subject. First, as seen above, the problem of moving from oppression to liberation is recast as a common field, inclusive of opponents. Second, during the course of struggle, no collection of individuals may be mistaken for the structure of injustice itself. In the case where it seems most likely that a collection of persons is the problem itself, King will insist that it is all the more necessary to address those persons in terms of the need to reconstruct a common system of justice. Here, King is saying that a collective evil is never precisely the same thing as a collection of people. Since evil is separable from persons in concept, King's philosopy of nonviolence seeks to achieve the separation in fact. King's logic of nonviolence strains against every temptation to treat collective evil as inherent to *any* collection of personalities.

As King addresses the challenge of Black Power, he understands the new insurgency as symptomatic of justifiable frustration. Indeed, it is extreme understatement to declare that a racist America is frustrating to its victims. Nevertheless, King presses the logic of nonviolence against two temptations. The first temptation is to declare white America irredeemable. The second temptation narrows the field of activity to black America only. The following three passages develop King's dialectical analysis of Black Power from concrete historical realities:

From the old plantations of the South to the newer ghettos of the North, the Negro has been confined to a life of voicelessness and powerlessness. Stripped of the right to make decisions concerning his life and destiny, he has been subject to the authoritarian and sometimes whimsical decisions of the white power structure. (King 1967: 36)

Although this thinking [Black Power philosophy] is under-standable as a response to a white power structure that never completely committed itself to true equality for the Negro, and a die-hard mentality that sought to shut all windows and doors against the winds of change, it nonetheless carries the seeds of its own doom. (King 1967: 44)

The hard cold facts today indicate that the hope of the people of color in the world may well rest on the American Negro and his ability to reform the structure of racist imperialism from within and thereby turn the technology and wealth of the West to the task of liberating the world from want. (King 1967: 57)

In these passages, structure denotes white power or racist imperialism that would confine and silence African Americans, assume inequality is appropriate for them, and use technology to impose dependence upon the darker people of the rest of the world. It is impossible to expect that suffering populations would not revolt. It would be morally obtuse to declare that they should not struggle. King seeks to guide the struggle toward revolutionary ends intended to eliminate the suffering.

Black Power could pattern its insurrection after the example of the American Revolution—and who could find fault with that?—but King seeks higher possibilities. As with classical structural analysis, King finds contradictions in the American-style revolution that cannot be sustained—lies that cannot live forever. As King sees it, African Americans are in a unique position to undertake a new kind of revolution that would reform an entire global structure from "within." A new order must be cast in the mold of nonviolence if it is not to replicate, albeit in negative, the image of the old.

Having completed his philosophical review of Black Power, King returns to treat the persistence of white power. For King, the genesis of America's racism lies in economic motives that encourage one party to seek advantage over another:

> Since the institution of slavery was so important to the economic development of America, it had a profound impact in shaping the social-political-legal structure of the nation. (King 1967: 72)

> Soon the doctrine of white supremacy was imbedded in every textbook and preached in practically every pulpit. It became a structural part of the culture. And men then embraced this philosophy not as the rationalization of a lie, but as the expression of a final truth. (King 1967: 75)

> Yet no one observing the history of the church in America today can deny the shameful fact that it has been an accomplice in structuring racism into the architecture of American society. (King 1967: 96)

The structure of racism and poverty promotes powerful interests of profit. This economic structure corrupts cultural and political values in order to diminish the personalities of the exploited, even with the complicity of the church. In the end, racial inequality is rationalized as justice, even divine justice.

We find two other terms used synonymously with structure, namely, *system* and *status quo*. In both cases, King insists that collective categories do not relieve one of having to answer questions about moral responsibility.

> If the society changes its concepts by placing the responsibility [for evil] on its system, not on the individual, and guarantees secure employment or a minimum income, dignity will come within the reach of all. (King 1967: 87)

> When evil men conspire to preserve an unjust *status quo*, good men must unite to bring about the birth of a society undergirded by justice. (King 1967: 89)

As we can see, King's logic of nonviolence insists upon structural conceptions. So long as poverty and unemployment remain systematic features of the economy, no amount of exhortation to "get a job" will eliminate the indignities shared by millions. And so long as there are people who work full-time to keep such structures in place, some others must labor for justice.

If justice is not to be achieved by blaming the victims of exploitation, neither will it be achieved by blaming "evil men" for their conspiracies. King is consistent with his principle of approach. Having rejected an individualistic account of inequality, King will also reject an individualistic attack upon its perpetrators or beneficiaries. As we have seen, this rigorous distinction between systems and structures, on the one hand, and individuals or persons, on the other hand, is an important axiom in the logic of King's philosophy of nonviolence. Note that we do not need to invoke the word of God in order to see that structural evils do not inhere in persons. In fact, as we have seen earlier, the concept of God is a sword with two edges—one side sharpened for greater equality, the other for greater inequality—depending upon the mode of faith that is exercised. King's rigorous ethic is sufficient to suggest philosophical reasons as to how one may confront a collective structure of evil and, at the same time, demand reciprocal love.

When King turns to the dilemma that remains for black America, he refers to "structured forces in the Negro community" that have failed to develop their potential for aiding liberation (King 1967: 124). The irony that black institutions themselves could be "structured" reveals an especially tragic dimension to King's suggestion that there is a dilemma at hand. In other words, some black institutions themselves have come to share interests with the structure that funnels the black masses into poverty and unemployment. Black institutions, too, may abet the evils of racism and poverty, either by their active support of the status quo or by their refusal to wage massive confrontation. This is not to be confused with the charge that black institutions practice "reverse discrimination"; what King says is that black organizations may secure the privileges of a few by relinquishing the interests of the many. King reminds advocates of black institutions that they must renounce structured interests and struggle aggressively in behalf of justice:

> Structures of evil do not crumble by passively waiting. (King 1967: 128)

[Booker T.] Washington's error was that he underestimated the structures of evil; as a consequence his philosophy of pressureless persuasion only served as a springboard for racist Southerners to dive into deeper and more ruthless oppression of the Negro. (King 1967: 129)

All these questions remind us that there is a need for a radical restructuring of the architecture of American society. . . . A new set of values must be born. (King 1967: 133)

The structure of white power or racist imperialism implicates black institutions, and has been tragically underestimated by institutional leaders.

When King outlines a general plan for the future, he concentrates on the need for "structural change." Indeed, King reminds us that African Americans have made distinctive contributions to structural understanding: "Negroes have illuminated imperfections in the democratic structure that were formerly only dimly perceived" (King 1967: 138). Having illuminated such features, African Americans are well prepared—if not uniquely suited—to rid democracy of its structural imperfections. As King contemplates a course of action, he suggests that African Americans must build alliances with groups who have developed an interest in structural change. Such groups may be found among labor, unionists, the poor, and welfare recipients. As we saw in the last chapter, King has high hopes for such a coalition: "The total elimination of poverty, now a practical possibility, the reality of equality in race relations and other profound structural changes in society may well begin here" (King 1967: 142).

In the aftermath of his campaign in Chicago, King does not trust "decaying political machines" to make a future of "deep structural changes," especially not the "changes we seek." Nor does he, after Selma, trust the decaying alliances of the civil rights movement: "It evokes happy memories to recall that our victories in the past decades were won with a broad coalition of organizations representing a wide variety of interests. But we deceive ourselves if we envision the same combination attacking structural changes in the society. It did not come together for such a program and will not reassemble for it" (King 1967: 151). Eliminating poverty, establishing equality among races, and other reforms will be won by a new coalition of persons, organized for a new kind of structural change. The last sentence of his penultimate chapter concludes the main argument of the book, calling for the immediate elimination of poverty in the United States.

King's concluding remarks in his last monograph concern the building of a "World House" to shelter a new kind of community "undergirded by justice." King quotes the eminent process philosopher Alfred North Whitehead: "a major turning point [has come] in history where the presuppositions on which society is structured are being analyzed, sharply challenged, and profoundly changed" (King 1967: 169). And King sees possibilities already in formation:

> Once the aspirations and appetites of the world have been whetted by the marvels of Western technology and the self-image of a people awakened by religion, one cannot hope to keep people locked out of the earthly kingdom of wealth, health and happiness. Either they share in the blessings of the world or they organize to break down and overthrow those structures of government which stand in the way of their goals. (King 1967: 176)

In the passage above we see how religion is called to its ethical duty. It is the task of the religious to awaken self images to their own value. Such consciousness will resist being trampled under the heels of social malignancy. In meeting after meeting, King and his co-leaders lifted their nonviolent troops from the pews of churches, aided by religious forms of oratory, music, and text. And this is one good reason why our usual appreciation for nonviolence is so heavily weighted with religious connotations. What else do we call the sense that there is something besides ourselves worth sacrificing for, if we do not call it religious? And what do we call the sense that there is unrecognized value within ourselves? We shall return to these questions in a later chapter. Secular forms of nonviolence thus have their challenge before them. Without a religious dimension, how does one participate in the kind of value-laden risk demanded of nonviolent confrontation? And yet religious defenders of nonviolence also have their challenge. How many forms of worship, parading under the banner of religion, thrive upon supremacies—or complacencies—of many kinds?

Although it is quite beside the point of this book, King's theology is informed by the work of his mentor, Benjamin Mays, who observes in *The Negro's God* that a "constructive" idea of God is emerging out of the black church (Mays 1938). According to this constructive idea, God is a kind of power that enhances personality. The task of the church, as broadly hinted by Mays, will be to work out a constructive conception of God as the church becomes more concerned with social reform. This conception of God, says Mays, avoids the shallow pragmatism of otherworldly religions that have indeed become opiates to the masses. This "constructive" conception of God, for Mays, also avoids the outright atheism of persons who are in revolt against social opiates. For Mays and King alike, the quest for personality is religious rather than humanist, because personality cannot be reduced to human efforts. Something is *given* to humans, and this fact demands religious attention. But these considerations need no special emphasis here.

King admits that the liberation of human personality is a complex task: "We have ancient habits to deal with, vast structures of power, indescribably complicated to solve" (King 1967: 184). Thus, the structural approach to poverty, racism, and war is the only serious approach available. "True compassion is more than flinging a coin to a beggar; it is understanding that an edifice which produces beggars needs restructuring" (King 1967: 187). The earth will become a World House when poverty is no longer possible, when racism is banished from our collective habits, and when violence is no longer deployed as a systematic weapon against democratic initiatives.

NINETEENTH-CENTURY PRECEDENTS

As King says, the concept of structure has been richly developed within an African American tradition. For instance, in 1845, Frederick Douglass, in his first autobiography, contemplates the fate of his enslaved grandmother. She spends her life producing wealth that is legally expropriated from any claims she might make. The riches of the plantation are transferred, according to American custom, from one master to the next—awarded to strangers who appropriate the wealth, but who do not value the laborer. As a final insult, the masters take all the credit for building a great nation. Horrified by the immorality of this economic system, Douglass asks, "Will not a righteous God visit?" Thus our genealogy of the concept of structure might begin with this African American manuscript circa 1844.

After Douglass, we might turn to the valedictorian's address delivered by W. E. B. Du Bois to his fellow graduates at Harvard, class of 1890. His topic was Jefferson Davis, president of a pro-slavery Confederate States of America:

> I wish to consider not the man, but the type of civilization which his life represented: its foundation is the idea of the strong man—Individualism coupled with the rule of might—and it is this idea that has made the logic of even modern history, the cool logic of the Club. It made a naturally brave and generous man, Jefferson Davis: now advancing civilization by murdering Indians, now hero of a national disgrace, called by courtesy the Mexican War; and finally the crowning absurdity, the peculiar champion of a people fighting to be free in order that another people should not be free. Whenever this idea has for a moment escaped from the individual realm, it has found an even more secure foothold in the policy and philosophy of the State. (Du Bois 1968: 147)

The spirit of the structural approach is evident as Du Bois seeks to understand civilized conditions that contribute to uncivilized institutions. Individualistic categories are rejected with outright scorn because their consequences have been so disastrously suffered. Racism and imperialism are already condemned by their features, even if they are not yet scientifically defined. With auspicious speed, the words of Du Bois were flashed across the telegraph wires of America, and a new generation declared its voice.

Du Bois speaks to an audience immersed in a theory of "Teutonic origins." According to this theory, the human species is of two distinct origins: one out of Africa, the other Teutonic. Furthermore, all the world's civilized progress may be attributed to the Teutonic breed.

Back of the infamous and virulent theory of the Teutonic origins of civilization lies an idea, says Du Bois. This idea of individualism, compounded by the rule of might, yields a familiar ideology that is systematically deployed to rationalize the uncivilized actions of individuals and nations alike:

> The strong man and his mighty Right Arm has become the Strong Nation with its armies. Under whatever guise, however a Jefferson Davis may appear as a man, as a race, or as a nation, his life can only logically mean this: the advance of a part of the world at the expense of the whole: the overwhelming sense of the I, and the consequent forgetting of the Thou. It has thus happened that advance in civilization has always been handicapped by short-sighted national selfishness. (Du Bois 1968: 147)

As violence advances a cause, it handicaps civilization, because violence contradicts wholeness of community. Violence does not distinguish between structures and persons. When the violent claim victory, even ideas are taken by force: "The vital principle of division of labor has been stifled not only in industry, but also in civilization; so as to render it well nigh impossible for a new race to introduce a new idea into the world except by means of a cudgel" (Du Bois 1968: 147).

The strong individual becomes, in fact, the ideal individual. The strong race becomes the ideal race. Short of a cudgel, how does one find a tool to reason with such people?

> To say that a nation is in the way of civilization is a contradiction in terms and a system of human culture whose principle is the rise of one race on the ruins of another is a farce and a lie. Yet this is the type of civilization which Jefferson Davis represented: it represents a field for stalwart manhood and heroic character, and at the same time for moral obtuseness and refined brutality. These striking contradictions of character always arise when a people seemingly become convinced that the object of the world is not civilization, but Teutonic civilization. (Du Bois 1968: 147)

If this is an example of the spirit of the structural approach—holding the system responsible, not the individual—Du Bois has not yet

situated the system within scientific categories. If this speech anticipates King's nonviolence, the concepts are not yet refined. Instead of
a wicked person we blame a wicked civilization. This shift of emphasis
helps us understand wicked people a little better, but not much. We
note the violence, but we do not isolate this variable for systematic
consideration.

Speaking to a white audience steeped in Teutonic-origin theory,
the young Du Bois borrows nearly all the ontological presumptions
behind such supremacist thought. For the sake of argument, Du Bois
stipulates that Teutonic origins are responsible for civilization as we
know it: there is such a thing as Teutonic civilization, it has made a
difference in our world, and it presents a type of civilization to be
judged in accordance with standards of common sense. Accepting all
this—and matter/spirit dualism, too—Du Bois rejects the claim that
Teutonic civilization has been a good thing. Du Bois entertains the
popular Teutonic ontology of the day, as today's intellectual acknowledges ontologies both white and Western, not for mathematical
precision, but in appreciation of historical force. The "cool logic of
the Club" may not be clear logic, but it has real effects. Whether white,
Western, or Teutonic, a kind of category—totalizing and self-serving—is being honored by strong men and strong armies to rationalize
their tyranny. This is how poor fictions become real ideologies. The
Club will have its fictions, and if you are "like Du Bois," the Club will
inflict them upon you. For Du Bois at Harvard, the work of commencement is to show the Club—in terms that it will understand—
that its fictions are ignoble in the extreme.

The ongoing work of analysis, however, requires a new ontology,
and so this student of William James reports that he "conceived the
idea of applying philosophy to an historical interpretation of race
relations. In other words, I was trying to take my first steps toward
sociology as the science of human action" (Du Bois 1968: 148). If
Du Bois yet accepted Teutonic ontology for the sake of argument, he
was also seeking a new approach—the point being no longer to
understand the Club, but to overcome its systematic grip. Beginning
with the 1899 study of The Philadelphia Negro and continuing through
the annual Atlanta University Publications of the first decade of the twentieth century, Du Bois undertakes a period of intensive observation

and analysis. Then, during the first decade of the National Association for the Advancement of Colored People, as Du Bois edits the organization's magazine, *The Crisis*, he wages a war of intensive polemics against "color prejudice." These works lay the foundation for a concept of the color line.

From the point of view of a civilization now awash with social studies, the problem of *The Philadelphia Negro* must seem at first trivial or dated: "It is my earnest desire to pursue this particular form of study far enough to constitute a fair basis for induction as to the present condition of the American Negro" (Du Bois 1899: iv). Today, there is no end to such studies. An entire bookshelf could be dedicated to studies of Negro Philadelphia, Black Philadelphia, Philadelphians of African American Heritage, and so forth, not to mention studies of other cities in the United States. It would no longer be sufficient to collect a fair basis of data for rudimentary inductions. There would be hypotheses to test, assumptions to refute, and new methods to try.

If Du Bois seems naive in 1899, as critics, including the later Du Bois, agree, there are three mitigating factors that ought to be considered. First, we see that the field is fresh; second, Du Bois has not yet developed a critical theory of class; third, the ontological assumptions of supremacist thought will here be put to the test, and so Du Bois is not quite flailing aimlessly away. The reigning presumptions regarding the Philadelphia Negro have been derived from the bigotry of Teutonic theory—stretched before us are neighborhoods teeming with indolent, criminal, and ill-born masses who owe their wretched condition to their innate inferiority. The problems of the Philadelphia Negro, therefore, are not really the problems of human beings. Perhaps, since 1899, we have seen some progress in our theoretical approach to the ghetto, but not without the help of Du Bois:

> I will trust this study with all its errors and shortcomings will at least serve to emphasize the fact that the Negro problems are problems of human beings; that they cannot be explained away by fantastic theories, ungrounded assumptions or metaphysical subtleties. They present a field which the student must enter seriously, and cultivate carefully and honestly. And until he has prepared the ground by intelligent and discriminating research,

the labors of philanthropist and statesman must continue to be,
to a large extent, barren and unfruitful. (Du Bois 1899: iv–v)

This text, signed from Atlanta University, June 1, 1899, announces
that it shall provide a necessary groundwork for the theory and
practice of social progress. The labors of the social and political
philosopher continue to be futile without such meticulous sifting of
fact. King's philosophy of nonviolence rests upon such bedrocks of
scholarship.

As with his analysis of Jefferson Davis, Du Bois cautions that the
Philadelphia ghetto can be fully understood only in the context of
Teutonic civilization: "to know the removable causes of the Negro
slums of Philadelphia requires a study that takes one far beyond the
slum districts" (Du Bois 1899: 6). Yet, having said this, Du Bois
concentrates his analysis on the ghetto itself. In other words, when
Du Bois first turns to study color prejudice, he will be more interested
in the effects than the cause. The choice Du Bois makes here is crucial
to our understanding of structural analysis. Contrary to a kind of claim
that seems to have a life of its own, Du Bois discerns that color
prejudice can be studied in areas where not a bigot is in sight. The
effects of color prejudice, in other words, may not be confined to the
direct or immediate experience of a bigoted act. Indeed, to study the
behavior of bigotry directly would today still be productive, but it
would barely touch what is interesting or important about color
prejudice. What interests Du Bois is life on the other side of the
tracks—a side of social reality that is surely constructed wherever a
ghetto exists. It is disingenuous to claim that color prejudice has no
effect upon ghettos. The kind of white violence that drove King from
the suburbs of Chicago is the precondition that establishes a ghetto's
walls and puts the ghetto under siege. As King would have the
sidewalks and neighborhoods of white America opened up in order
to let the ghetto out, Du Bois entered the ghetto with a methodical
eye for the kind of reality that was inscribed upon the ghetto within.

Du Bois sorts the people of the Philadelphia ghetto into four
classes: criminal, poor, middle class, and aristocrat. The middle class,
for Du Bois, is the "rank and file of Negro working-people" who feed
the "slums" from one hand as they feed the "upper class" from the

other. "Here we see questions and conditions which must receive the most careful attention and patient interpretation" (Du Bois 1899: 7). Chief among the concerns Du Bois presses is the predicament of black aristocrats—those who, like himself, may boast of superb achievements and abilities:

> Scattered throughout the better parts of the Seventh Ward, and on Twelfth, lower Seventeenth and Nineteenth streets, and here and there in the residence wards of the northern, southern, and western sections of the city is a class of caterers, clerks, teachers, professional men, small merchants, etc., who constitute the aristocracy of the Negroes. Many are well-to-do, some are wealthy, all are fairly educated, and some liberally trained. Here too are social problems—differing from those of other classes, and differing too from those of the whites of a corresponding grade, because of the peculiar social environment in which the whole race finds itself, which the whole race feels, but which touches this highest class at most points and tells upon them most decisively. (Du Bois 1899: 7–8)

The peculiar social environment in question denies these worthy aristocrats their due estimation.

Neither the achievements nor the character of this class are of the slightest interest to anyone outside the ghetto. Du Bois, for instance, although employed by the University of Pennsylvania, notices that his name is not listed when the faculty register is published. "I would not have known where to place or what to call him," explains one official (Lewis 1993: 180). Any faculty member who carries the qualifications implied by a Harvard Ph.D. would feel the sting of such exclusion.

Du Bois wants us to know how exclusion plagues the black aristocracy. In this "peculiar environment," which demeans achievement, ambitions become pathetic rumblings and grumblings. Du Bois provides a patient assessment:

> Many are the misapprehensions and misstatements as to the social environment of Negroes in a great Northern city. Sometimes it is said, here they are free; they have the same chance as the Irishman, the Italian, or the Swede; at other times it is said, the environment

is such that it is really more oppressive than the situation in the Southern cities. The student must ignore both of these extreme statements and seek to extract from a complicated mass of facts the tangible evidence of a social atmosphere surrounding Negroes, which differs from that surrounding most whites; of a different mental attitude, moral standard, and economic judgment shown toward Negroes, than for most other folk. That such a difference exists and can now and then be plainly seen, few deny; but just how far it goes and how large a factor it is in the Negro problems, nothing but a careful study and measurement can reveal. (Du Bois 1899: 4)

Indeed, King's confrontation with the great Northern ghetto of Chicago presented difficulties not quite the same as, nor altogether different from, conditions he had battled in the South. Perhaps nonviolence cannot be vindicated until it returns to this obdurate reality and finds the means to remedy it.

We saw earlier that King could not discuss structure without discussing history. Neither can Du Bois examine the peculiar condition of black aristocrats without first showing how historical developments have been disastrous to their aspirations. Twice in its history Philadelphia was hit with waves of mass migration. Each time, because of the resulting aggravation of color prejudice, the black aristocrat of Philadelphia was swept to ruin:

Thus we see that twice the Philadelphia Negro has, with a fair measure of success, begun an interesting social development, and twice through the migration of barbarians a dark age has settled on his age of revival. These same phenomena would have marked the advance of many other elements of our population if they had been as definitely isolated into one indivisible group. No differences of social condition allowed any Negro to escape from the group, although such escape was continually the rule among Irish, Germans, and other whites. (Du Bois 1899: 11)

In hard times, as in other times, the black Philadelphian could not escape from a race-bound identity. When the "barbarians" happened to be masses of freed slaves from the South, then the black aristocracy of Philadelphia were herded together with them. When the "barbarians" were white ethnics, no black citizen was safe. In either case, the aristocracy found double discouragements to reward their achievements. Here we see how Du Bois continues to deploy chivalric categories of feudal history, the better to disturb one's comfort with such accounts, if not to overthrow them completely. Moreover, we anticipate with numerous historical examples the very problem that King sought to address in his Chicago campaign. If white ethnics could work their way into middle-class neighborhoods and cling to small turfs of success, then why not black Americans, too?

Du Bois reports that state-approved color prejudice had for centuries been the norm, even in the City of Brotherly Love: "as early as 1693 we find an order of the Council against the 'tumultuous gatherings of the negroes of the towne of philadelphia, on the first dayes of the week'" (Du Bois 1899: 11–12). And socially approved prejudice, even if not law on the books, has always had harrowing results. "That the riots [of 1834] occurred by prearranged plan was shown by the signals—lights in the windows—by which the houses of whites were distinguished and those of the Negroes attacked and their inmates assaulted and beaten" (Du Bois 1899: 27). During pre-Civil War riots, "a successful effort was made to deprive free Negroes of the right of suffrage which they had enjoyed nearly fifty years" (Du Bois 1899: 30).

Du Bois observes in 1899 that a new age in economic history threatens to confound the further development of black Philadelphia: "New methods of conducting business and industry are now rife: the little shop, the small trade, the house industry have given way to the department store, the organized company and the factory" (Du Bois 1899: 45). In this new world, the virtues of Benjamin Franklin's Poor Richard have become quaint. Machinery is all electric, if not gas, and the craftsman has become a replaceable technician. These developments aggravate the economic malaise imposed upon black ghettos:

> how much more sensitive the lower classes of a population are to
> great social change than the rest of the group; prosperity brings
> abnormal increase, adversity, abnormal decrease in mere num-
> bers, not to speak of other less easily measurable changes. Doubt-

less if we could divide the white population into social strata, we would find some classes whose characteristics corresponded in many respects to those of the Negro. Or to view the matter from the opposite standpoint we have here an opportunity of tracing the history and condition of a social class which peculiar circumstances have kept segregated and apart from the mass. (Du Bois 1899: 49)

Here is a prelude to the great race–class problem. Poor blacks share many traits with poor whites, especially in times of boom and bust, but the black poor are subject to a peculiar disadvantage that keeps them segregated and apart namely, the color of their skin. If the advancement of capitalism promises higher peaks for some, it also threatens lower valleys for others. Du Bois investigates the ways in which black poverty differs from white, especially in times of economic bust.

The black ghetto is always more than just a poor neighborhood, and Du Bois will be interested in the differences. In black ghettos, for example, the careful observer notes peculiar traits not shared by poor whites:

Scanning this population more carefully, the first thing that strikes one is the unusual excess of females. This fact, which is true of all Negro urban populations, has not often been noticed, and has not been given its true weight as a social phenomenon. (Du Bois 1899: 53)

[Between 1820 and 1840] the opportunities for work were gradually restricted for the man, while at the same time, through growth of the city, the demand for female servants increased, so that in 1840 we have about seven women to every five men in the country, and sixteen to every five in the city. (Du Bois 1899: 55)

The feminization of the ghetto is accompanied by another peculiar trait:

The colored population of Philadelphia contains an abnormal number of young untrained persons at the most impressionable age; at the age when, as statistics of the world show, the most crime is committed, when sexual excess is more frequent, and when there has not been developed fully the feeling of responsibility and personal worth. (Du Bois 1899: 55–56)

And so, after a fair collection of data, Du Bois may tender the following induction peculiar to the black ghetto of Philadelphia: "We find in Philadelphia a steadily and, in recent years, rapidly growing Negro population, in itself as large as a good-sized city, and characterized by an excessive number of females and young persons" (Du Bois 1899: 57). Yes, King and others will attempt to link the common curse of poverty that spans the color line, but this does not suggest that real differences should be overlooked. Groundwork studies completed by Du Bois require that we not fall uncritically into color-blind models of poverty.

As Du Bois collects facts relevant to color prejudice, he anticipates a common query from the land of opportunity. Don't poor whites and blacks have the same chance to advance their careers through scholarship or industry? After all, Du Bois is employed by a large, predominantly white university. Are not the same opportunities available to other qualified black aristocrats?:

Young women of the colored race are qualifying themselves for public teachers by taking the regular course through our Normal School. No matter how well qualified they may be to teach, directors do not elect them to positions in the schools. It is taken for granted that only white teachers shall be placed in charge of white children. (Du Bois 1899: 94)

Given such evidence, Du Bois concludes that "the Negro problem in Philadelphia is no longer, in the main, a problem of sheer ignorance" (Du Bois 1899: 95). Du Bois accumulates overwhelming evidence that failures of ghetto poor, like achievements of supremacist leaders, are the inevitable and tragic result of systematic color prejudice:

Every one knows that in a city like Philadelphia a Negro does not have the same chance to exercise his ability or secure work according to his talents as a white man. Just how far this is so we will say later; now it is sufficient to say in general that the sorts of work open to Negroes are not only restricted by their own lack of training but also by discrimination against them on account of their race; that their economic rise is not only hindered by their present poverty, but also by a widespread inclination to shut against them many doors of advancement open to the talented and efficient of other races. (Du Bois 1899: 98)

In these statistics and tables we have first to notice the large proportion of those people who work for a living; taking the population ten years of age and over, and we have 78 per cent of the Negroes of the South Ward, and 55.1 per cent for the whole city, white and colored. . . . 16.3 per cent of the native white women of native parents and of all ages, in Philadelphia are breadwinners, their occupations are restricted, and there is great competition; yet among Negro women, where the restriction in occupation reaches its greatest limit, nevertheless 43 per cent are bread-winners, and their wages are at the lowest point in all cases save in some lines of domestic service where custom holds them at certain figures; even here, however, the tendency is downward.

The causes of this peculiar restriction in employment of Negroes are twofold: first, the lack of training and experience among Negroes; second, the prejudice of the whites. (Du Bois 1899: 109–111)

The twofold causes of repression may be reduced to one dominant cause, since "lack of training and experience among Negroes" when compared to other racial types is one indicator by which "prejudice of the whites" is measured. What is clear from these statistics? That black populations work more. That black women work more than white women. That, generally speaking, the black population is working harder, against greater odds, and getting less for it. If wage slavery has a meaning, here it is.

As Du Bois suggests: "the peculiar distribution of employments among whites and Negroes makes the great middle class of white people seldom, if ever, brought into contact with Negroes—may this be a cause as well as an effect of prejudice?" (Du Bois 1899: 110–111).

Du Bois was not the first to find evidence that the color line was oppressive, nor was King the last to experience the racism of white America. Between Du Bois and King we find time-wearied corroboration of fact and time-honored inductions of principle. Yes, Du Bois admits that skill levels are depressed in the black ghetto, but he refuses to conclude that this is a result of native inferiority. In a nation where distributions are uniformly skewed in favor of whites, the distribution of skills is also pinched from aspiring black workers. Color prejudice has direct effects on the conditions one finds inside a ghetto's walls.

"Already a white labor union movement is beginning to crowd the Negro," reports Du Bois in 1899, "to ask for legislation that will strike him most forcibly and in other ways to bring organized endeavor to bear upon disorganized apathy" (Du Bois 1899: 116). In making this observation, Du Bois works against one background assumption that feeds color prejudice: things get done if one gets organized; if black Americans cared more, they would be better organized. This background assumption, however, obscures the truth on two counts. First, it ignores the blatant prejudice that has long energized organizing efforts from the white side of the color line. Thus, "getting organized" has involved some rather undemocratic principles that hardly count as moral examples of uplift. Second, there is an historical naiveté in the presumption that black Americans are not organized simply on account of a lack of initiative. A more knowledgeable position would take into account the deliberate statutory obstacles and often violent discouragements that have impeded the development of black organizations. From the black side of the color line, "getting organized" was not an unmixed civic opportunity. Even in King's day, civil rights workers had to work under cover of "prayer meetings" to avoid undue harrassment from local police.

In the end, for Du Bois, the individualistic principle, or racist principle, or nationalist principle, which becomes a principle of human nature for Teutonic civilization, is understood to be the cool principle of exclusion:

> The real motives back of this exclusion are plain: a large part is simple race prejudice, always strong in working classes and intensified by the peculiar history of the Negro in this country.

Another part, however, and possibly a more potent part, is the natural spirit of monopoly and the desire to keep up wages. . . . So to-day the workmen plainly see that a large amount of competition can be shut off by taking advantage of public opinion and drawing the color line. (Du Bois 1899: 129)

The employers in this matter are not altogether blameless. Their objects in conducting business are not, of course, wholly philanthropic, and yet, as a class, they represent the best average intelligence and morality of the community. A firm stand by some of them for common human rights might save the city something in taxes for the suppression of crime and violence. . . . Without doubt, in many cases, the employer is really powerless; in many other cases he is not powerless, but is willing to appear so. (Du Bois 1899: 129–130)

Du Bois understands white workers with slightly more sympathy than white employers. The former are expected to act on their interests, as they shrewdly calculate the value of exclusion. The latter, however, representing "the best average intelligence and morality of the community," are expected to take a "firm stand" for "common human rights." Both classes, however, do something more than discriminate on the basis of color. Each class also acts out of an economic motive that makes color prejudice a matter of self interest. With the introduction of this calculus, the notion of color prejudice begins to develop into the structure of racism.

In his analysis of white attitudes, Du Bois is still entertaining a romantic distinction between aristocracy and mass that emphasizes a *noblesse oblige* that ought to operate among white classes and the black "talented tenth" alike. Du Bois asserts that, in their day-to-day struggle for economic survival, middle classes have more flexibility than lower classes to moralize about their wider responsibilities. Indeed, this assessment is remarkably accurate and explains much about the fits and starts of American reform movements. To the extent that white middle classes assume the luxury of moral reflection, to just such an extent do reform movements flourish. Let the same classes begin to feel their luxuries pinched, however, and their calculations quickly retreat to the decimal points of self-interest. So long as progress on the race question depends upon the beneficent feelings of the middle class, therefore, progress will have structural limits. This dilemma is the very same problem faced by King after Selma. His experience in the suburbs of Chicago demonstrated that white moral introspection ended when black demands entered the suburban housing market. Thus, King was forced to recast his coalition of reform. With the best of intentions, Du Bois implicates himself in the lie that one can be serious about removing "the odium of race" while being smug about the structure of class. King's last monograph confronts this lie head-on.

The early work of Du Bois, with its "four grades" of black Philadelphia—"the criminals, the poor, the laborers, and the well-to-do"—is a valiant attempt to argue for a nobler kind of discrimination (Du Bois 1899: 311). Thus, "the object of social reform should be so to diversify Negro employments as to afford proper escape from menial labor for the talented few, and so to allow the mass some choice in their lifework" (Du Bois 1899: 141). This can only be accomplished after white America gives up its "strong tendency . . . to consider Negroes as composing one practically homogenous mass" (Du Bois 1899: 309). Appropriating, if you will, a four-class structure for the Philadelphia ghetto, Du Bois is chiefly interested that black upper classes be appreciated for their achievements. "Nothing more exasperates the better class of Negroes than this tendency to ignore utterly their existence" (Du Bois 1899: 310).

Furthermore, Du Bois will parry the backhanded jab that, coming from some would-be ally, pretends to exonerate the black aristocrat from racist categories, exclaiming, "but I don't think of you as black!" Such exclamations depend on the hidden premise that black implies an undesirability from which the present party is excluded. In other words, color prejudice exiles black talent into a conceptual nether-world where talent cannot be black. Whites, on the other hand, may take pride, as the highest achievements of white individuals are touted *as white achievements*, even when they are very rare. Any white boy *could* be President, and Einstein is considered proof of any white boy's genius. Answers Du Bois: "In many respects it is right and proper to judge a people by its best classes rather than by its worst classes or middle ranks. The highest class of any group represents its possibilities rather than its exceptions, as is so often assumed in regard to the Negro" (Du Bois 1899: 316). Why, then, is black talent not viewed *as black achievement*? Why must black achievements of intellect be treated as white-inspired? Why do scholars, when confronted with black genius, ask, "Where did he get it?" Black talent exposes the self-contradictory presumptions of white supremacy. It is easier for the supremacist to make an exception to the rule of black inferiority than to grapple with his ensuing quandary.

Of course, it is easy to smirk about the pains of the petty bourgeoisie. So-called aristocratic achievements often do not seem worth their precarious gildings. Du Bois, walking the streets of Philadelphia in his immaculate attire and his pompous posture, must have cut a figure easy to ridicule from many sides. Viewed from the outside, knowing nothing of what it means to earn a middle-class opportunity the hard way, the petty bourgeoisie character is least of any class entitled to sympathy or respect. *The Philadelphia Negro* turns out to be a kind of confession in which Du Bois tells the story of the professional bourgeoisie, what we might call "working professionals," who know very well how much they give up to their profession every day and what they get in return. One hundred years later, that confession still rings true.

The precarious anxiety of the petty bourgeoisie indeed becomes the definitive consciousness of our age. At its worst, it is nothing but jealous, judgmental puffery, loathing the poor for their desperation, the rich for their leisure. At its best, however, it is the life of aspiration itself. As pure aspiration, indeed, it *never* arrives. What Du Bois personified, however, was the amazing strength of this aspiring class. It would push and push again, despite the shambles that were more often than not paid in return. And Du Bois warned that the fragile psychology of this class has little else to sustain it than the quiet recognition of worth among peers. Indeed, it is easy, fashionable, and often helpful to mock the self-sustaining spirit of the petty bourgeoisie. Crush this spirit, warns Du Bois, and you risk crushing life itself.

In this regard, King and Du Bois bear the brunt of a common misunderstanding. Here were two reformers in suits, personifications of petty bourgeois status, never quite as successful as they should be when it came to the problem of the masses. And both pressed especially hard in areas that would most benefit the middle classes. This dogmatic criticism has its obvious force. Nevertheless, it is a strange double standard that points to middle-class achievements among "race classes" as easy targets of ridicule and at the same time disparages a seeming lack of aspiration among "race masses." In the face of such flexibility, it is easy to see that ridicule is all that is offered. The limited uplift achieved by Du Bois and King far outweighs the downward drag of our ever fashionable race cynics.

Furthermore, the dialectic of middle-class aspiration, so evident in the work of Du Bois and King, illuminates the crushing devastation of the Chicago movement. It was King's purpose to open Chicago housing so that aspiring, middle-class African Americans could take their place among their class peers. But Chicago was as vicious as Alabama on this point. Although King had traveled a thousand miles, he was still walking the streets of Dynamite Hill, in Birmingham, Alabama, where Angela Davis grew up. When King marched through white neighborhoods in an effort to secure housing for aspiring black classes, he encountered displays of public viciousness that seethed with hatred. Once again, the dogmatic critics may have their field day, but the fragile hopes of middle-class aspiration were met with vile rebuke in Chicago. And we can see that the image of Chicago stands for a century of human torment that Du Bois first documented in 1899.

THE CENTURY OF THE COLOR LINE

We have seen how the chief concern for Du Bois—what he means by the "removable causes" of the Philadelphia ghetto—is the peculiar effect of color prejudice. This is why he would write a few years later in The Souls of Black Folk (1903) that the problem of the twentieth century is the problem of the color line. And this is why he spent ten years at the beginning of the century documenting the effects of race prejudice and the possibilities of black talent for the annual Atlanta University Publications. By 1905, Du Bois et al. reported scientific progress:

> We believe that there has grown in the last ten years a larger scientific spirit in dealing with the Negro problems and a demand

for verifiable knowledge, rather than mere opinion, as a basis for
sound judgment and philanthropic effort.

The investigators of the last ten years seem on the whole to
indicate: (a) A progressive differentiation of the Negro race into
social and economic classes. (b) A slow recognition that this fact
makes it more and more unjust to characterize the race as if it
were a unit. (Du Bois 1898–1917 10: 8)

These conclusions reaffirm those of The Philadelphia Negro project and
support the widely held assessment of Du Bois as a kind of elitist
preoccupied with the development of "the talented tenth." We miss
the point of Du Bois' lasting contribution in this regard, however,
unless we seee how the Du Boisian concept of the black talented tenth
poses a challenge to the traditional class prejudices of Teutonic
civilization. If Du Bois does not yet have a critical theory of class—in
other words, a theory of class organically related to the economic
processes of our "new age" of capitalism—he nevertheless retains a
commonsense aversion to greed, whether Teutonic or not. Thus, when
Du Bois conceives of a black talented tenth, he does not mean to
connote the reigning examples of elite Teutonic habits, popularized
by Veblen's Theory of the Leisure Class.

The Atlanta University Conference of 1907 made resolutions
about the role of the talented elite within black economies. The
conference agreed to emphasize "tendencies among Negroes toward
co-operative effort." It would be important to hold before black
Americans "the ideal of wide ownership of small capital and small
accumulations among many, rather than great riches among the few"
(Du Bois 1898–1917 12: unnum. p.). Here are these remarkable
resolutions, reported in full:

> The conference regards the economic development of the Negro
> Americans at present as in a crucial state. The crisis arises not so
> much because of idleness or even lack of skill as by reason of the
> fact that they unwittingly stand hesitating at the cross roads—one
> way leading to the old trodden ways of grasping fierce individu-
> alistic competition, where the shrewd, cunning, skilled and rich
> among them will prey upon the ignorance and simplicity of the
> mass of the race and get wealth at the expense of the general well

being; the other way leading to co-operation in capital and labor, the massing of small savings, the wide distribution of capital and more general equality of wealth and comfort. This latter path of co-operative effort has already been entered by many; we find a wide development of industrial and sick relief, many building and loan associations, co-operation of artisans and considerable co-operation in the retail trade. Indeed from the fact that there is among Negroes, as yet, little of that great inequality of wealth distribution which marks modern life, nearly all their economic effort tends toward true economic cooperation. But danger lurks here. The race does not recognize the parting of the ways, they tend to think and are being taught to think that any method which leads to individual riches is the way of salvation.

The conference believes this doctrine mischievously false, we believe that every effort ought to be made to foster and emphasize present tendencies among Negroes toward co-operative effort, and that the ideal of wide ownership of small capital and small accumulations among many rather than great riches among a few, should persistently be held before them. (Du Bois 1898–1917 12: unnum. p.)

For more than one hundred pages, in the report that follows the above resolutions, Du Bois reviews West Indian history, where, "we find the most direct survival of African economic customs" (Du Bois 1898–1917 12: 19).

Out of this lengthy discussion there emerges, in true Du Boisian style, "a larger form which I have elsewhere called Group Economy. It consists of such a cooperative arrangement of industries and services within the Negro group that the group tends to become a closed economic circle largely independent of the surrounding white world" (Du Bois 1898–1917 12: 79). If there is to be a talented tenth, it will be known for its imaginative experiments in cooperative organization—or group economy—not for its ability to monopolize private assets or public power. Likewise, when King speaks of black liberation, he does not fail to encourage a broader revolution of values.

But what are the chances in this century to produce black elites with cooperative leadership skills? In 1912, the *Atlanta University Publi-*

cations report the following resolutions with respect to the black craftsman:

> 1. Negro American skilled labor is undoubtedly gaining ground both North and South.
> 2. This advance however is in the face of organized opposition and prejudice. The organized opposition is illustrated by the determined effort of the white locomotive firemen to displace Negro firemen, not for inefficiency or any cause but race and color. Race prejudice is shown by both employers and laborers in every line of skilled labor where the Negro is seeking admission. On the other hand, in the Miners' Union and in some building trades where the colored man has an assured footing, he is well treated and is achieving economic independence.
> 3. What, then, should be the black man's attitude toward white laborers and the labor movement? Some people advise enmity and antagonism. This is a mistake. The solution of all laborers, white and black, lies in the great movement of social uplift known as the labor movement which has increased wages and decreased hours of labor for blacks as well as white. When the white laborer is educated to understand economic conditions he will outgrow his pitiable race prejudice and recognize that black men and white men in the labor world have a common cause. Let black men fight prejudice and exclusion in the labor world and fight it hard; but do not fight the labor movement. (Du Bois 1898–1917 17: 7)

By identifying a common cause shared by black and white laborers, the 1912 resolutions would seem to contradict the 1905 proposal for a black group economy. A classic problem emerges out of the strategic inconsistency that would call for national cooperation on the one hand and international alliance on the other. If the tension caused by the inconsistency of these approaches is difficult to resolve in theory, it is also difficult to make an actual choice in practice.

Can one "fight prejudice and exclusion in the labor world and fight it hard" while at the same time establishing "a closed economic circle largely independent of the surrounding white world"? This is the well-known contradiction between nationalism and internationalism. It is a troublesome problem for both theory and practice and defines many of the factions of the race–class approach. If Du Bois later came to more careful analysis of the labor question, he never gave up his nationalism. The color line was a material contradiction of civilization to begin with; how could one bring consistency to bear upon it?

The race–class question, for all its delineation of the contours of oppression, frustrates clear analysis. Is the significance of race increasing or declining? How much effort shall the black community spend in struggle with whites compared with energy that could be directed toward a group economy? After Du Bois has lived more than sixty years in the United States, he will not be able, in good conscience, to advise young blacks that they should turn their talents away from black institutions for the sake of eliminating color prejudice. After all, there is a real economic war at hand, and the African American community cannot afford to sacrifice its existing institutions for the sake of moral instruction. White America wouldn't get the point, anyway. In such a context, the hope earlier expressed by Du Bois that education would reduce white prejudice is a dream yet unfulfilled, sure to be obstructed wherever effective attempts are made.

Rather than make artificial dichotomies of live choices, Du Bois developed a complex strategy embracing several fronts of activity. White publics would be educated, group economy would be encouraged among blacks, and barriers to opportunity would be challenged in the wider, whiter world. This complex strategy, if not delicately balanced, easily degenerates into ideological dichotomies. As Harold Cruse has pointed out, the choice between self-help and integration crystallized into dichotomy over the next decades, and would eventually force Du Bois out of the NAACP. And I think it was the dichotomizing tendency of Black Power that also prompted King's critique. King never argued that self-help was wrong. As pastor to a black church and leader among black pastors, he knew very well the value of self-help. King shared with Du Bois a sense of the complexity of live options. I will explicate King's systematic program of social struggle in a later chapter. For the time being, it is important to realize that one need not reject agitation or integration in order to pursue self-help. A comprehensive and multifaceted strategy could work on various fronts of the struggle simultaneously. Nowhere is this better exemplified than in the early days of *The Crisis*.

Having completed impressive, if obscured, groundwork in social ontology, Du Bois in 1910 opened up a national publicity campaign from Harlem in the form of *The Crisis*, the monthly organ of the new National Association for the Advancement of Colored People. The crisis at hand, of course, was the crisis of the color line. And the name of the journal, echoing the eighteenth-century choice of Thomas Paine, emphasized a revolutionary spirit. Needless to say, Du Bois was ready with crisp, insistent prose:

> The object of this publication is to set forth those facts and arguments which show the danger of race prejudice, particularly as manifested to-day toward colored people. It takes its name from the fact that the editors believe that this is a critical time in the history of the advancement of men. Catholicity and tolerance, reason and forbearance can to-day make the world-old dream of human brotherhood approach realization; while bigotry and prejudice, emphasized race consciousness and force can repeat the awful history of the contact of nations and groups in the past. We strive for this higher and broader vision of Peace and Good Will.
>
> The policy of THE CRISIS will be simple and well defined:
>
> It will first and foremost be a newspaper: it will record important happenings and movements in the world which bear on the great problem of inter-racial relations, and especially those which affect the Negro-American.
>
> Secondly, it will be a review of opinion and literature, recording briefly books, articles, and important expressions of opinion in the white and colored press on the race problem.
>
> Thirdly, it will publish a few short articles.
>
> Finally, its editorial page will stand for the rights of men, irrespective of color or race, for the highest ideals of American democracy, and for reasonable but earnest and persistent attempts to gain these rights and realize these ideals. The magazine will be the organ of no clique or party and will avoid personal rancor of all sorts. In the absence of proof to the contrary it will assume honesty of purpose on the part of all men, North and South, white and black. (Du Bois 1910–1940 1.1: 10)

When Du Bois speaks for "reasonable but earnest and persistent attempts" toward both "the rights of men" and "the highest ideals of American democracy," he means to include "agitation." The term echoes Frederick Douglass, who often counseled agitation in order to advance America's highest principles. The general approach also anticipates King's definition of nonviolence as "the persistent application of peaceable power to offenses against community." As Du Bois serves as a link in a methodical tradition of struggle, he also announces that "personal rancor" has no proper place.

While Du Bois understands how "honest critics mistake the function of agitation," he argues that agitation is needed, just as a dentist's drill is needed. So long as an awful system of race prejudice wreaks daily havoc upon millions, an NAACP will be needed "to tell this nation [about] the crying evil of race prejudice" (Du Bois 1910–1940 1.1: 11).

> What is the National Association for the Advancement of Colored People? It is a union of those who believe that earnest, active opposition is the only effective way of meeting the forces of evil. They believe that the growth of race prejudice in the United States is evil. It is not always consciously evil. Much of it is born of ignorance and misapprehension, honest mistake and misguided zeal. However caused, it is none the less evil, wrong, dangerous, fertile of harm. For this reason it must be combated. (Du Bois 1910–1940 1.2: 16)

Evil must be resisted. Though structures of evil are not precisely intentional, they nevertheless have real effects that must be fought in active and public ways. Here, again, new dimensions of the color line exceed the limits of race prejudice. Racism includes not only the intentional and conscious perpetuation of color prejudice but also its allies, "misapprehension, honest mistake, and misguided zeal." After three-and-one-half centuries of institutional inertia, the complex structure of racism is not always apparent to those who are its most active perpetrators.

Du Bois introduces the term *evil* in ways that will be appropriated by King. To begin with, there is no metaphysical timidity about the term. In the moral realm, evil is not so much wrong as detestable. Nevertheless, evil is not necessarily intentional. In fact, there are collective evils—King's "triple evils"—that may always be severed from any necessary connection with intentional personality. Du Bois promises to treat his opponents *as* if they had good intentions. Thus, the presence of evil challenges logic to formulate a path of resistance that isolates issues—not personalities—for constructive resolution: "It is precisely because the opportunity to earn a living, even for those equipped to do so, is not given to-day to thousands of colored people in the United States, that the National Association of Colored People exists" (Du Bois 1910–1940 1.3: 17).

Because such facts as those delineating the color line do not announce themselves, but must be painstakingly assembled, organization is necessary to any struggle:

> Some of the greatest catastrophes in history have come because the mass of men have been deceived and misled as to the truth of conditions by timid, well-meaning persons, who, knowing the awful facts, suppressed them systematically and spread the sweet and gentle lie. . . .
>
> Race prejudice is rampant and is successfully overcoming humanitarianism in many lines, and the determination of the dominant South to beat the black man to his knees, to make him a docile ignorant beast of burden, was never stronger than today. This is the truth. (Du Bois 1910–1940 1.6: 22)

Evil does have its active proponents; race prejudice in the United States is not a "divine thing against which it is perfectly useless to strive," but rather "a deliberately cultivated and encouraged state of mind" (Du Bois 1910–1940 2.1: 19). Likewise, as we shall see, King will emphasize the need to collect information as the first step of nonviolent confrontation. And King plainly recognizes the ongoing challenge to counter habits of race propaganda that have become pervasive features of American media.

To support the claim that race prejudice is often "deliberately cultivated and encouraged," Du Bois will use *The Crisis* repeatedly to document the mismanagement of information by the American press.

One of his reports appears under the headline "The Manufacture of Prejudice: Three American Fairy Tales from the Associated Press" (Du Bois 1910–1940 2.1: 35). Given that color prejudice depends so heavily upon a falsified flow of information, Du Bois is meeting the problem head-on in a project combining both theory and practice:

> There are people in the United States who say: "We have tried education as a solution for the race problem and failed, therefore," etc.
>
> We cannot too often insist that this is not true. We have never tried the experiment. We have begun the experiment—we have tried it here and there, but the United States has not to-day, and never has had, a complete rational system of elementary education for its myriads of black and white children, and this fact is perhaps the greatest arraignment of American democracy.

In terms that evoke the presence of John Dewey, a founding director of the NAACP, *The Crisis* will set out to educate the educator against race prejudice, as the white press, pulpit, and schools maintain their untiring disinformation campaigns favoring the usual Teutonic state of mind.

So long as media propaganda remains focused on race prejudice, Du Bois also continues to investigate other forms of Teutonic inclination, especially the values that get perpetrated with respect to business and private profit:

> The test, then, of business is philanthropy; that is, the question as to how far business enterprise is doing for men the things they ought to have done for them, when we consider not simply their present desires but their future welfare. Just here it is that past civilizations have failed. Their economic organization catered to fatal wants and persisted in doing so, and refused to let philanthropy guide them. Just so to-day. Whenever a community seats itself helplessly before a dangerous public desire, or an ingrained prejudice, recognizing clearly its evil, but saying, "We must cater to it simply because it exists," it is final; change is impossible. Beware; the epitaph of that people is being written.
>
>   It is just as contemptible for a man to go into the grocery

business for personal gain as it is for a man to go into the ministry for the sake of the salary.

There is not a particle of ethical difference in the two callings. The legitimate object of both men is social service. . . . Thus "from the blackening of boots to the whitening of souls" there stretches a chain of services to be done for the comfort and salvation of men.

Those who are doing these things are doing holy work, and the work done, not the pay received, is the test of the working. (Du Bois 1910–1940 2.2: 64–65)

This polemic prefigures King's moral indictment of both the status quo and its ideology of private profit. When King speaks of a "revolution of values," he includes such considerations as the value of labor and the responsibility of powerful interests. If communism, for King, has smothered the individual, then it is also true that capitalism, with its profiteering values, fails to nurture a healthy community.

LITTLE KINGDOM OF SALT

As the question inevitably arises, "but what can we do about it? the present system is all we know," Du Bois invites the imagination to Africa and "The Little Kingdom of Salt":

In the heart of the desert of the Sahara there is a tiny oasis, about six miles long and two broad. Here lives and prospers a curious community of black men whose little Kingdom has hardly ever been visited by whites. . . .

The habits of order and economy among these people and the necessity of carefully preserving property so hardly acquired has developed not only their intelligence and power of initiative, but their sense of solidarity or commercial welfare in a very high degree.

Beggars are quite unknown in the community. Every inhabitant is part proprietor of the public property, represented by the salt wells, the date palms and the gardens. There is always food for

every one, more or less plentiful, to be sure, a trade is good or
bad. (Du Bois 1910–1940 2.3: 119–120)

Implicit in this mythical community "hardly ever visited by whites"
is a vision of black group economy especially suited to the struggle
against Teutonic class structure. Unfortunately, however, Du Bois
situates his alternative economy in terms that are rapidly disappearing
from economic reality. The scenario above is valuable for an economy
of craft and agriculture, but Du Bois was also witnessing the last
golden age of the family farm. Global formations of capital would
soon make a mockery of the village ideal. Little kingdoms of manufacture, like all feudal categories of reality, were rapidly disappearing,
opening new floodgates of urban dispossession.

Upon his return from the First Universal Races Conference of
August 1911, Du Bois speaks ontologically about the "fundamental
fallacy involved in taking a static instead of a dynamic, a momentary
instead of a historic, a fixed instead of a comparative point of view
of people" (Du Bois 1910–1940 2.4: 157). The black ghetto had been
illuminated by the improved comparative approach, and the problem
of the color line in general would be less obstinate if the peculiarities
of black life could be viewed in the context of race prejudice—a
dynamic process of comparative confinement and exclusion over a
long period of time.

Seen in this way, the race question becomes, in turn, part of a
larger process of exclusion—the exclusion of labor from profit. As we
saw earlier, this larger question has long been recognized, nor did it
come as a surprise to King. As if bound by some universal law of logic,
the question of race entails the question of labor, and any complete
confrontation of racism must include class allocations that devalue
the laboring hand. "Back of the despising of life lies the contempt for
men who live. They are not ends, but means—'hands' for doing my
work, 'masses' for me to contemplate, 'niggers' for me to keep down"
(Du Bois 1910–1940 2.4: 159). Thus when Du Bois reflects again on
the Races Conference, he notes, "the labor question was hardly
touched in its main modern phases, although a strong, masterly
argument was made to show that the economic foundations of
imperialism were as weak as those of the slave barons of the South

and as wicked" (Du Bois 1910–1940 2.5: 208). The labor question, once again, conveys a shared interest among "hands, masses, and niggers." There's something imperialism shares with slavery that is weak because it is structurally wicked. What cannot stand in the light of justice must fall.

Accepting the "strong, masterly argument" concerning parallels between imperialism and slavery, Du Bois is conceptually receptive to socialist thought, but he is nevertheless wary of the behavior of the socialist parties:

> Of all recent forward movements the Socialists have rung truest on the race question in their theoretical statements. But here they have usually stopped. "Why do not Negroes join the Socialists?" they ask. They do not ask such silly questions of white folks: they go and see why they do not join. . . . All of which goes to show that the Negro problem is the door which bars progress in the United States and which makes us liars and hypocrites. (Du Bois 1910–1940 2.6: 244)

We see an emerging appreciation for socialist theory in the wake of the Universal Races Conference. Are socialists in turn prepared to appreciate the problem of the color line? Du Bois is wary, given his view of the practical hypocrisy of this theoretical vanguard.

While white socialists mutter that black masses are not interested in the class revolution, Du Bois and the NAACP will continue to enlist all "people of good will" to fight race hatred. If Du Bois occasionally entertains notions related to the labor question, he does not change the broad terms of his campaign. Because he has failed to make the turn toward class analysis, Du Bois confronts the problem of World War I with logic that is inadequate to the task. Working from a moralistic assumption that allied motives are more pure than German intentions, especially with respect to color prejudice, Du Bois prescribes military service in support of the lesser evil: "Undoubtedly, then the triumph of the allies would at least leave the plight of the colored races no worse than now. . . . On the other hand, the triumph of Germany means the triumph of every force calculated to subordinate darker peoples" (Du Bois 1910–1940 9.1: 28, 30). Thus, it is possible for Du Bois to describe black soldiers from Senegal as sons of Africa "fighting to protect the civilization of Europe against itself" in a war that could do much to alleviate race prejudice (Du Bois 1910–1940 9.1: 26–27). And this is how the race analysis of *The Crisis* and its editor comes into conflict with a new journal in town, *The Messenger*, edited by Chandler Owen and A. Philip Randolph.

As we begin to turn away from Du Bois toward Randolph in our narrative development of King's logic of nonviolence, we see how certain categories may be developed from the ongoing struggle of the color line. If we read history with an eye to nonviolent precedents, then we can discern how much of nonviolence theory has been produced at the cutting edge of agitation. When Douglass speaks of high ideals, he is not shirking his duty to struggle. When Du Bois eschews personal rancor and studies systems of social malaise, he is not seeking detachment from the confrontations that must be waged. As words like *spirit* and *love* enter into the complex conception of a struggle earnestly waged, we want to avoid reactions that would displace such concepts from their contexts. And when King comes to emphasize the impoverishment of labor, we can see how this "social-ist" insight is as old as Frederick Douglass.

Wending our way toward Randolph, we are looking to explicate the second of King's triple evils, poverty. With Du Bois we have seen how the evil of racism is identified as the problem of the century. And we have seen how the economic question, or the question of labor, is always a companion to the color line. It remains to be seen, however, how the modern turn toward mass production will demand a con-ceptual shift in terms of struggle across the color line. In our narrative thus far, Du Bois has analyzed society along lines appropriate to an economy of manufacture. Although powerful infrastructures have been laid by the great industrialists of the gilded age, the American worker was not yet converted into the mass wage laborer. With Randolph, and the transformations wrought by World War I, we shall have to insist that terms of struggle grapple explicitly with the emergence of a new form of economy called capitalism. Gone forever are the old material conditions that led craftsmen and plantation farmers to wage open war for equality. As wealth is forfeited from individual farms and crafts to collective corporations, what slim vision will sustain democracy as a relationship among peers? More-over, we know very well how the age of manufacture handled the question of African America. Now that capitalism has arrived to concentrate the power of elites even further, what hope might inform progressive aspirations?

What we see in these early works of Du Bois is how the color line leads toward complex questions of economic organization and stra-tegic flexibility. In the crisis of the color line, however, choices too often become dichotomies, and preferences are labeled as divisions that weaken the broad front of struggle. Either one is for the middle class, or one is for the mass. Either one is talking to white people, or one is helping black people. Self-help or integration. Total confronta-tion or abject pacification. Love or power. Yet the complexities of these issues in thought are always exceeded by the crush of a complex reality. Somewhere between the disarray of thought that refuses to grapple with structural terms and the doctrinaire orthodoxy that insists upon some single answer—between these extremes, we find King's pluralistic analysis of structure in terms of race, class, and violence. The result of this pluralism is a philosophy of struggle that would include every helpful voice and accept any helpful collabora-tion. Whether he was speaking to white America or black America, King called for recognition that racism, poverty, and violence defined common terms of injustice that could neither be separated, denied, nor ignored.

As for the well-known spiritual dimension of nonviolence, we find that it insists upon a kind of compassion for the most unlikely victims of oppression—the oppressors themselves. If Jefferson Davis deserves sympathy, it is because the lie that he lives is the curse of a heritage that he does not transcend. If a better Jefferson Davis is possible, something else is needed beyond the moral exhortation to "get a life." Sympathy and structural analysis are twins, born of the same desire to see better persons emerge. Here is what Du Bois says in his famous appeal on behalf of the NAACP, "Join or Die":

Freedom is a state of mind: a spiritual unchoking of the wells of human power and superhuman love. Is there anything in America that is so strangling brotherhood and narrowing humanity and encouraging hatred, lust and murder as race prejudice? Is there any conceivable crime that it does not daily excuse? Any conceivable humanity that it may not defy? If you want freedom, then join this association and fight race hatred. (Du Bois 1910–1940 7.3: 133)

Behind this appeal to pledge money and energy in behalf of organized opposition to race prejudice is a metaphysical declaration. True, the headline for this polemic, "Join or Die," calls attention to a brute material urgency that daily threatens some new lynching. And the rhetoric calls attention to the fact that tough-minded organization is needed. The lead sentence, however, connects the reader to an ontology of love and personality that necessarily defines the possibility of liberation. Within the polemic of this tough-minded organizer, we find that freedom has ideal qualities that speak to the needs of spirit. Again, we find remarkable precedent for King's logic of nonviolence, organically connected to the daily needs of a struggle that was headquartered in Harlem.

Chapter 3

———·———

STRUCTURE AND CLASS

> One of the few experiments in the attachment of emotions
> to ends that mankind has not tried is that of devotion so
> intense as to be religious, to intelligence as a force of social
> action.
>
> —JOHN DEWEY

A. PHILIP RANDOLPH, RALPH J. BUNCHE, AND THE CONTEXT OF CLASS ANALYSIS

King was not yet born when A. Philip Randolph challenged Du Bois and inaugurated Harlem's radical renaissance. Yet King would live to reenact the intellectual turmoil that was caused when analysis of capitalism confronted the race question, head to head. It is sometimes argued that King took a Marxist turn in later campaigns, but this chapter serves to remind us that King had been talking to Randolph for many years—they flew to Ghana together in 1956, marched to Washington together twice, and worked closely on labor issues. Before any of these contacts, Randolph had long since translated the terms of African American struggle into concepts that would engage economic dimensions of exploitation.

As we saw in the preceding chapter, Du Bois inaugurates our development of the concept of structure by calling attention to color prejudice as a systematic influence upon the lives of black citizens who live in ghettos of exclusion. No doubt the life of the ghetto is not to be reduced to the exclusions of color prejudice—no real person is anyone else's negative image—but the effects of color prejudice are palpable, even when accompanied by wealth and achievement. The quality of success is transformed when color prejudice intervenes as a kind of background radiation, always there to remind you. And the quality of poverty is twisted into a new kind of knot. In his play for universal respect, Du Bois proposes military service as a means to lift the level of appreciation that black Americans might enjoy in their own country, but even this will have tragic effects. The milieu of color prejudice intensifies with evidence of black heroism. The positive role model is ineffective as a strategy unto itself. Only after a more fundamental transformation of American society is effected will the example of military service be allowed to stretch the fabric of the popular mind. In recent years, it was not military service alone that distinguished Colin Powell, because military service had long been performed by many blacks before him. Something else had been transformed by the civil rights era that made Powell's military service available for appreciation in a way never before possible—and made it possible for him to rise to the number-one position in the military.

It was a transformation of collective relations that reformed race prejudice in America, more than the other way around. For this reason, the structural dimension of racism must emerge into consideration. Our contemporary retreat from affirmative action is but the latest evidence that the structure of racism is poorly understood. "Color prejudice is aggravated by structural remedies," argue the forces of retrenchment, precisely in contradiction to the evidence that history presents. "Let black Americans only prove their merits to white superiors, and advancement is sure to follow!" That argument, however, died on the battlefields of World War I.

What we bring forward from the early work of Du Bois says two things. Color prejudice has structural effects beyond the immediate impact of any bigoted act, and it is not at all alleviated by evidence of black achievement. What King did was this: he traced the structural effects of color prejudice into their public manifestations and by means of nonviolent action forced changes in these arrangements. In the process, some forms of color prejudice lost their footing and fell. What concerns us in this chapter is the logic that traces the effects of color prejudice into the economic structures of capitalist civilization. The concept of structure is the tool that one uses to leverage arrangements of inequality into retreat. Thus, it is the structural approach that signifies a conceptual victory worthy of some reflection if democratic theory is to advance.

What we must pose in counterpoint to the early work of Du Bois, without suggesting that Du Bois never learned from his mistakes, is the incompleteness of color prejudice as a theoretical tool. For this reason, it is time to linger with Randolph and his radical critique. We learn from Randolph how to extend our analysis of color prejudice into the matrix of interests that one finds operative in a capitalist economy, where signs of black achievement are taken not as promise but as threat. A collective struggle is being waged under capitalist terms in America, and this provides economic incentive why black talent must either be neglected, defined as not black, or perceived—with paradoxical intensities of relief and anxiety—as black only. This may suggest the curious conclusion that racial prejudice is not racial at all, but purely economic. Yet, in the end, we shall want to affirm that race prejudice is real, even if it has important economic dimensions.

When King declared moral war on the triple evils of racism, poverty, and war, he did not say that poverty was all there really was. True, King planned a Poor People's Campaign and moved directly into the economic issues that brought him finally to Memphis, Tennessee. But these activities did not negate the declaration made by Du Bois that the problem of the century was the problem of the color line. If, for instance, there is a class dimension to be added to our current construction of affirmative action, it should not be supposed that black "classes" face no problem at all. When the logic of race and that of class get played off against each other, beware making the black middle class reprise its role as America's excluded middle. No, the progression of thought I mean to indicate in this chapter is more dialectical than that. And so I will present concluding remarks around the figure of Ralph Bunche.

For Bunche, the race–class debate reduces to class terms of economic exploitation. Lost is the sensitivity gained by Du Bois for the special dimension of exploitation reserved for deployment along racial lines. Bunche will stipulate that intensity is a true factor that enters into the calculation, but he cannot convey the intimacy of what that intensity implies. If Bunche is more mathematically satisfying, then we pay a price for such abstraction that is ultimately too expensive. In the rough-and-tumble world that these theories are supposed to serve, color prejudice is no mere intensity, as if the rest of us could imagine just a slightly more difficult day on the job. No, there is a distinctive kind of cut that racial prejudice makes that cannot be subtracted as if from two sides of a single equation. There is no white worker who can truly legitimately say, "but I know what you're talking about, my life is just that way." So I want to emphasize that King never took that mathematical turn. For King, class analysis provided a necessary dimension for any struggle of justice. But, as we are learning in Somalia and Bosnia, ethnicity is poorly treated as some accidental factor. One of the last pictures circulated of King showed him standing in front of a poster that said "Black is Beautiful."

Until white workers become educated on the intricacies of political economy, black workers have choices to make. Shall black workers begin to organize where all general theories of politics suggest—among those who provide the strongest base of support? Or shall black workers refuse to organize until there are enough white comrades to share the burden? The race–class question is this kind of empirical beast. And white public opinion responds with a two-point approach that is doubly disabling from a black point of view. In the first instance, white citizens declare that black problems should be addressed by blacks first. In the next moment, after blacks have gathered for collective struggle, whites cry racism. Bunche's logic abets such double-edged criticism. Thus, King will be not quite the integrationist that Bunche would prescribe. As mighty as King's integrative efforts may have been, they were rooted in nationalistic cultural institutions like the black church and Randolph's union of railroad porters.

Here is a fine point of King's logic of nonviolence that has been dulled from twin misuse. On one side, King's logic is said to prescribe rigorous integration at every level of struggle—but this side ignores the predominance of black talent that always surrounded King. On the other side, King's logic is said to be a black development only—

and this side ignores two things. First, the general logic of nonviolence may yet be applicable to exploitation among poor whites, women, gays, lesbians, or others. Second, King always welcomed help from anyone who could see the general issue of justice that was at stake. Thus, King's logic of nonviolence would not exactly reject Bunche's conclusions about the general problem of exploitation in the world, but the struggle against exploitation is always made from some perspective, and this is not always a good reason to forego nationalistic lines of organization. We shall revisit these issues later. In the end, however, we will see how King acknowledges the analytic merits of Bunche but adopts a plan of struggle more closely resembling the work of Randolph.

The general lesson of King's structural pluralism allows the logic of nonviolence to make sense of emerging struggles in a flexible way. Although King defended gay organizers, he did not anticipate the emergence of a gay–lesbian liberation movement. Likewise, the feminist movement exceeds the specific formulations that King articulated. Nevertheless, when King refused to reduce black struggle to just another kind of poverty, he laid foundations for appreciating why it is that sexism and homophobia present legitimate challenges of their own. We may say the same for Michael Lerner's recent insistence to take anti-Semitism more seriously. Emerging from the experiential inventories of our daily lives, each of us knows best how oppression feels to us. In the struggle to lift these burdens from each other's backs, King's logic of nonviolence is constructed to respect, to hear out, to defend the right of various groups to emerge and define themselves as rising classes. If we can avoid the temptation to reach for what Laurence Thomas (1993) calls "invidious comparisons," then we can help our neighbors where we find them.

CLASSICAL FOUNDATIONS
OF STRUCTURAL THEORY

"During the Christmas holidays of 1949 I decided to spend my spare time reading Karl Marx to try to understand the appeal of communism for many people," wrote King in his first movement book, *Stride toward*

Freedom (King 1957: 92). Rejecting communism as "basically evil" because of its metaphysical materialism, ethical relativism, and political totalitarianism, King nevertheless found points that were compelling. Following a lead suggested by Archbishop of Canterbury William Temple, King presented communism as a Christian heresy that grasped essential Christian truths but also melded with other opinions that had to be rejected. Among the Christian truths expressed by communism was its yearning for a classless society. "The Christian ought always to be challenged by any protest against unfair treatment of the poor, for Christianity is itself such a protest, nowhere expressed more eloquently than in Jesus' words: 'The Spirit of the Lord is upon me, because he hath anointed me to preach the gospel to the poor; he hath sent me to heal the brokenhearted, to preach deliverance to the captives, and recovering of sight to the blind, to set at liberty them that are bruised, to preach the acceptable year of the Lord'" (King 1957: 93–94).

"I was deeply concerned from my early teen days about the gulf between superfluous wealth and abject poverty, and my reading of Marx made me ever more conscious of this gulf," continued King. Indeed, King had been impressed by American poverty ever since the soup lines of the Great Depression. There was something about Marx that raised King's consciousness. "Moreover, Marx had revealed the danger of the profit motive as the sole basis of an economic system: capitalism is always in danger of inspiring men to be more concerned about making a living than making a life. . . . Thus capitalism can lead to a practical materialism that is as pernicious as the materialism taught by communism" (King 1957: 94–95). If modern-day capitalism was not quite the same beast portrayed by Marx in 1859, King nevertheless found durable truths in communist literature and was frank about it during a decade that was especially harsh on communism.

As King's last campaigns became more concerned with economic justice, his earlier writings would serve to remind us that King had been grappling with the problem of capitalism at least since 1949. But more than this, we may want to see how King operated in a world already heavily influenced by Randolph's work in this area. When young pastor King arrived in Montgomery, for instance, and sought to take up leadership of the local NAACP, he found that leadership already firmly in the grasp of E. D. Nixon, a stalwart community fixture and member of the Brotherhood of Sleeping Car Porters (BSCP). And the BSCP was synonymous at the time with its outspoken founding leader, Randolph. This chapter thus contributes to our understanding of King's logic of nonviolence by demonstrating how that logic was informed by conceptions of economic justice that had been pioneered by Randolph.

In many ways, the practical shift of tactical targets that characterized King's last years was prefigured in the theoretical challenge that Randolph had presented to Du Bois some fifty years before. The fight against race prejudice would have to take capitalism and class conflict more seriously. Following his intellectual skirmish with Du Bois, Randolph was recruited into the labor movement, where he worked for decades as head of the Brotherhood of Sleeping Car Porters. As a labor leader, Randolph was an early advocate of the march-on-Washington tactic. As organizer of the 1963 March on Washington, he framed the event as a march for "jobs and freedom." Furthermore, as Bayard Rustin recalled, "Randolph understood that the upcoming phase of the civil rights movement would involve economic justice" (Rustin 1987: 425). When King prepared in 1967 to move toward a "poor people's campaign," he took direction from Randolph's 1966 Freedom Budget, itself an update from a full-employment bill that had been gutted by Congress in 1946 (Pfeffer 1990: 288). With these facts in mind, it is no wonder that King, like other civil rights leaders of his day, would call Randolph, "the Chief" (Rustin 1987: 418). We return to Harlem in 1917 in order to recuperate that original challenge, as class analysis meets the struggle of the color line.

One of the early facts that will concern Randolph, co-editor of Harlem's radical magazine, The Messenger, is the rioting of black soldiers who are returning home from World War I to a country that is not improving along the color line. Du Bois had been wrong to say that the black soldier would be fighting to save the West from its racist self, and The Messenger was eager to explore the error. When returning white soldiers used their wartime skills to organize a new kind of violence against black communities, black soldiers returned fire. The ensuing "riots" were evidence that renewed racism would be met with redoubled resistance. The editors of *The Messenger* found these phenomena perfectly explainable from a scientific point of view:

> The country is all alarmed over the rioting of Negro soldiers. We are not surprised or alarmed at the perfectly human tendency. It was Lester F. Ward who said, in his "Human Dynamic Sociology," "Human nature is uniform. Like causes produce like effects as well in the social as in the physical world."
>
> How true is this! No one seemed to have been surprised or certainly alarmed, over the rioting of white troops in East St. Louis. Nor have we heard of any of those troops being punished—notwithstanding the fact that they rioted, pillaged, plundered and massacred under the eyes of all the authorities and before tens of thousands of citizens.
>
> Negro troops are just human. Provocations with them have a limit. The facts have not been stifled but every one acquainted with conditions in this country knows that they have restrained themselves well under the taunts, insults and abuses so unsparingly heaped upon them.
>
> We have especially admired the discipline of the Negro troops at Chicago who held off 500 white disturbers in a fine, soldierly discipline, without any unnecessary violence. We do not advocate or condone criminality or lawlessness among Negroes. We condemn it. But we cannot fail to explain it. Extenuating circumstances are always legitimate evidence in minimizing or justifying an act.
>
> The Negro is probably the best and most loyal soldier in the United States. He does his duty in a fine, manly, courageous way. But the government has failed too often to do its duty by the Negro soldier.
>
> Do not expect the supernatural from the Negro soldier. He has feelings, race pride and ambitions like other men. If you prick him, he bleeds. If you tickle him, he laughs. In a few words, the Negro soldier is just *Human*. (Randolph 1917 1.11: 6)

The steady voice of reason from Harlem shows its affinity for Du Boisian analysis, emphasizing environments, insisting that black problems are human problems, eschewing double standards. Furthermore, the analysis of The Messenger purveys a nonviolent inquiry that seeks to understand the systematic conditions that lead to violent eruptions. These riots will not be stopped by preaching to the rioters themselves; rather, lasting peace will be achieved by a transformation of powder-keg conditions. But The Messenger will not overlook the error of Du Bois for his position on the world war. Black soldiers returning from the war find themselves not the object of national gratitude, but of renewed, and re-armed, prejudice.

Du Bois had been wrong to predict that the sight of black soldiers would engender a softer attitude among whites; meanwhile, the war had produced a progressive dynamic in the rising expectations of blacks. After fighting "to make the world safe for democracy," black soldiers were in no mood to accept continued prejudice at home. The Messenger's editors mocked the obvious hypocrisy of the slogans that had carried African Americans to war: "It is unfortunate that no Negro has been able to carry his mind to Germany yet—so insistent are the demands upon his efforts to make the world safe for democracy in that part of the world known as the United States" (Randolph 1917 1.11: 19). And the editors of The Messenger were eager to articulate a new voice for these rising expectations.

Randolph's Messenger could not exonerate Du Bois for making an erroneous call about the marginal effects of a great war, because, from the point of view of the new analysts in town, the bad call revealed a critical weakness of theoretical approach. Du Bois had reasoned from moralistic grounds that innate hardness of heart could be softened by examples of black dedication. That did not happen. Thus, Randolph insisted upon a new ground of analysis based upon interests. And from such a point of view, the war must have grim consequences:

The real bone of contention in the war is darker peoples for cheap labor and darker people's rich lands. Africa alone is rich in gold, copper, rubber, cocoa, oil, dates and diamonds. India produces great stores of cotton and foodstuffs. The islands of the United States are rich—indeed prolific—in the production of sugar, coffee and tobacco. China has extensive coal mines and oil wells.

Not only is a great wealth of natural resources to be had in these countries. These countries have an abundant supply of labor.

These are the tools of the capitalist—undeveloped resources and undeveloped peoples—cheap land and cheap labor.

Most liberal and radical movements have failed to secure the support of Negroes because they generally break down at that point of contact. The Negro problem has been the shoals, the Scylla and Charybdis on which the radical movements have foundered. (Randolph 1917 1.11: 10)

If liberal and radical movements were built upon recognition that capitalism exploited land and labor, these movements were also slow to understand the aggravating conditions of the color line. On the other hand, race movements built upon recognition of the color line had been equally slow to locate their own position within a dynamic of capitalist exploitation. Thus, a race movement had advocated participation in a pro-capitalist war, while the labor movement advanced race prejudice. Together, these strategies guaranteed mutual defeat.

As Randolph saw it, black Philadelphians at home served with Senegalese natives abroad as cheap labor for a global system of exploitation. The tragedy of the system was doubled when black citizens of both continents were enlisted in armies to defend the dynamics of their oppression. By taking sides in World War I, the darker people of the world were dying to choose between warring, would-be masters. Analysis no longer focused on color prejudice as an accidental impediment to universal progress; rather, color prejudice was understood as an active and necessary rationalization of global imperialism. Teutonic civilization may have been rooted in ancient habits of greed, conquest, and pride, but, in the "new age" of industry, it was also harnessed to the interests of a new kind of state, requiring a new analysis of process and conflict.

Randolph's attention to economic structure enables him to explore the ways that war serves to reinforce the exploitation of cheap labor. Although this correlation is especially bad news for black workers, it may be worrisome enough for white workers to induce in the latter a practical motive for solidarity. And here Randolph seeks to soften white attitudes by demonstrating that exploited workers of all races share a common struggle of class conflict:

To safeguard labor standards is the difficult work in all wars. There is a spurious attempt to appeal to the patriotism of the laborer to work for less while the capitalist and employer continue to raise the prices of their commodities. The Negro is in peonage in peace times—to a great extent, so to reduce his standard in war time puts him back into actual—if not nominal slavery. White and black, laborers must recognize their common interest in industry, in politics, in society, in peace. They should join hands not from any abstract altruistic motive, but for their mutual advantages. Neither should allow a horde of scabs and strike-breakers outside of the union when it is possible to have them within the union. Besides, so long as the white dog and the black dog—laborers— fight over the bone, the third capitalist dog will surely run away with it while the contention ensues. (Randolph 1917 1.11: 11)

Whereas Du Bois had once appealed to white classes to respect black aristocrats, Randolph would encourage white masses to seek solidarity with black workers. Randolph's argument relies not chiefly on good will but common interest. The war is squeezing workers of life and liberty. Unless workers awaken to their interests, the war to secure global democracy will result in widespread disempowerment for common citizens. Against this chaos of war, Randolph seeks a logical path to advance labor and "preserve and extend democracy and liberty within the United States" (Randolph 1917 1.11: 11). Since war provides a poor context for progress in democracy, white and black workers share an interest in peace.

The debut issue of The Messenger thus provides a conceptual outline for a critical theory of class, which structures our understanding of race prejudice and speaks to an audience more working class than black. Moreover, because this analysis is born in time of war, The Messenger is especially sensitive to the antidemocratic dynamic of violence. A milieu of violence shackles liberation, and The Messenger will not play loose with suggestions for further violence:

Mr. Common Man, before you can put away something for rainy days, you have got to put away those who bring you rainy days.

No, No, we don't mean for you to do anything rash.

But you have got to stop electing men who want the war

profiteers to keep their profits. You have got to run your government yourself and you have got to run it for service—not for
profits. As long as we vote as we do, "To eat or not to eat," that
will be the question. (Randolph 1917 1.11: 13)

Randolph does not remind the reader that the rainy-day makers tend
to be white, because he is appealing to white workers. Nor does he
advocate nondemocratic means for liberation, because he is too
familiar with the state of war. Like Du Bois, Randolph insists upon an
ethic of service and a politics of agitation. The ballot, not the bullet,
is his call.

Turning to an audience of black preachers, The Messenger asks
religion to play a progressive role. If the church would struggle against
racism, it must also struggle against exploitative systems of profit. For
Randolph, support of working-class interests has become a matter of
principle in the black worker's struggle for human rights. Thus,
Randolph finds it unconscionable when black preachers refuse to
encourage the collective empowerment of labor unions:

A very interesting report was made on the Negro preachers' stand
on Unionism, which shared a lamentable incapacity on the part
of Negro Apostles of Christ to appreciate the most elementary
phases of the question, and their disinclination to look kindly
upon the working class of the Negroes receiving more wages.

Let our so-called ministers of human suffering take note.
Poverty is the most appalling kind of suffering. Low wages pro-
duce poverty. The Union is the only remedy for low wages.
(Randolph 1917 1.11: 14)

The new analysis also challenges the church to update its conception
of evil and its doctrine of salvation. Here, with The Messenger, the evil
of poverty is exposed, and the church is invited to join issue. When
Marxist analysis is advanced by Randolph, a curious transformation
takes place, and the church is treated as a persuadable, possible ally
in the struggle for workers' rights. And more, we find in the early
work of Randolph a nonviolent spirit of inquiry that actively promotes
peace as a companion to justice.

CLASS ANALYSIS MEETS RACE

"He who does not pursue his interest will lose his interest," declared *The Messenger*, "Such has been the case of the Negro" (Randolph 1917 1.11: 15). Certainly Douglass had understood that interests entailed agitation, and so had Du Bois, but Randolph understood it with specific reference to the laboring class. Decades earlier, Du Bois had talked about the idea of a strong man who, in defining the possibilities of Teutonic civilization, denied the advancement of civilization itself. In the first year of *The Messenger*, Randolph in turn protested an idea of industrial democracy that opposed the value of democracy itself. Whereas Du Bois had protested the ideology of the strong man by showing that it contradicted wholeness, Randolph objected to the ideology of the free market because it contradicted the democratic premise of social control:

> A scientific examination of our present economic system will reveal that the cause of our present national weakness lies in implicit and abiding reliance on the efficacy of our national, economic vermiform appendix—the "laissez-faire" doctrine, or "let alone" policy.
>
> And, although over three-fourths of the countries of the world either own and operate all or some of their railways, we permit a few senile individuals, like conscienceless highwaymen, to take toll off the common citizen and to accumulate such colossal fortunes as to menace the free institutions of democracy, by coercing or intimidating public opinion.
>
> Moreover, the railroads have more than a domestic or national significance. (Randolph 1917 [2.6]: 15)

Freedom, for Randolph, is something embedded in social practice, not something conceived as free from social meddling. And here the double danger arises, that masses who leave power uncontested also invite a climate of public opinion opposed to their own interest. As King would point out, accumulations of power very soon translate into ominous blocs of public esteem. In other words, the ideas of the age honor the interests of the ruling class. Moreover, since the capitalist ruling class is increasingly transnational, the longer workers accede to capital's demands, the less effective will their voices sound when they raise questions at a national level.

One exasperating tragedy of free market ideology is the way in which it induces the mass of its believers to act against their own collective empowerment. And the ideology of the free market becomes all the more tragic once Randolph shows how the masses act against their own interest as a matter of so-called principle. By "letting alone," indeed, by insisting that capital accumulations not be "interfered with," the masses, in principle, abandon democratic control of social change. Yet, markets are only legitimate, suggests Randolph, when they are *democratically controlled*. Furthermore, the dynamic of the modern market operates on an order very different from what has gone before:

> The advent of the steel and iron age wrought a significant change in political theory. The Manchesterian-textile-politico-economic philosophy was replaced by the Birmingham-iron-and-steel-imperialistic philosophy. Countries shifted from producers of consumers' goods to producers of producers' goods. In short, hats and shoes gave way to rails and steel cars.
>
> Formerly, the several countries competed with each other in selling natives trousers in the same territory; German merchants could offer their wares in British South Africa; English merchants could sell their wares in German South-west Africa.
>
> But when King Steel strode into the undeveloped fields of the world; bribed and intimidated petty kings of small principalities into granting spheres of economic influence and established railways with foreign capital, world politics assumed a new aspect. (Randolph 1917 [2.6]: 15)

The masses "leave alone" the markets so that free markets may "respond to popular interest." Even if this model were applicable to a capitalism of competing consumer goods, it is dangerously naive when applied to capital put into the service of imperialism. Meanwhile, the possibility of true economic democracy, in either theory or practice, is suppressed and ignored in the name of popular free-market ideologies.

In the end, the *laissez-faire* principle entails brutal consequences for the masses. By "leaving alone" the fortunes of capitalists and their enterprises, the masses license ever larger accumulations of power, the better to stage international cataclysms of war in which the masses would do most of the dying:

> No longer was competition between two powerful countries in the same territory tolerated. The railways in Africa, India, China, are a sine qua non to the development of the oil, coal and iron mines. The desire for exclusive control in awarding franchises for railroad building causes the various Western European Powers to seek political suzerainty over the unexploited lands. The sharp international rivalry which ensues, fosters, breeds and engenders suspicions, jealousies and bitter antagonisms against each other.
>
> Thus, it is plain to one that, one of the dominant and controlling factors, in the scheme of world politics for creating wars, is the extension of private capital in foreign undeveloped fields, in the form of railroads. (Randolph 1917 [2.6]: 15–16)

The dialectic of transnational capital thus exposes new grounds for war. Within the space of a few paragraphs, Randolph has tossed his readers onto a new heap of problems. The innocent sounding *laissez-faire* doctrine has developed in stages, from bucolic competition among manufacture-age merchants, to industrial monopolies that produce infrastructures of capital goods, and finally to international armed conflicts that masquerade as national interests. But what if?— what if "letting alone" were a principle *not applied* by the masses to owners? What if railroads were developed and sustained out of working-class interest? What if the principle of "taking care" or "market tending" were the one most favored by the masses wherever capital deployments were concerned? Randolph's preoccupation with railroad theory prefigures his lifetime commitment to railway labor and provokes new questions about the meaning of that railroad lawyer who presided over the American Civil War.

These are grim facts of a global predicament as they may be constructed from a democratic perspective, especially from the perspective of black labor:

Indeed, world politics have entered a stage where grim, silent, passionate forces are hurrying humanity along, like leaves in a torrent. But as human will and intellect have tamed the fierce powers of lightning and the storms, it will also master, organize and direct the tumultuous energies that are now stirring its own deeper nature and breaking in to the battle cry of destructive action, conquest, expansion, glory and might. (Randolph 1917 [2.6]: 16)

With words that prefigure King's nonviolent idealism, *The Messenger* prepares ground for its claim to being the "Only Radical Negro Magazine in America" (Randolph 1917 2.7: cover). In other words, what *The Messenger* is, *The Crisis* is not. Meanwhile, a pacifist method of inquiry takes shape, as Randolph's call for economic democracy seeks to transform the consuming and working masses into the controlling interests of society. Not only would worker participation in new forms of capital satisfy national democracy, it would also contribute to international peace. Indeed, this vision helps to define the great Harlem Renaissance: "The New Negro is awakening. After having been the political Rip Van Winkle of America for fifty years, sleeping in the cesspools of Republican reaction, he has at last opened his eyes" (Randolph 1917 2.7: 8).

The new international class analysis of African American interest leads Randolph to reassess the loyalty that black masses had long paid to the party of Lincoln: "The Republican party is the party of plutocracy, of wealth, of monopoly, of trusts, of big business. But the Negroes—99 per cent of them—are working people. They have nothing in common with big business and their employers. They ought to belong to the workers' party. And that is the Socialist party" (Randolph 1917 2.7: 8). Gone are most of the reservations that Du Bois expressed about the Socialist Party, and Randolph hints that Du Bois has been working closely enough with Socialist Party members to see that they are trying to erase the color line. Yet, fairness requires our retrospective acknowledgment that the Socialist Party was not a lifelong affiliation for Randolph. One biographer notes that socialism simply did not speak the language of the people (Anderson 1973: 147), a criticism that echoes the insistent judgment of Harold Cruse that American culture demands its own language of struggle, not imported categories from Europe (Cruse 1967). But, then again, the contemporary voice of Cornel West, and his affiliation with the Democratic Socialists of America, reminds us also that these questions remain unsettled, if not unsettling. In my own opinion, the disarray of socialist theory in the United States is precisely the legacy of the color line, which prevents common interests from articulating a common voice. Why is there no socialist labor party of consequence in the United States? I answer that the most significant barrier is racism.

Traditional structural analysis since Marx has always worked to uncover consequences that are never announced as direct intentions. "Bloody legislation," for instance, long rationalized for the greater good, is criticized for its special interests. Likewise, Randolph turns attention to vagrancy laws that prohibit conspicuous rootlessness, not only because the poverty of vagrancy is an ideological offense, but also because vagrancy represents the last freedom of the impoverished to escape servitude to menial employment. When the vagrant happens also to be an organizer, no deep psychology is needed to understand why the state should want him arrested:

> The object of vagrancy laws of recent date in this country is to break up the radical labor movement. . . . Upon these vicious vagrancy laws peonage in the South was built up. . . . The radical press must emphasize that the use of the four billion dollar profits which our millionaires received last year for the payment of decent wages would set into play all the labor which the country needs. (Randolph 1917 2.7: 10)

The classical analysis of "bloody legislation" is Americanized to show how the state enforces a status quo of mass peonage and elite profits. This is how patriotism becomes "a little barrack behind which scoundrels hide their profits" (Randolph 1917 2.7: 11). On occasion, King was faced with court injunctions and local codes that banned public demonstrations. More than once, King was accused of being an outside agitator. When Randolph talks about well-known Southern codes that collaborated to keep organizers out, how much better do we understand the context of remarks that sought to question King's patriotism when he defied such codes.

When *The Messenger* reports the "government's seizure of 58 labor agitators and its threatened seizure of about 8,000 more for the purpose of deporting them," the editors assert, that from a "scientific" point of view, such actions are "perfectly normal." Weren't Socrates, Jesus, and Marx abused in turn by the state? Haven't others more recently and more close to home been equally abused? The following passage seems to anticipate the kind of criticism King would receive when he "meddled" in the affairs of Birmingham:

> In the United States deportation is very old. So general has it been that only those of us who have observed Southern conditions can thoroughly appreciate it. Magistrates, police commissioners and judges commonly try Negroes in the South and give them sentences to leave the town, city, county or state in five hours, twenty-four hours, one hour, a half hour. Nothing is more likely either for a Negro agitator. The Negroes are told that this "Yankee nigger" is trying to get you all in trouble. And the Negro agitator is told that "we white folks get along perfectly peacefully with our 'niggers' and they are satisfied until you 'Yankee niggers' put notions of social equality in their heads." Then sentence for the agitator follows. The Negro agitator will get one of three things— first, sentence to jail, probably followed by lynching; second, sentence to jail to be transferred to a peonage farm or labor swamp; and third, sentence to leave the place, that is, deportation. (Randolph 1917 2.8: 2)

Agitation for equality, whether for class or race, has always been a death-defying calling in the United States. And this is because structures of inequality are structures of violence, very often state-administered violence. When King answered his critics, in a letter from the Birmingham jail, that he had a right to go anywhere to agitate against injustice, he was answering for generations of predecessors who had been agitating on Southern soil.

The long tradition of agitation produces deep philosophical consensus. When the editors of *The Messenger* reflect upon the predicament of deportation, for instance, they provide a classic outline for an apologist of agitation:

> Personally, we believe in deportation. We differ with those who control this government only in what is to be deported. The agitator does not produce the discontent. He may heighten, intensify and extend it. He may give organization and direction to the action adopted by the discontented. But the real discontent is produced largely by the conditions. Without the conditions his agitation would spring forth stillborn. What the reactionaries of this country need to do is to deport the unspeakable conditions under which the people are living. (Randolph 1917 2.8: 2)

Despite the sporting approach, the editors are disciplined thinkers, wanting to deport systems, not people. And it will be these same systems that carry the blame for trouble, not the agitators who confront the system with its truth. As King will write from the Birmingham jail: "Actually, we who engage in nonviolent direct action are not the creators of tension. We merely bring to the surface the hidden tension that is already alive. We bring it out in the open where it can be seen and dealt with" (King 1964: 85).

RANDOLPH VS. DU BOIS

As we have seen, much of what Randolph had to say was a direct challenge to the leadership of Du Bois and The Crisis magazine. This was perhaps never so explicit as in Randolph's call for a new kind of leader: "Thus it is obvious that the hope of the Negro lies, first, in the development of Negro leaders with a knowledge of the science of government and economics, scientific history and sociology; and second, in the relegation to the political scrap heap, those leaders whose only qualifications are the desire to lead and the intent to do good" (Randolph 1917 2.7: 18). If this allusion to Du Bois seems veiled, it is made bare only a few pages later. While the "distinguished" Du Bois receives credit for being "courageous, fearless, cool and honest," he is not the knowledgeable leader.

Having dismissed more than a decade of social studies published by Du Bois, the editors do not fault the man so much as the education: "Greek, Latin and classicism were stressed at Harvard. None of the older Negro leaders have had the modern education." In his autobiography, Du Bois will concur with the editors, who go on to say that "political science is new to the old Negro leaders, while the brand taught in the universities is largely mischievous and reactionary" (Randolph 1917 2.7: 27–28). Working their way to a clearer conception of purpose, the editors of The Messenger promote their next issue as "The only Magazine of Scientific Radicalism in the World Published by Negroes." And they state their mission to be "scientific education" (Randolph 1917 2.8: inside front). The implication that neither Du Bois nor his Crisis could be considered scientific was a bold claim, indeed. Faced by a postwar reality that was not proceeding in the direction predicted by Du Bois, the editors of The Messenger declare that their new philosophy is the only reasonable response available. New standards of analysis take Du Bois by surprise. In his autobiography, he confesses that in 1917 he finally got acquainted with Marx.

In 1918, a global structure had emerged from one world war that seemed to make further world war inevitable. Thus, the editors of The Messenger turned with a sense of urgency to analysis of world politics at the "Peace Conference":

> Our subject suggests that the securing of peace is the object of this conference. But, peace is a state arrived at through a process of give and take, carried on, of course, between the victor and the vanquished. . . . This, however, is a conference of the Allied countries and not a peace conference between the belligerents. . . . A "League of White Nations" has been formed to carry on wars, in the future, according to approved rules of humanity.
>
> There must be no more Belgiums. There may be Congo massacres of innocent Africans by Belgians though. There may be Memphis and Waco (Texas) burnings of Negroes. Hush! Don't raise the race issue. (Randolph 1917 2.8: 5)

As the war was fought to secure domination over darker peoples and their lands, a so-called peace is constructed to consolidate that domination. Thus, peace has been defined in terms that will fail to restrain violence along the color line. Under such terms of peace, unnecessary violence is defined as the kind of thing suffered by white allies. This definition of peace is not bound to respect the rights of white losers or black victors. Self-interest, not human interest, is the structure of the new world order:

> Will this conference bring peace and prevent future wars? The answer to this question is: that the same causes that produced the war just ended are latent in the foundations which are being built by the agents of imperialism in this conference. So long as there is a bone before hungry dogs, they will fight over it. So long as there are weaker peoples and undeveloped countries and stronger people and developed countries, those conditions must needs be prolific and productive of wars. If the peace conference does not break up in a war, it will be followed by wars, at no distant date. There are *peace* conferences and *piece* conferences. (Randolph 1917 2.8: 5)

When the editors of The Messenger frame their global interests, two features of nonviolence emerge: first, that there is a difference between peace (arrived at through reciprocal arrangements) and quiet (imposed by a dominant faction); second, that human rights atrocities have domestic manifestations along the color line that deserve attention on a par with international conflicts. Even today, the discipline of peace studies is embedded within a language of international conflict that effectively overlooks important categories of conflict.

If the editors of The Messenger are eager to exploit the errors of Du Bois, retrospect allows us to see how much the new logic in Harlem depends upon principles long affirmed by Du Bois. For Du Bois, wholeness also stood in moral contrast to domination by a part. In criticism of the alleged peace that obtains between developed and undeveloped countries, Randolph throws down another premise already declared by Du Bois—that the black world cannot be treated separately from the white. Our understanding of the black ghetto necessarily leads us to consider forces that exist outside its perimeter. Conditions of the "undeveloped" neighborhood imply a certain type of relationship to neighborhoods that are "developed." Violence is embedded as much in the orderly habits of developed neighborhoods as in the disorder of the undeveloped. The conditions of the former are purchased at the expense of the latter, revealing terms of social order that ever verge upon combustion.

Black soldiers returning home following "the war to save democracy" find themselves confined within familiar structures of peonage and prejudice. "Returning soldiers must put their thinking caps on," advises The Messenger. "For now is the time to use brains, not bullets" (Randolph 1917 2.8: 6). This conceptual model eschews violence, values peace as a process of give and take, and encourages philosophical reconstruction of our ethical theories:

> It was, indeed, regrettable that nationalistic atavism ruled the actions and utterances of the Socialists gathered at Berne. . . . The "bad nation" theory raised its ugly and menacing head to do violence to one of the cornerstones of the Socialist philosopher—the economic interpretation of history. The bad or good nation theory is as untenable and unsound as the bad or good man theory. Internationalists are not interested as to which nation applied the fuse to the international magazine, which all of the nations are responsible for creating, which exploded in 1914 and set the world afire. All of the great powers, capitalist nations, are responsible for this war. . . . The law of mutual repulsion is, presently, ruling national psychologies. When the storm of elemental passion passes, the law of mutual co-operation will raise a new international out of the ashes of this world debacle. (Randolph 1917 2.8: 6)

Unlike the bad-civilization hypothesis that Du Bois had used to counter the good-civilization hypothesis of the Teutonic supremacists, Randolph approaches nations through an economic theory of global structure. The worrisome nature of ideology, however, remains the same. "National psychologies" are still being ruled by "the law of mutual repulsion."

The ideological component of exploitation is a recurring problem for structural analysis. White America is not psychologically organized for equality, said King. White America is self-deluded by race prejudice, said Du Bois. For Randolph, white America and black America share a vast ignorance of class interest. "White and black workers alike, lack intelligent leadership which is responsible to them. Of course, the Socialists answer these requirements, but this the people must be taught; they don't know it. They are still the victims of the prostitute, kept capitalistic press and the subsidized capitalistic schools"(Randolph 1917 2.8: 8). Within the consensus that American psychology is perversely mismanaged, Randolph makes a distinctive contribution. Using his single-minded method of analysis, Randolph criticizes collective consciousness from an economic point of view.

Randolph's economic critique departs from Du Bois very clearly when the focus turns to lynching. What, for Du Bois, had been treated as a phenomenon of race prejudice, Randolph analyzes as an important question for labor. Randolph's approach is announced by the didactic headline "Lynching: Capitalism Its Cause; Socialism Its Cure":

> Today lynching is a practice which is used to foster and to engender race prejudice to prevent the lynchers and the lynched, the white and black workers from organizing on the industrial and voting on the political fields, to protect their labor-power.
>
> Why do I affirm this and how is it done? This brings me to the consideration of capitalism as a cause of lynching.
>
> Now, just a word as to the reason for inquiring into the cause. . . . Because in order to remove the effects of a disease, physical or social, you must first remove the cause. (Randolph 1917 2.8: 9)

The reason for study—to find the removable causes of social disorder—was the same reason given by Du Bois as he approached the black ghetto of Philadelphia. Whereas Du Bois concentrated at the level of color prejudice, this being the removable cause, Randolph sees color prejudice in turn as having a removable cause in class conflict. The remarkable analysis below is so clear in its exposition and so little remarked upon in our literature of today that I think it is important to present at length:

> For clarity of exposition I shall divide the causes into two classes, and I shall treat them in the order of ultimate and immediate or occasional causes.

But, before proceeding to build our structure of the real causes of lynching, we shall do the excavation work by clearing away the debris of alleged fallacious causes.

First, it is maintained by most superficial sociologists that "race prejudice" is the cause of lynching.

But the fallacy of this contention is immediately apparent in view of the fact that out of 3337 persons lynched between 1882 and 1903, there were 1192 white persons.

Leo Frank, Frank Little and Robert Prager, all white men, are instances of recent date.

Second, it is held by some that "rape of white women" is the real cause. Again the argument is untenable when it is known that out of the entire number of persons lynched, during the above-state period, only 34 per cent. can be ascribed to rape as a cause.

Third, still others contend that the "law's delay" is the controlling cause. This also is without force when the fact is known that men have had their day in court—taken out and lynched, despite the fact that they (the accused) were convicted or acquitted. Leo Frank is an instance in proof. Thus much for what are some of the occasions but not the causes for lynching.

We shall now consider the real and positive causes of this national evil.

As to the Meaning of Capitalism

Capitalism is a system under which a small class of private individuals make profits out of the labor of the masses by virtue of their ownership of the machinery and sources of production and exchange. For instance, the railroads of this country are owned by less than 600,000 stockholders who employ more than 3,000,000 persons. The ownership of the railroads by the 600,000 stockholders enables them to make billions of profits out of the labor of the 3,000,000 workers. Now there is the crux of the problem. A business is carried on for profits. Labor is the chief item in the expense of production. It is to the interest of the employer to work the laborer as long hours and to pay as low wages as possible. On the other hand, it is to the interest of the laborer to get as high wages and to work as short hours as possible. Hence, the conflict between the capitalists and the workers. The desire and the power of the owner to make profits from the means of wealth production, which labor must use in order to make wages with which to live, is at the basis of this conflict.

Let us see how it applies to our proposition in question.

We will now review its economic aspects.

During the Civil War one-third of the man-power of the South was killed off. The Civil War resulted in the abolition of property rights in Negroes. Free labor was abolished. For 250 years the slave-owning class had the right, sanctioned by the government, to use the Negro as a horse, a machine. And the invention of the cotton gin had forced the market value of the slaves up. Huge fortunes had been made and the slave-owners had lived in luxury, ease, comfort and splendor off the labor of Negroes.

This crop-lien system is profitable to the white bankers of the South. Both white and black farmers are fleeced by this financial system. But white and black farmers won't combine against a common foe on account of race prejudice. Race antagonism, then, is profitable to those who own the farms, the mills, the railroads and the banks. This economic arrangement in the South is the fundamental cause of race prejudice, which is the fuse which causes the magazine of capitalism to explode into race conflicts—lynchings.

Prejudice is the chief weapon in the South which enables the capitalists to exploit both races. (Randolph 1917 2.8: 9–10)

Speaking about systematic features of capitalism, Randolph will grant that black workers are more exploited than white, but his analysis proposes that working classes of both races share a common class interest. Because the class consciousness of white and black workers is damaged by lynching, ruling groups will not prevent lynching, because it is in their interest to oversee a divided, psychologically mangled, working class.

Whereas Du Bois accentuated the differences between white poverty and black poverty, Randolph analyzes common causes. Nevertheless, when it comes to proposing a hypothesis of struggle, Randolph follows Du Bois in articulating a specific program for African Americans: "The reconstruction program for the Negro must involve the introduction of the new social order—a democratic order in which human rights are recognized above property rights" (Randolph 1917 2.8, Supp: 3). By the time King is writing his last book, he too will argue that African Americans may be the last hope of the world.

Of the philosophical virtues that accompany analysis of the color line, a prevalent disposition is confirmed with Randolph. Social analysis, regulated by the principle of justice, will be accompanied by strategic proposals. In the May–June issue of 1919 the editors announce that "it is becoming evermore apparent, as an examination of the Negro problem is made, that the solution is economic justice and not economic charity. . . . This is a new era now, and the Negro has done with tips and with charity. His new demand is justice" (Randolph 1917 May–June 1919: 6). Randolph's new social order will overcome "industrial conscription," "peonage," "the company store," and "tenant farming" (Randolph 1917 2.8, Supp: 3–4). "The time is ripe for a great mass movement among Negroes. It ought to assume four distinct forms, viz., labor unions, farmers' protective unions, co-operative business, and socialism" (Randolph 1917 May–June 1919: 8). How do these particular forms work together for Randolph as a complete program for a mass movement? He seeks solidarity among city workers and farm workers alike, cooperative consciousness among merchants and managers, and a socialist approach to political policy. Furthermore, the operative strategy calls for a mass movement.

As the editors of The Messenger exercise their flexible analysis of class conflict in application to perennial features of a capitalist milieu, they do not ignore the farm crisis. Here, as elsewhere, Randolph and co-editor Chandler Owen find signs of the larger struggle for economic democracy. "The recent indictment of A. C. Townley, President of the Farmers' Non-Partisan League, the prohibition of many of the League's meetings, and the general cheap charges of disloyalty, non-patriotism, et al, against the League, reveal that organization to be thoro-going, democratic and useful" (Randolph 1917 2.7: 13). The partisan definition of friend—as one who is known by the enemies he keeps—yields to more class-interested reasons for favoring the agrarian radical:

The city worker is robbed by being overcharged for his flour from the very wheat for which the farmer was underpaid. The city worker is underpaid for making the very overalls and shirts for which the speculators and financial pirates overcharge the farmer. The fight must be made not against the speculator, but the system which produced and perpetuates the speculator. The old order must go. (Randolph 1917 2.7: 13; emphasis in the original)

Here is precedent for King's logic of nonviolence, as Randolph recommends struggle against the *system* of speculation, not against speculators themselves. And The Messenger's explicit concern with agrarian reform reminds us that some dimensions of the logic of nonviolence were not explicitly taken up by King but were left for others, such as the late César Chávez and the ongoing struggle of the United Farm Workers. For specific historical reasons, King was increasingly forced to urbanize his program of reform. In retrospect, we may want to see how rural agrarian conditions are equally challenging and share a mutual interest in the overall quest to reform racist imperialism from within.

IMPERATIVES OF RADICAL THEORY

Having announced their strategy to meet the democratic needs of the age, the editors take stock of prospects for success. Oppression along the color line is acute, especially at the hands of working-class whites. Black radicals will have to rid white workers of their oppressive habits. The radicals will also have to convince black masses that color prejudice is a tool that separates black workers from their white brothers and sisters, and that white workers, too, are kept in a state of delusion by pulpit, press, and school:

Here, the Negro radical's task is doubly huge and difficult. They must educate the radicals to the realization of the fact that capital is ever weaving a net work of lies around Negroes, and, to educate Negroes so that they may understand their class interests. Negroes must learn to differentiate between white capitalists and white workers, as yet they merely see white men against black men. This makes the Negro both a menace to the radicals and the capitalists. For inasmuch as he thinks that all white men are his enemies, he is inclined to direct his hate at white employers as he is to direct it at white workers. (Randolph 1917 May–June 1919, Supp: 20)

Whereas Du Bois would educate whites that there were class differences among African Americans, the better to ease prejudice against the talented tenth, Randolph would educate blacks that there are class differences among whites, the better to end racial hostility against the white proletariat.

A strange involution of projects renders the work of Du Bois quaint for its convolution of talent and aristocracy—for its acquiescence to the diminished value accorded the working masses by the scales of capitalist ideology. The strategy of Du Bois, which would counteract Teutonic arrogance by proving the merit of a black aristocracy, runs the danger of confirming and reinforcing Teutonic arrogance of class. Du Bois senses this himself when he insists that the talented tenth should value public service above private gain. In fact, Du Bois is careful to avoid making white elites any sort of model for black elites. But in his effort to distinguish "the better classes," Du Bois abets an ideology that presumes that class distinction is more a measure of individual talent than of collective conflict.

Du Bois himself had endorsed each item of Randolph's program: unions, cooperatives, and socialism. But only Randolph explicates the connections that make these forms into a complete program for social reconstruction. And this is precisely the sort of logic that is fully employed by King in his later years. True enough, other people had proclaimed truths that were endorsed by King, but few mastered or even attempted the comprehensive vision achieved by King. Thus, it was not without philosophical implications that Randolph introduced King at the 1963 March on Washington as "the moral leader of our nation."

The internationalist approach of The Messenger has been noted for its attention to world peace, but the value of a global approach is also relevant to the struggle for racial equality at home. Half a century before King published his vision of a World House, Randolph was developing a tradition of international analysis:

The international method of dealing with problems is the method
of the future. . . . Almost all democratic problems have been
settled through force of international opinion. . . . Our Civil War
was won by the North, because Karl Marx, the founder of Socialism, and Frederick Douglass, who had more character and intelligence than any of our present day old crowd leaders and other
persons interested in universal democracy, appealed to the public
opinion of England to oppose the system of chattel slavery which
still obtained in the United States. . . . The beneficiary of a system
cannot be relied upon to change that system from which he
receives his benefits. . . . The Negro in the United States cannot
expect much assistance from those who control this government,
because the manufacturers and capitalists whom President Wilson
says are the government of this country, are making huge profits
out of the cheap labor of Negroes. (Randolph 1917 Aug. 1919:
5–6)

Acting again as a corrective to the strategic vagueness of Du Bois'
campaign against racial prejudice, the editors of The Messenger want to
make lynching an international issue. Axiomatic to Randolph is the
thesis that people who share interests in a system cannot be relied
upon to lead reform of that system. If profit in America feeds upon
racism, then forces outside America will be needed to encourage
change.

Domestic pressures can also be applied. Lynching can be opposed
at home by self-defense, and it can be made an international problem if
African Americans are prepared to use the "economic force" of their
labor power (Randolph 1917 Aug. 1919: 8–9). Randolph suggests
that a general strike should be initiated by black workers. This will be
the kind of "argument" that will convince folks of the folly of racial
prejudice. What will be left to say when all African American labor is
withdrawn from its daily contribution? (See Lester Turner Ward's Day
of Absence.) All the polemics of The Crisis and The Messenger together would
not win the world to the African American cause any sooner. Somehow, polemics and theories of moral suasion must be augmented by
powerful programs of action. The logic of nonviolence soars to
imaginative heights!

To prevent race riots, The Messenger encourages self-defense and more African Americans on police forces. But this is a rare kind of piecemeal approach for the editors. To really end race riots, the editors propose a more comprehensive strategy:

> Lastly, revolution must come. By that we mean a complete change in the organization of society. Just as the absence of industrial democracy is productive of riots and race clashes, so the intro- duction of industrial democracy will be the longest step toward removing the cause. When no profits are to be made from race friction, no one will longer be interested in stirring up race prejudice. The quickest way to stop a thing or destroy an insti- tution is to destroy the profitableness of that institution. The capitalist system must go and its going must be hastened by the workers themselves. The capitalists are the beneficiaries of race riots. The same is true of war. The workers entail huge burdens of expense and lose their life and limb. Make wars unprofitable and you make them impossible. This is the task of the workers, white and black, and especially the imperative duty of the white workers by virtue of their numbers, their opportunity and their intelligent class consciousness. (Randolph 1917 Aug. 1919(2.9): 21)

As the editors work their reconstruction upon a system that is understood economically, the call for democracy is translated into economic categories as well. "Industrial democracy" widens the scope of racial struggle beyond the elimination of race prejudice. The point now is to bring into existence an economic order that cannot divide and conquer.

Du Bois developed intuitions along the lines of economic analysis as he explored the role of the talented tenth within the community and researched African economic practices. But Randolph situates the struggle with more specific awareness of classical structural analysis and thus marks a departure from the pioneering social ontology of Du Bois. As reviewer William N. Colson wrote, "It was upon the foundation of liberalism created by Mr. Du Bois' personality that the awakening of 'The New Negro' had its genesis. . . . As some one has said: 'The hope of peace has passed from liberalism to labor' " (Randolph 1917 2.4–2.5: 11).

BUNCHE'S WORLD VIEW

If this book were about Du Bois or Randolph, there would be much more to tell. But the purpose of this chapter is to gather only that necessary evidence from each thinker to construct a concept of structure that may be situated within its African American genesis and so illuminated that we may better understand the concept as it comes to be developed by King. We are done, then, with Du Bois and Randolph. How might we summarize our results with respect to structure in an African American tradition? There is another thinker who provides the necessary summation. Thus, we turn to Ralph J. Bunche and *A World View of Race* (1936).

Classical structural theory since Marx has been keenly interested in the impact that capitalism has upon class relations. And the classical model has always emphasized the international common interests that workers share in their conflict with capital's owners. But the classical model did not sustain any systematic consideration of the role that would also be played by race. In the hands of European theorists, the decisive conflicts were between nations and classes; race and ethnicity deserved no further note. With Du Bois, however, the color line was no secondary phenomenon—it was *the problem* of the century. And we have seen how Du Bois centered his project upon the elimination of racial prejudice. But the great race–class question cannot be posed until Marx meets Du Bois, or until Randolph makes it impossible to talk of race prejudice in isolation from class conflict. Racial prejudice, like jingoistic patriotism, turns out to be a great aid to the further exploitation of labor. In the work of Ralph Johnson Bunche, the theoretical turmoil of the race–class question is put into its most harmonious form.

Ralph Johnson Bunche is one of America's invisible people. Who remembers that he was the first black American to win the Nobel Peace Prize for his work in the Middle East? How often is he cited in our various discussions of racism? Yet, Bunche provides a classic synthesis of thought about the problem of racism. And it will be no surprise to learn that this distinguished diplomat, who devoted his energies to the United Nations, was a committed internationalist. *A World View of Race* is dedicated to the proposition that national distinctions and racial distinctions can only hamper our human quest to be free. For Bunche, there was one great global battle between the exploiting and the exploited before which all other distinctions fade. Thus, with Bunche, we have a complex theory of global economics that incorporates the dimension of racism. And this is an achievement for theory. But racism loses much of its distinctive character under the piercing analysis of Bunche, and, in the end, King will not accept such rationalism.

It is the internationalist commitment of Bunche that defines his theoretical strength and illustrates an ideological weakness. There is great wisdom in the observation that the world is a field divided only by the difference between exploiters and their victims. We can learn much from such a theory. But Bunche also declared his beliefs long before the spectacle of national liberation began redrawing the world map. During the nationalistic struggles, the concept of nation was given a liberating function previously thought to be impossible from a rationalistic point of view. For international peace to thrive, national identities must be subordinated—this much is true. But colonialism had set conditions for nationhood that could best be contested upon nationalistic grounds. Throughout Africa, Asia, and South America, liberation was organized on the premise of national self-determination.

Ultimately, there is reason to agree with Bunche that international order is not entirely consistent with nationalistic forms of identity. But the provisional flux of liberation suggests that identities are socialized at a complex national level and that these identities cannot be homogenized by rational rulings. Even as King articulated a great dream of integration, he addressed a divided audience. As much as it may be true that some mathematical equivalent joins black workers to white in a global crisis of exploitation, the lived experience of the structure of racist imperialism demonstrates that some workers must unite along nationalistic lines if they are to gain any ground at all. A quest for coalitions between black workers and white labor is one thing, but to refuse to recognize where black workers are is a kind of rationalism that even King's integration cannot accept.

As Bunche approaches the global problem of the color line, he begins with a philosophical overview. On what grounds might one raise the question of race in the first place? What warrant grants the right to search the world for racial justice? For Bunche, the terms of quest may be found in the language of enlightenment:

> The concept of human equality and the doctrine of natural rights were cradled in the modern Western World. These ideals embodied the political promise of the future; indeed, they formed the warp and woof of most modern political institutions. There was no limit to the promise which such doctrines held forth to peoples and classes which had been abused and oppressed for centuries. The "civilized" West of the nineteenth and twentieth centuries became a great testing ground for those principles which were counted upon to free the great masses of people from suffering and bondage.
>
> In the practical history of our modern world however, the ideal doctrine of the "equality of man," (along with most of its ideals), has fallen upon hard times. True, we continue to pay lip service to the "sacred" concept of the "natural rights of man" and its international corollary, the "rights of peoples." But the dominant peoples and powerful nations usually discover that such concepts cut sharply across their own economic and political interests. So, with those favored groups, who know well how to use them for their own profit, such doctrines come to assume a strange role. (Bunche 1936: 1)

For Bunche, a grim new phase of struggle has emerged because the force of old concepts has waned. Equality is no longer honored by ever new practical applications. In the long struggle between rising aspirations and settled interests, the doctrine of equality has been hired into the service of favored groups.

True enough, the concepts of enlightenment were hardly deployed with universal purity over the centuries; nevertheless, a certain language was developed to legitimize and extend the historical institutions that emerged. And it seemed in retrospect that human rights had served a helpful function. Now speaking from an American perspective in the grip of Jim Crow and depression, Bunche examines the prospect for further progress. The concept of equality seems to have fallen under the control of entrenched and favored classes:

It is convenient for them to be able to preach this conventional idealism and humanitarianism while practicing at the same time economic and political exploitation. However, it was the doctrine of human equality which formed the theoretical foundation for the revolutions which released the American middle class from English tyranny and the French bourgeoisie from feudalism. Orators, text-books and state papers in present-day Europe and America still faintly echo the equalitarian concepts of Locke, Rousseau and Jefferson. But the vital issues involved in the practices of our contemporary political and economic life more and more imply the inequality of peoples. One of the rocks on which the noble philosophy of human equality has run afoul takes shape as the frightful bogey, *race*. No other subject can so well illustrate the insincerity of our doctrines of human equality and the great disparity between our political theory and our social practice as that of race. (Bunche 1936: 1–2)

The problem of race, then, becomes the best example for showing how far social practice will admit the influence of political theory. Upon the question of the color line, political theory becomes strangely useless. Whatever equality ever meant, surely it never meant race.

If we can grasp the insincerity of racism for a democratic milieu, and the persistence of its rationalizations as decades pile up, we will be equipped to understand the predicament of social ontology as we find it. To begin with the hardened cases first, supremacist practitioners are very often quite bold in their abandonment of liberal principles. Their tastes are more classically aristocratic, preferring a sense of human nature that is from the outset determined by innate or meritorious hierarchies. From this point of view, the rhetoric of democratic equality was always more effusive than real—the better to clear such tender veils from the eyes and look upon the world with the kind of vigor meant for ruling minds:

The ruling classes among the dominant peoples of the Western World find it expedient, therefore, to hark back beyond Locke, Rousseau and Jefferson to the more limited and comforting philosophy of "equality" advanced by the Greek philosopher Aristotle:—"some men are born to serve and some to rule."

In a world such as ours some such creed of inequality is both inevitable and indispensable. For it furnishes a rational justification for our coveted doctrines of blind nationalism, imperialism and the cruel exploitation of millions of our fellow-men. How else can our treatment of the so-called "inferior races" and "backward peoples" be explained and rationalized? (Bunche 1936: 2)

As Du Bois had observed in 1899, our professions of democratic revolution only serve to hide how much we believe in differences among people. An honest self-awareness would quickly show us how far we have yet to reconstruct our assumptions of human nature.

As Randolph observed time and again, the premise of individual difference is a valuable rationalization to those interests that continue to dominate laboring masses. Bunche wants to make the further point that racial prejudice is a superlative example of the kind of group prejudice that is rationalized by inequality:

The fundamental assumption upon which the modern theory of inequality is based is that of obvious "difference" among groups of people. This apparent difference has been developed into an elaborate theory of race. Our rulers, our men of action, have found in this theory a device which well serves their purposes of domination and exploitation. The theory of race, endowed with a false dignity by pseudo-scientific treatment, thus serves to justify economic policies, to bolster up political ambitions, to foment class prejudices and many other types of social antagonism among both groups and nations. In this way the concept of race plays an increasingly dominant role in the political and economic affairs of our modern world. In large measure, however, it is the product in the first instance of wishful thinking, and in the second instance of blind passion and willful, pseudo-scientific distortion. On close inspection these passionate, dogmatic theories of race and human inequality, which are employed to support political and economic motives in many parts of the world, are exposed as shameless subterfuges thriving on ignorance and hysteria.

That is why it is impossible to understand the issues of modern world politics interpreted merely in simple terms of nations or domestic politics interpreted solely as groups engaged in economic and political competition. Race itself has become an effective instrument of national politics. A careful analysis of the role played by race affords us an important clue to world affairs. Fortunately there is a body of scientific knowledge on the subject of race which can be profitably explored. With this knowledge in hand we can more readily understand the true implications of the role played by race in the bitter political and economic conflicts besetting the world in which we live. This is the task to which we now proceed. (Bunche 1936: 3)

Bunche issues the customary warning against pseudoscience and its supremacist interests—a warning that will be repeated by King and that has not yet lost its relevance. Bunche, however, like King after him, can do more than polemicize against supremacist ideology, because there is already available to scholarship an alternative body of literature.

Fewer than four decades after The Philadelphia Negro, a new generation can review "a body of scientific knowledge on the subject of race." Under these circumstances, Bunche does not have to begin gathering the "basis of facts" in the way Du Bois began. And here the unfairness of Randolph's attack upon Du Bois is evident. Science is a cumbersome process of interlocking contributions. Neither Randolph nor Bunche would have been able to soar to their theoretical heights had it not been for meticulous foundations of fact supplied by Du Boisian documentarians. By the mid-thirties, in the wake of a New Negro and a Harlem Renaissance, Bunche may proceed upon the achievements of a scientific community already enriched by fact and theory. He may, therefore, after succinct examination, report that "existing racial divisions are *arbitrary, subjective and devoid of scientific meaning*" (Bunche 1936: 7). Bunche makes it clear that race is an arbitrary trait, interpreted and deployed by powerful interests. Bunche hovers near the further inference that all such divisions are equally arbitrary, subjective, and self-interested.

When race loses its scientific standing as on objective classification, and is shown to be an arbitrary weapon of group prejudice, the social questions of race are redefined. Instead of asking what in the nature of darker people destines such a group for slavery, peonage, or menial labor, one asks what in the structure of class conflict works to suppress the African American and subvert her class interests:

> One significant deduction that can be made from knowledge of these modified theories of race is the tremendous importance of environmental and social conditions for the individual or the group. The inherent ability of any individual or group is dependent for its realization and expression upon the presence of proper conditions for its cultivation. Thus social, economic and political systems, by determining the financial resources, educational and all other opportunities in the society, are intimately tied up with the physical and psychological character which the individual or group will develop. And *social race* becomes as important a factor as *physical race* or biological heredity. (Bunche 1936: 13)

The supremacist, however, prefers to play dumb to social environment, and appeals, dogmatically, to the biological determinism of genes or the cultural inheritance of poverty. The popular school of social Darwinism exploits the genetic doctrine of biology in order to prevent scientific investigation of socially perpetuated inequalities. Bunche grapples with these virulent doctrines as global crisis deepens into the gulch of a new world war.

The emerging scientific view is challenged, under pressure of emerging technologies, to transform racial phenomena into terms that more accurately reflect the salient features of modern structures of power: "*Group antagonisms are social, political and economic conflicts, not racial, though they are frequently given a racial label and seek a racial justification*" (Bunche 1936: 23). "Modern races may have no scientific validity, the term 'race' may even be pseudo-scientific, but 'racial problems' are ever with us," because

> race is a social concept which can be and is employed effectively to rouse and rationalize emotions; because race, having no scientific definition, is sufficiently flexible in its social meaning to make it an admirable device for the cultivation of group prejudices.
>
> The true historical explanation is that the conquering peoples constituted themselves the ruling class and relegated the con-

quered group to an inferior status. Thus race became a badge of social superiority, and in time the dominant race assumed for itself qualities of moral, intellectual and political superiority, as well as economic privilege. (Bunche 1936: 25–26)

Although there is no biological or intellectual inferiority between races, there is social inequality, and social inequality is caused by oppressive features of political economy, not by inherent characteristics of any sort.

A peculiar complexity of group prejudice—as Du Bois suggested—is that the violence that perpetrates social inferiority often succeeds in subduing even the idea of equality:

So long as the dominated race passively accept their lower status in the society, there prevails a sort of benevolent racial prejudice in the form of paternalism, and racial conflict will not become acute. In every such society there are a number of forces at work encouraging the group under the heel to submit without active protest. For example, historically, organized religion has often encouraged the subject peoples to accept humiliating and under-privileged status by preaching the necessity of obedience and the acceptance of things as they are, while holding forth the promise of better things in the life to come. Unquestionably, the Negro Church is responsible, to a considerable degree, for the much advertised docility of the American Negro. (Bunche 1936: 26)

As King complained, there are "structured forces" within the African American community that are obstacles to empowerment. And, as Bunche explained, we can expect such patterns wherever "a benevolent racial prejudice in the form of paternalism" prevails.

What will later become known as "the culture of poverty" is thus much illuminated as Bunche continues his analysis:

The determination of the dominant racial groups to maintain their "superior" status, expressed in race prejudice, keeps the minority racial groups from attaining political, social and economic equality. The process works in a vicious circle. The prejudice of the dominant group is rationalized on the basis of "inferiority" or backwardness of the minority or weaker peoples. The resulting racial or "color line" which usually assumes the form of segregation, severely restricts the social opportunities of the "inferior" peoples, makes it impossible for them to attain the fuller life, or to rise above their "inferior" status, and thereby emphasizes and perpetuates the consciousness of difference between the groups. Such attitudes are usually group attitudes. (Bunche 1936: 27)

As Du Bois asked, is not segregation both a cause and effect of color prejudice? Group prejudice and group oppression, with their flexible rationalizations, become reflexive habits of social life, contributing to a cycle of oppression among the dominant, docility among the dominated.

Thirty years before King announced his plea for guaranteed income or employment, we find Bunche confirming that principle, which was already implicit in Randolph's socialism:

When society makes it no longer necessary to compete for jobs and economic status in order to earn daily bread; and when society guarantees economic security to all peoples, regardless of race, color, or cultural affinity, then alone will the chief source of group conflict be removed. It will not be so easy then to employ the device of race to stir up emotions in support of false economic and political policies, for the basic "drive" of prejudice will no longer be present. (Bunche 1936: 32)

King does not credit Bunche, nor does Bunche credit Randolph, and yet there is a common conceptual model of struggle emerging from the theories of these thinkers.

One of the chores that must be tended with each of the thinkers of the Heroic Age of American Philosophy is to show how racism and inequality define the rules of social process, not the exceptions yet. As Bunche says, "Such violent flare-ups as race riots and lynchings are not mere isolated cases of bad group relationships, but stem from the widespread oppression of one group by another through legal and illegal means" (Bunche 1936: 35). Furthermore, there is a common observation among many thinkers that resistance by black

America offers what little hope the world has for a revolutionary vanguard:

> The Negro race is the most oppressed of all racial groups and appears to be best able to resist and survive racial persecution. Consequently, the result of the struggle of the Negro race for emancipation from inferior economic and political status will do much to determine the future nature and extent of race prejudice and conflict throughout the world. (Bunche 1936: 36)

As Randolph exhorted black America to introduce democracy into global economics, Bunche suggests that black America might have a great role in reducing the twin evils of racism and violence. This brings us close to the end of our historical investigations about structure, because we are nearly to the point where we can assert to have demonstrated a concrete concept and history underlying King's term *racist imperialism* and its triple evils of poverty, racism, and war.

As Bunche notes, "Modern imperialism has given added impetus to the tendency to classify human peoples as 'superior' and 'inferior' for race has been a convenient device for the imperialist" (Bunche 1936: 38). Describing the behaviors of imperialism around the world, Bunche articulates a litany that differs from that of Du Bois and Randolph only in the choice of examples, not in the quality or character of the deeds. Africa is "raped" in the name of "Christian religion" and "advanced European culture"; Ethiopia receives such "blessings" as "brutal suppression" and "greedy economic exploitation"; in the end, "approximately one-third of the human race is directly subject to imperial domination" (Bunche 1936: 38–39):

> Imperialism is an international expression of capitalism. The rapid growth and expansion resulting from the development of industrialism and capitalism led the peoples of industrial countries to seek raw materials and new markets all over the world. This led to more general group contact, and because of the base motives of imperialism, to more widespread racial conflict. The invasion of a territory by a more powerful race results not only in racial conflict but makes more difficult the struggle for existence of the

weaker race. In addition the culture and social structure of the latter race tend to be disorganized. (Bunche 1936: 40)

Writing a veritable preface to Walter Rodney's classic How Europe Underdeveloped Capitalism, Bunche concentrates on imperialism's role in Africa:

By what devices is Africa governed? In the history of the contact of Europe with the African two extremes of policy have been applied to him. The one, based entirely on greed, regarded him as the essentially inferior, sub-human, without soul, and fit only for slavery. The other, based entirely on sentiment, regarded him as a man and brother, extended to him the equalitarian principles of the French Revolution and attempted to "Europeanize" him overnight. Both desired to get as much from him as possible. Both were unscientific and devoted little attention to the needs and the desires of the African. (Bunche 1936: 46)

"Will it be good for him?"—a Texas prison guard muses upon the question in a short story by Du Bois, "Jesus Christ in Texas." Will the labor of the prison yard be good for the prisoner? The question is unfathomable to all enforcers of inequality. "Will it be good for them?" This is the one question never asked as imperialist structure manipulates menial labor.

What hope, then, can be offered for those who do not get what's good for them? Bunche is not easily optimistic:

The plain fact is that the contemporary international order, characterized by its capitalist-imperialist organization, has no possibility of effectively controlling the destiny of such peoples and areas. For the international order cannot override the existing vested capitalist interests which muster the forces of the state for their protection. As the world is now organized, these interests cannot be overcome for they are intimately tied up with the class-relation of capitalist society. The same forces which protect them are the exact forces which protect and promote the interests of the capitalist within the capitalist state to which he claims allegiance. Just as the capitalist state in its internal affairs maintains a legal and constitutional system designed to protect absentee ownership and safeguard those property rights which make the capitalist supreme, just so, in the realm of external affairs, the state's authority, by the very nature of his relationship to it, must be employed to impose that type of supremacy over other peoples. (Bunche 1936: 64)

As it was axiomatic with Randolph, those who benefit from a system cannot be relied upon to change that system. But Randolph had assumed that international pressure could supersede national interests. Bunche observes that the further away one goes for help, the more one finds that class antagonisms have already arrived, leaving workers of the world in desperate disarray.

If the people who profit from a system are bound to protect it, and if, in any case, radical analysis holds systems more responsible than individuals, what remedy remains available to revolutionary hope?

It is only when this supremacy and privilege are dissolved and when it is no longer within the power of the privileged property-holding class to determine the institutional life and habits of the modern state, that there can be hope for the development of an international order and community which will promise the subject peoples of the world genuine relief from the heavy colonial burdens of imperialist domination. At the present their outlook is not bright: the international order and their race are both arrayed against them. (Bunche 1936: 64)

Revolutionary theory confronts the fact that the oppressed themselves cannot be taken for granted as allies for reconstruction. Thus, who can be optimistic about the chances for structural relief? In this quandary, Bunche returns to the liberal Du Bois:

Du Bois attacked [Booker T.] Washington vigorously, but not on the basis of the fallacies inherent in Washington's economic philosophy, nor on his intense and misleading racialism, but on the grounds that he was compromising with the Southern whites and the Northern industrialists in the struggle for political and civil equality. The same attitudes are generally typical of the Negro

organizations engaged today in the fight for Negro liberation—
the NAACP, the Urban League, the Negro Business League, and
others. They all turn a deaf ear to contentions that the plight of
the Negro business man or the Negro worker in this country is
inevitably and inextricably tied up with the plight of the white
business man or the white worker; that race merely determines
the intensity of the problem of the members of the race, not the
quality. (Bunche 1936: 83)

The world view of race, therefore, takes the intense experience of the
color line and scientifically reconstructs from it the quality of class
conflict. For Bunche, the race–class question revolves around the
distinction between intensity and quality.

Du Bois observed that the intensity of race prejudice can be most
keenly sensed from the perspective of the black elite. This is where a
pure and arbitrary intensity of feeling divides class interest and
separates black from white out of no other reason than one's skin-
color heritage. But the quality of black oppression is not shared
equally among black masses and elites. If elites concentrate on the
intense phenomenon, at the expense of qualitative analysis, they
actually play into the interests of racist imperialism. By emphasizing
what's important to black elites, one evades the question of what's
important for black masses. So long as one evades the question of the
masses, imperialism rests unchallenged. One can work on color
prejudice and never leave the confines of the middle class. To work on
poverty, hunger, and day-to-day police brutality, however, requires a
revolutionary orientation. "The truth is that the mere solution of the
so-called 'race problem' would still leave unsolved about all of the
fundamental problems affecting the disadvantaged Negro. It may well
be asked how much better off would the Negro be if it were possible
for him to throw off his racial identity and suddenly turn white"
(Bunche 1936: 85). The talented tenth could get along quite well in
a world without color prejudice. The masses, if still masses in quality,
will have less reason for enthusiasm.

The Negro turned white would be entitled to the ballot also. But
it may well be doubted that this would mean much to him in an

age when democracy with all of its fussy trappings is being universally debunked and discredited. Paper rights and political privileges have not protected millions of the white population from abject wage-slavery, if indeed they can find the chance to sell themselves into it; they have carried the ballot to the bread lines. Social equality has not offered many opportunities for the white hunky to marry himself out of poverty. (Bunche 1936: 85–86)

Because Bunche does not want to be misunderstood, he concludes: "One of the latest and soundest views of the American race problem, and, for that matter, the race problem throughout the world, regards it, then, as merely one aspect of the class struggle" (Bunche 1936: 89).

KING AND THE RACE–CLASS QUESTION

With Bunche's conclusion, the dialectic of the race–class question has been flung from the concept of racial prejudice to the concept of class struggle. Within this supple realm one may stake out the actual contours of King's structural analysis. Certainly, class conflict is emerging into view against the background of racial prejudice. Nevertheless, King's text is saturated with racial categories. There is a "Negro Dilemma" at hand and a "White Backlash." While white America is addressed and analyzed, black America is advised on its choice of future allies. King is moving into the class conflict from a racial base. He has a foot firmly in each mode of analysis.

The problem of the century is the problem of the color line, said Du Bois. What he meant is both easy and difficult to say. In the easy sense, Du Bois was talking about terrorism, exploitation, and poverty deployed against populations of color the world over. In the more difficult sense, he wanted to say that among the causes of these events there was one common removable cause: color prejudice. Randolph observed that among the causes of color prejudice itself was the removable cause of capitalism. Later, Bunche argued that the color line of the century is one among many global manifestations of imperialist oppression.

Du Bois, in time, declared for the Communist Party and removed himself to Africa. The scholar–militant, who, half a century earlier, had begun researching African forms of economy, moved to Ghana. As Plato once moved to Syracuse, or Marx to London, Du Bois moved to Ghana, the better to encourage a righteous order among men. Meanwhile, from Atlanta, King was confronting the jailers of Georgia and Alabama, learning the lessons that would bring him from civil rights to economic rights. *Where Do We Go from Here: Chaos or Community?* is largely concerned with this transition. As the demonstrators at Birmingham and Selma had dramatized *race* conflict, next time King would have them dramatize the terror of *class* conflict. But there was not to be a next time. A "racially motivated" assassination protected America from its most shattering self-realizations.

As we will see in the next chapter, King was confident that African Americans had "forged their own tactical theory of nonviolent direct action" and that this tactic "had proved to be the most effective generator of change" for the civil rights movement (King 1967: 17, 18). The challenging work of the future would turn nonviolent direct action toward a movement for economic rights. If nonviolent direct action was to have importance outside the American South it would have to prove its worth elsewhere.

Yet, in much of his last book, King offers a defense of nonviolent direct action still attached to the terms of the race movement. Again, King's last monograph takes a pluralistic approach, moving into a language of economic struggle but never dismissing terms of racial justice. The shooting of James Meredith, in fact, entrenches the language of race. And much of King's last monograph is concerned with the phenomenon of Black Power, which was born in the immediate aftermath of Meredith's wounds. How does one overcome *racial* terror in Mississippi? This great Faulknerian theme was taken up as the central problem of the Meredith shooting.

In the heat of the march there was agreement that the civil rights movement must move forward, that Meredith's shooting had created an opportunity to escalate the racial focus of the civil rights struggle. There was general agreement that the end in view was more black power. The famous disagreement between factions of the Meredith march centered around questions of means. Black Power challenged the tactic of nonviolent direct action, and demanded that the movement become more racially separate, more nationalist. Thus, the shooting of Meredith was all the additional evidence needed to prove that the victories of the civil rights campaign had intolerable limitations. No one could call the civil rights movement a success. What was wrong? At the time of the shooting, King recalls offering many conjectures; meanwhile, his Black Power opponents had conjectures of their own.

The Black Power movement said the civil rights revolution was not concerned enough about the black masses because the civil rights movement was not black enough. The movement must be black only, the better to deal with race, and it must reject nonviolence, the better to confront the violence of racist imperialism. Having accepted the reigning terms of definition for the civil rights movement, Black Power strategists wanted to concentrate on race with renewed vengeance. King was largely responsible for setting the terms of the civil rights movement, and the Black Power debate was evidence of the strategic limitations of a civil rights struggle in an imperialist milieu.

During the Black Power debates of the Meredith march, King still accepted many of the race-struggle assumptions. One year later, King came to a more considered evaluation: "One unfortunate thing about Black Power is that it gives priority to race precisely at a time when the impact of automation and other forces have made the economic question fundamental for blacks and whites alike" (King 1967: 49–50). To overcome the recalcitrant effects of racial prejudice one would have to theorize the race question along with the question of class. "In this context a slogan 'Power for Poor People' would be much more appropriate than the slogan 'Black Power' " (King 1967: 50). King was not arguing for integration as an "integrationist" who simply supposes that it is wholesome for little black boys to be able to hold hands with little white girls—and, if it happens, the sky won't fall. [Rather, King argues for integration as a means to coerce a greater sharing of opportunities from an imperialist structure.]

The call for integration as an antidote to imperialism is a conscientious choice, based upon structural analysis that affirms that racism is a counterpart of economic exploitation. Economic exploitation may be said to thrive upon systems of collective self-interest, whereas integration can only thrive in a milieu of collective common interest. The philosophical challenge for King is to systematically recast structures of collective self-interest into structures of collective common interest. The method of nonviolent direct action is distinctive for the radical priority it places upon such structural reform.

If it is mathematically correct to talk about the declining significance of race, it is also politically naive. Perhaps it is true that, insofar as black masses are concerned, problems are less and less to be cured by erasing color prejudice and more effectively solved by eliminating poverty and unemployment. But it is politically naive to separate black poverty and unemployment from color prejudice.

And yet it is important to issue a warning to theorists who would dismiss nationalistic struggle on the grounds that utopia must be international. King never repudiated Black Power in such an outright fashion; rather, he understood how such movements are sincere responses to the persistence of a color line. King even allowed that such nationalistic alliances had positive merit and could be modeled, for instance, upon Jewish examples. Nationalism, however, tilts in the direction of essentialism, and thus toward inevitable violence. When the principle of exclusion becomes a preoccupation, magnified more by bitterness than by shrewd experience, then dogmatism has triumphed over intelligent strategy, and one is left flailing at paranoid projections, no longer capable of liberating a really miserable world.

Once again, the recent work of Cornel West develops a delicate balance along Kingian lines. When West speaks of progressive nationalism, he encourages reflection upon the values and limitations of shared contours of struggle. On the one hand, black Americans may share a collective experience that informs precious dimensions of identity and struggle. But as soon as these shared resources are constructed in exclusive terms, problems begin. White observers are usually quite sensitive to the implications of black nationalism, and thus miss the legitimate context of such leanings. The Farrakhan question comes up only long enough to detect the edge of exclusion, and this detour enables all to avoid the task of confronting the legitimate concerns that underlie his base of support.

Thus, the very quick dismissal of Farrakhan only feeds the frustration among African Americans that nobody really wants to listen. Is it exclusion as a principle that white America fears, or is it exclusion when practiced by blacks? Given the history of white America and its pundits, it is difficult to imagine that white critics honestly fear the principle of exclusion in itself. Farrakhan thus becomes the victim of a double standard, and for that reason he is defended. If ever criticisms of Farrakhan were to go hand in hand with acknowledgment of ongoing exclusions on the white side of the fence, then we could all concentrate on the issues of progressive nationalism—how identities both black and white can serve as foundations for democratic renewal. To pretend, however, that Farrakhan is the worst we've ever seen is to ignore the very message that makes Farrakhan most instructive. Who in white America has never been to dinner with a bigot? Archie Bunker we can love. Only Farrakhan is worthy of our hate. Instead of demonizing Farrakhan, the logic of nonviolence compels us to recast the field of analysis so that responsibility is widely shared. One must see clearly how, since 1968, conditions in black America have in many respects actually *gotten worse*.

One last question remains as we turn from the work of Du Bois, Randolph, and Bunche. The early King shared with these thinkers an optimism that words like *equality* could encourage change so long as the hypocrisy of popular usage could be exposed. But in the end, King saw that hypocrisy was not a single phenomenon of doing one thing and saying another. After all, think about it, hypocrisy can result from either enthusiastic ignorance or a studied pose. In the case of enthusiastic ignorance, the "inadvertent" hypocrite can be transformed through a process of reflection. The enthusiasm of the ideal can be applied to the ignorance of practice. A person who truly values equality can see that certain behavior is not consistent. But another kind of hypocrisy takes hold when the pose of equality becomes a mask for the deeply seated conviction that equality will not work. And this is the kind of hypocrisy that especially exasperated King in his last years. If justice cannot be pursued, it can be redefined—perhaps even to the point where justice is measured by the advancement of already favored classes.

In a proliferation of neo-isms, intellectual terrain was widely reconfigured in the aftermath of King's assassination. Underpinning the new discontent was a crush of disappointment and embarrassment concerning sixties-style ideals. That the pursuit of such ideals would always be life-risking was built into King's theory of nonviolence, because King understood what made structure real. In the post-King era, thought has been variously engaged in escape from King's conclusions. Perhaps there is a way to simply think our way into a new world order without confrontation or cost. Perhaps there is a way to use violence so that the other side does all the dying. Or, finally, perhaps there is a way to say that the present world order is not all that bad, leaving us a few decades to relax and reap the profits of the land. Yet, one full generation later, the legacy of the King era comes back to haunt. In the post-structural era one desperately wishes that change could cost less, that cleverness were enough to outwit the order of things, that nonviolence might be relative. In the end, however, the real work must somehow spill into the streets where favored interests do not stand idle. At moments such as these, not only does King's philosophy invoke aspirations of equality against structures of violence, but King also stands ready with a tonic of love. As paradoxical as this prescription seems, it is the best answer that King can muster for a torment that cannot be wished away.

Chapter 4

———•———

NONVIOLENT DIRECT ACTION

The war against war is going to be no holiday excursion or camping party.

—WILLIAM JAMES

HOWARD THURMAN AND THE ETHICS OF LOVE

Without a doubt, King pursued action—nonviolent direct action. Images from the King years recall a great turbulence. Movement in those days was a noun to be reckoned with. Yet, King seemed never quite swept away. Somehow, through the rush and the push of events, King maintained a reflective composure. With persistent faith, against pummeling opposition, King held to his idealist conviction that mind could give form to matter. Certainly, King's idealism knew disappointment, surprise, discouragement, and terror. But in the face of all these realities, King also affirmed a kind of higher law that sheltered hope, love, and choice. Against structures of injustice, but never discounting their force, King mounted confrontations. And to tell the truth about it, from King's point of view, profound activism had deep roots in systematic inquiry—or philosophy, if you will. Action thus takes higher meaning and value in relation to intelligent ethical reflection. When it comes to justice, there is nothing so brutish as pure action, nothing more pitiful than pure thought.

Working from the perspective of his Christian heritage, King built a theory of action upon principles suggested by the great mystic scholar Howard Thurman. For Thurman, the example of Jesus indicated how one could begin to order a world of chaos, moving outward from individual personality. The integrity of this inner order could then be pressed into service, confronting the world with truth and love. As we shall see, Thurman found in the life of Jesus an example of prophetic existence. After all, Jesus was a Jew who was nurtured by Jewish traditions. The Jewish prophetic tradition exemplified personal integrity in the face of social decadence—a great refusal, if you will. As Thurman and King drew upon their Christian heritage, each avoided Christian chauvinism. Both had reverence for reverence, but never insisted that the only authentic reverence was Christian.

King had much in common with Thurman. Both were Southern-born, educated at Morehouse College, and chose the ministry as vocations. Thurman had journeyed to India, where he met with Gandhi. A torch of nonviolence thus passed directly through Thurman's hands. As fellow clergymen, Thurman and King shared concerns for social conditions sometimes thought to be outside the purview of religion. Thurman brought the torment of headlines inside his church, where a healing spirit might visit and bring peace. In the aftermath of the murder of Emmet Till, for instance, he declared in church, "There is a higher law than Mississippi's." He was an innovator in forms of worship, and for a time he ministered to an experimental, racially pluralistic congregation in San Francisco, under the auspices of the Fellowship of Reconciliation.

Clearly, King's philosophy of action does not end with Thurman's invitation to truth-telling, courage, or love, but these principles provided ethical criteria. The art of action that King developed would strive to insinuate these ordering principles into collective manifestations that would also shrewdly transform brute structures of injustice. Thus, the ends and means of justice were not to be separated, even under conditions of desperate struggle. After two chapters of explication on the concept of structure, the reader is not likely to forget the kind of practical challenge that defined King's world. Structural reform of America's social relations would be real work upon obdurate material, and it would assume warlike commitments in terms of organization and resources. These facts must not be forgotten, because they could never be forgotten by King. When King talked of truth, courage, and love, it was always from within the momentous challenge of the movement, not from outside. He carried Thurman's book during the Montgomery bus boycott, but not for the sake of dispassionate disquisitions. For King, Thurman's book was a handbook for survival.

In addition to taking up the well-known ethical principles of nonviolence, and the street actions that take shape, this chapter seeks to explicate the ways in which King was seeking a general logic of liberation that posited methods, aspects, contexts, and strategic aims for nonviolent liberation. Here the logic of nonviolence dwells upon general classifications that would help guide strategic discussion and thought. Just as the classification of general branches of knowledge has been a millennial preoccupation among philosophers, we may say that King was working to classify branches of liberation. The mass action program, central to the logic of nonviolence, is situated in four dimensions of context. The first dimension speaks to an ethical context regulated by courage, truth-telling, and love. The second dimension places direct action within a four-step process of inquiry and activity that aims at structural confrontation and reform. These first dimensions are well-known contributions. Not so well known, however, are two other dimensions of context that King is just beginning to develop in his last monograph.

What is the relationship between direct action and education? What purpose do cultural activities serve in a process of liberation? In his last monograph, King opens a very important inquiry by proposing a six-faceted classification of liberation activity. As with the pluralism of King's structural account, we shall find also a pluralism of social activities that may serve the complex needs of a struggling community. To speak intelligently of these issues is difficult work, but crucial to liberation. As King's pluralism in other areas avoids crippling dichotomies of thought, so does his conceptualization of various aspects of struggle serve to mediate between various clusters of talent. The classroom is placed in relation, not in opposition, to the street. Likewise with other aspects of struggle. Nonviolent movements demand a context of healthy nurture that must be provided by struggling communities. King is serious about his efforts to make the most of various energies that thrive in a multidimensional community. One dimensional struggle is no answer worthy of life.

Moreover, King was also beginning to outline a tripartite approach to power. Speaking of ideology, economy, and politics, King was not evading the challenge to amass black power. In fact, King was trying to survey reliable roads. This book is insufficiently long to offer a complete elaboration of these potential levers, but it is important to show how King sketched the outlines of his complete system. The logic of nonviolence does not end with metaphysical defenses of first principles, but rather also suggests a research project for systematic analysis. And this feature of King's logic of nonviolence remains remarkably unnoticed by critics and defenders alike. Here King may yet lend influence to theory and to scholarship.

In this chapter we shall see how King continued to develop the concept of direct action during his later years. But, more than this, we shall also see how King's concept of action is necessary to his theory of justice, because, in an ever imperfect world of human arrangements, justice is revealed in struggle. True, King valued action because it was effective, and he was developing new concepts of action in order to become more effective, but King was seeking a particular kind of effectiveness that exemplified a rigorous theory of justice. Thus, King's concept of action leads to his concept of justice, and this chapter's examination of action prepares the way for considering justice as a final term of importance for King. Whatever fellow citizens might want from one another, common nationhood implies a relationship that should be enhanced, not diminished. Thus, for King's logic of nonviolence, justice and action were terms that had to remain interconnected if community, not chaos, was to animate human affairs.

King's last monograph is one more philosophical attempt on his part to develop the concept of action within a systematic framework. As with King's earlier writings, we find in his last monograph a four-step process that guides the ethical use of direct action. Writing about Operation Breadbasket, King sketches the general method that regulates his nonviolent approach to action. First, information is gathered, then goals are formulated, and then negotiations are undertaken for the purpose of social reconstruction. Only when initial negotiations fail does one resort to some form of nonviolent direct action, in order to speed negotiations to a fruitful conclusion. In the case of Operation Breadbasket, then directed by Jesse Jackson, black churches worked to secure jobs from companies that made profits from black consumers. But the general method was also the same one used by King in his more famous campaigns.

Although the drama of direct action leaves impressions of demonstrations as ends in themselves, King's practice of nonviolence always contextualized direct action within a framework of deliberative democracy. These are well-known features of King's nonviolence that are commonly taught in nonviolence workshops. Yet, the popular conception of King's nonviolence does not usually grasp the ethical analytical process that gives shape to the street protest. Thus the power of nonviolence is widely assessed without attention to the contextualizing groundwork. If King gets credit for leading great protests, he is less appreciated for the intelligence with which he chose the grounds, timing, means, or issues that the protest would address. Along the way, King was always in the process of developing a general theory that would guide these considerations toward justice. In Montgomery, King was thrust into leadership of a movement that he did not start. But in Birmingham and Selma, King was more or less master of the events and their respective agendas.

If conceptual groundwork is important to nonviolent action, then our review of the concept of structure has not been a diversion. The genius of nonviolent direct action is made most apparent only when we appreciate how the tactics of a particular movement have been chosen in response to critical analysis of the structural problems at hand. The boycott of Montgomery's buses was an action that would bankrupt the bus company. The action was chosen to pressure a structure of segregation at its vulnerable point. Although King did not initiate that boycott, his leadership provided a systematic direction that we now call his logic of nonviolence. Later, he would develop that philosophy further in various struggles against other problems of injustice in the South. In Birmingham, King's leadership helped demolish the structure of Jim Crow segregation. In Selma, voting rolls were opened. These campaigns seemed to vindicate the hope that nonviolence could not know defeat. In both cases, targets were strategically chosen in consideration of revolutionary structural change. And in both cases, King operated within a general theory aimed toward justice. In Chicago, however, King met new difficulties.

Without turning this book into a superfluous account of history, the paragraph above is meant only to remind the reader that the art of nonviolence amounts to much more than the ability to organize street demonstrations. The why, the where, and the when of such demonstrations is most brilliant when—as with King—the issues are framed for maximum reconstruction of social arrangements. Here the genius of King or Gandhi is widely missed. At the conclusion of Gandhi's famous march to the sea in 1930—when he stood on the beach and sprinkled a few grains of salt between his fingers—the genius of the moment cannot be divorced from a strenuous structural analysis. How does such a gesture instigate the collapse of an entire colonial system? Not without keen analysis. Likewise, when Gandhi invented modern-day nonviolence in South Africa, the fact that he first marched with a column of coal miners in 1913 is crucial to the philosophical importance of the event. The challenge for nonviolence in the coming millennium is just this sort of challenge. What should be the precise points of confrontation, and why should those be considered as paramount?

In the last years of King's life, nonviolence was losing its tenuous hold on the American imagination. By summer's end in 1968, one could only gaze bewildered at the crises and rebellions that ruptured domestic tranquillity. There were culture wars, as well, being fought on college campuses that would transform the curriculum of higher education. Power, ethnicity, and gender would begin to emerge as essential themes of cultural postmodernism. At first, many of these movements eschewed nonviolence as a discredited and defeated reformism. Even for the antiwar movement, there were "good guns and bad people." Meanwhile, in macroeconomic terms, a heated and hopeful boom during the postwar period in the United States gradually cooled into the calculated cynicism of 1980s lifeboat ethics. Realism—that loaded term—was deployed in the service of individual interests, and the baby boom was soon giving way to the "me" generation.

If these social and political changes have undermined the viability of King's philosophy of nonviolence, then I hope to show that the predicament is not inescapable. By reviewing King's theory of nonviolent direct action, I hope to show that it is sufficiently flexible to bridge differences in the environments one might encounter. In other words, King's philosophy of nonviolent action provides a critical method for social change, applicable to ongoing global inequities, even if difficult to apply. Moreover, I want to suggest that King's attention to process is one mark of his distinguished contribution to the development of social and political philosophy. If it is a commonplace to recognize the increased importance of process-oriented conceptions, then I encourage reflection on King's philosophy of nonviolence, because King has something to teach us about justice as a human process of struggle.

The purpose of this chapter, then, is to set out King's systematic defense of nonviolent direct action and to situate the process within its ethical context as a disciplined quest for justice. Already presumed by the following arguments are two points hopefully demonstrated in previous chapters: that equality is a worthy pursuit and that structures of inequality pervade our social environment. Given these premises, some kind of confrontation is needed. As inequality was found to limit self-esteem and respect among citizens, so the pursuit of equality shall be regulated by a quest for fellowship and reciprocity. As material questions of equality are pursued with vigor, it shall not be forgotten that wider issues of community are at stake. Reminders of this wider purpose shall in fact be raised by those who place themselves at greatest risk. In this context, "we shall overcome" does not mean that we shall sing our way to victory, nor does it mean that we shall overcome *you*. Rather, it means that we shall confront structures of inequality with our bodies, and we shall overcome injustice. In other words, it signifies the process of seeking out justice through action.

What in the world is one to do, given a dream of equality and the reality of inequality as we find it under conditions of so-called industrial democracy? King's answer is coherent and comprehensive, yet admits its experimental foundations. To maximize the minimum, or minimize the maximum, in an algebra-like calculation of human relationships is King's prescription for hell. To repeat the decent claim that one always respects others, and treat the pronouncement itself as justice well done, is King's definition of sentimental liberalism. To vote one's pocketbook is to enthrone profit and practical materialism. To call for one big movement ignores the delicate logic of coalitions. Power without reciprocity yields not peace, but quiet. To act without analysis or to analyze without action—neither remedy will satisfy the complex requirements of justice. In a fragmented world of specialties and special interests, corrupted by the opulence and oppression of a status quo, King's conception of justice is insistently holistic, persistently active, and inviolably social. In sum, we find in King's logic of action a systematic and state-of-the-art articulation of what justice means.

JESUS AS ETHICAL MODEL

As we search for a context that may help us to understand the moral and ethical discipline of King's nonviolent method, this chapter introduces Thurman's classic work, Jesus and the Disinherited, first delivered as a series of lectures in 1948 at Huston College (now Huston–Tillotson College) in Austin, Texas. In the book, Thurman seeks to explicate the ethical insights of the Jewish prophets, as interpreted through the life of Jesus. The ethical example of Jesus continues to have relevance for people who find themselves backed up against the wall. How ought impoverished ethnic or religious minorities respond to the material and spiritual assaults of imperial oppression? The example of Jesus suggests a response of courage, truth telling, and love. The value of such an ethic resides in its ability to restore psychological and spiritual order within a milieu of ethical chaos. As I argued in the introduction to this study, there can be no doubt that King was familiar with Thurman's thesis, almost immediately upon its publication, some five years before King put the book into his briefcase during the Montgomery bus boycott. This is one borrowing that the editors of the King papers do not specifically identify.

As we listen to Thurman's exposition of the life of Jesus, it will be important to remember that his words are not chosen for a sermon but for a college lecture. Thus, it is still possible to emphasize the secular development of these concepts in order to demonstrate King's engagement with contemporary categories of social and political philosophy. Even in reference to Jesus, I will show how the significance of the example may be articulated almost completely in terms of ethics. Moreover, the defense of nonviolence that King offers in his last book is addressed to secular audiences—Black Power advocates and white liberals alike.

As the concept of nonviolent direct action unfolds before us, we will see how it plays a crucial role in King's philosophy of nonviolence. We will see especially how nonviolent direct action satisfies a need to assert psychological health and ethical values within a milieu of racist imperialism. As we have see, injustice is more than a material arrangement. Questions of spiritual disorder cannot be ignored. Material maldistributions result in real spiritual consequences that in turn present real problems for struggling people. Somehow this spiritual malaise must be directly addressed. Hence, it is important to establish a foundation of psychological health. It is also important to King that ethical questions be raised in forthright confrontation to unethical practices. By attending to these concerns, the logic of nonviolent direct action challenges complex assumptions about ideology and class structure. Truth is asserted where false consciousness was thought to prevail. Power is organized by forces assumed to be powerless. And long nights of struggle are fortified by the strength of love.

Of war, it has been said that its techniques are simple, yet its goals are difficult to achieve. With nonviolence, similarly, elegant theory confronts immense challenges of fact. In the Chicago campaign of 1966, fact had three faces: Mayor Richard Daley, the glacial solidarity of white neighborhoods, and the revolutionary expectations aroused by the movement that King led. When King called off a culminating march to Cicero, Illinois, and accepted Mayor Daley's document for fair housing, he thereby shattered the credibility of nonviolence altogether. In the face of unified white hostility, nonviolence had marched to its Rubicon but did not cross. As vindicated as King may have felt by the agreement with Daley, as worried as he may have been about the human cost in violence that would have been extracted in

Cicero, or as impressed as he was with the support he was gaining among marchers, all his accomplishments as the master practitioner of nonviolence were quickly dismissed as outdated in the aftermath of the Chicago campaign. From his own point of view, the campaign had been halted in time to save lives and establish a beachhead for further struggle. From the point of view of his Chicago supporters, however, nonviolence had proved its irrelevance.

What King's supporters in Chicago wanted was victory the old-fashioned way. Just in the way that the Birmingham campaign had broken the back of Southern segregation, King's supporters wanted to bust an entrance into white, middle-class neighborhoods in the North. By marching on Cicero—the city where Al Capone lived, but Ralph Bunche could not—Northern blacks might assert the vitality of nonviolence. But King blinked. In Birmingham, King had also been criticized for calling off the action in exchange for a promise to desegregate in sixty days. Yet, in Birmingham King was on home soil, compared to Chicago, and the force of his authority stood on a more stable foundation. While James Foreman could walk away from Birmingham in disgust at the outcome, history would ultimately declare that campaign a brilliant victory. In Chicago, it was like Foreman all over again, but this time history also walked out on King.

Something else was revealed in Chicago that defined the limits of the civil rights age. Whereas the Southern campaigns had aroused white sympathies for black participation in public life—at downtown lunch counters or voting booths—there was no reserve of sympathy to be tapped when the Chicago campaign moved the issue next door. In the end, the sacred nature of white neighborhoods was an idol that even King was too horrified to confront. And this specter, which haunted King's last days, also hastened his strategy in the direction of finding issues that white America could embrace. A Poor People's Campaign could perhaps help white people to see that the struggles of black America were only human.

If the controversy between Black Power and King "is not yet resolved" at the writing of his last monograph, "it is also true," argues King, "that no new alternatives to nonviolence within the movement have found viable expression" (King 1967: 18). In his argument with Black Power, King asserts that nonviolence is a powerful tool that Black

Power cannot surpass. Massive nonviolent direct action, argues King, is a tactic that has the rare power to confront the structure of racist imperialism. Black Power, he argues further, is little more than a slogan when compared to the comprehensive plan of struggle that may be deployed in conjunction with nonviolent direct action (King 1967: 31).

In his dialogue over Black Power, King stipulates many points of agreement, noting obvious limits to what the civil rights movement achieved. But King also warns that, in a moment of bitter disappointment, certain real achievements should not be overlooked. With full acknowledgment of structural challenges that remain, King encourages hope based upon tentative new developments. If the nonviolence movement was thrown into confusion by backlash, King was still able to assert that "excessive despair and dissipation of fighting strength have not occurred" (King 1967: 18).

Despite the rejection of nonviolence by Black Power advocates, King predicted that "there will certainly be new expressions of nonviolent direct action on an enlarged scale" (King 1967: 20). On the other hand, said King, "it cannot be taken for granted that Negroes will adhere to nonviolence under any and all conditions" (King 1967: 21). In anticipation of the common query from white liberals who wonder why all black leaders can't be nonviolent—a curious wistfulness, indeed—King warns that stubborn injustice has human consequences. "Nonviolence is a powerful demand for reason and justice. If it is rudely rebuked, it is not transformed into resignation and passivity" (King 1967: 21). It is important to note how King does not issue absolute condemnations when faced with a faction that would reject nonviolence. In this case, King is more intent on condemning the system that resists nonviolent pressure. Although King often declares his own ethical choice as nonviolence, he never presents that choice as a moral imperative that others are bound to follow.

Writing in response to critics who would say that nothing of worth has been accomplished by nonviolence, King sums up achievements that may be credited to the civil rights movement of the King years:

Negroes have irrevocably undermined the foundations of Southern segregation; they have assembled the power through self-

organization and coalition to place their demands on all significant national agendas. And beyond this, they have now accumu-
lated the strength to change the quality and substance of their
demands. From issues of personal dignity they are now advancing
to programs that impinge upon the basic system of social and
economic control. At this level Negro programs go beyond race
and deal with economic inequality wherever it exists. In the
pursuit of these goals, the white poor become involved, and the
potentiality emerges for a powerful new alliance. (King 1967: 17)

For these reasons, King argues that despair is unfounded, despite the
limited gains won and the tragic costs incurred by the civil rights
movement. Moving closer to the point of this chapter, King argues
that the civil rights movement has developed something of lasting
value apart from any considerations of improved conditions. The
movement, in short, has developed a process of social change that
may be fruitfully refined and deployed in pursuit of future goals. King
is talking, of course, about "the tactical theory of nonviolent direct
action" (King 1967: 17).

THE TACTIC DEFENDED

Whereas the tools of legal challenge had engaged the elites of the
NAACP during previous decades of civil rights struggle, nonviolent
direct action could now engage the masses. NAACP officials never
tired of reminding King that a court decision—not a boycott—had
desegregated Montgomery buses. Nevertheless, King could argue that
something spectacular had been revealed in the mass movement of
the Montgomery bus boycott.

King's opening argument for nonviolent direct action is surprising on two counts. To the critics who regard violence as legitimate
under certain circumstances, King argues that nonviolence is admirable for its psychological militancy. Nonviolence is thus an excellent
means of gathering massive anger and frustration, then releasing it
"under discipline to maximum effect." In response to critics who
emphasize the importance of public order, King argues that nonvio-

lence offers the most intelligent means of confronting social disorder. Despite the enormous pressures of Southern segregation, nonviolent direct action "caused no explosions of anger—it instigated no riots" (King 1967: 17). With these opening arguments, King gives form to a collective psychology of militancy, but distinguishes such turbulence from the chaos of riots. No doubt these arguments are surprising to advocates of violence and order alike. King is claiming to meet both criteria in excellent fashion. In the aftermath of disappointment and backlash following the Chicago campaign, however, nonviolent direct action was losing credibility as a militant psychological channel. And friends of order once again found it difficult to see how nonviolence instigated no riots.

If nonviolent direct action was a tool, it was a volatile device. The anger of nonviolent practitioners could grow beyond their strength to love. From this point of view, nonviolence would appear as a means of social control, not social change. Meanwhile, from the point of view of those who seek to maintain orderly social arrangements, the disruptive nature of nonviolence seemed so obvious as to be in need of no further reflection. From this point of view, King always had been a troublemaker. Thus, King was caught between two tightening pincers of criticism. The eruption of Black Power suggested that nonviolence was too tame, while the hostility of white backlash declared that nonviolence caused too much trouble. Amidst this growing pressure from opposite directions, King struggled to defend nonviolence.

As King reviewed the claims he had made for nonviolent direct action over the brief course of his career, he took blame for the naiveté of his representations: "I should have known that in an atmosphere where false promises are daily realities, where deferred dreams are mighty facts, where acts of unpunished violence toward Negroes are a way of life, nonviolence would eventually be seriously questioned" (King 1967: 26). Nonviolent direct action might once have transformed anger into hope, but sustaining such hope depended upon a rational judgment that results had met reasonable expectations. When suffering and disappointment entailed more pain than seemed justified by results, then the rationality of the nonviolence method fell under suspicion.

Not many people could share King's conviction that righteous campaigns invariably produce more pain than they should, that they always bring unmerited suffering to the campaigner, and that such unmerited suffering itself is a kind of price of redemption. Thus, he must reckon with increasing amounts of anger and frustration wherever suffering continues to exceed any "reasonable" perceived gain. As Hanes Walton (1971) charges in his book on King's political philosophy, King does not seem to give any satisfactory answer, apart from religious fundamentals, as to why struggling populations should persist with nonviolent direct action in the face of overwhelming discouragement. Because King's religious outlook seems fatalistic, his critics do not seriously address King's claim that confrontations with injustice are never fair.

King's claim is serious, indeed. When one enters into confrontation with social structures of injustice, one enters a zone of suffering. Under such circumstances, the cost of winning justice is never fair. Perhaps this is ultimately a religious understanding of justice as redemption in a world of sin, but it does not seem inaccessible to a more secular understanding. The pursuit of equality has its history. In a world of structured inequality (as discussed in previous chapters), one ought to know that systems of injustice do not yield to the righteous because of their powers of discernment. In his argument for persistent nonviolence, King is, in part, calculating with tough-minded realism the requirements of a healthy and effective process of structural reform. And it seems to me that King's important claim deserves a hearing. If it is true that confrontations with evil are never waged with impunity, then King accurately anticipates the deep spiritual struggle that must ensue. If one dismisses suffering as avoidable, whether by means that are more or less militant, then all of King's spiritual philosophy turns to rhetorical embellishment.

Consider the difference between the surface of a mirror and the shine of its gilded frame—one of these regions makes the reflection of struggle possible, the other makes a gilded ornament at the edges. And it is this kind of difference that separates King's ethic of love from the theories of his secular critics. Because of King's claim that suffering is inescapable—if you fight evil, you will pay!—a spiritual depth is forced upon King's nonviolence. Considerations of love become necessary preparations. For his secular critics, however, who evade the premise of suffering, talk about love is fine decoration for a nonviolent method. In this difference, the truly religious question emerges. What, indeed, are the foundations of courage and hope, what are the attractions of justice that an individual might bring to nonviolent confrontation? In the risk of one's own life, isn't some profound faith asserted? What King establishes as a premise of nonviolence is the reality of inescapable sacrifice. Thus, secular scholars of nonviolent activity may want to address the following question: where has the actual persistence of nonviolence *not* been accompanied by faith?

Granting the truth of King's observation that suffering inevitably comes to all activists and prophets of justice, it may nevertheless be said that King is evading another issue that adds a tragic burden to any nonviolent movement—the recognition that mistakes have been made within the movement itself. Even when it is agreed that some suffering is inevitable in the face of structural forces, it is not easy to live with the admission that some strategic decisions were poorly called. In the wake of Chicago, this is the admission King cannot easily make; therefore, King is unable to directly confront one grave source of tribulation. In some sense, all the movement's suffering and frustration must be explained in terms of racism and injustice, for such movements would entail no suffering, to speak of, if racism and exploitation were not *palpable* forces. But those movements are also put under the double burden of carrying the weight of their own mistakes and their own in-group conflicts. And these are factors that King does not emphasize—perhaps because the self-perceived weight of his own miscalculations is a burden he dare not reveal. But as anyone acquainted with the day-to-day responsibilities of struggle can attest, King is neither the first nor the last activist for whom the weight of personal errors and interpersonal conflicts may become as burdensome as the larger issues themselves.

Considering the additional burden of in-group errors and conflicts that are sure to crop up during campaigns of nonviolence, what lessons might be relevant from King's own philosophy? In this case, it seems that we may strengthen the practical case for King's ethic of love. A violent psychology of bitterness can just as well turn inward as outward. Habituated to hatred, where does a struggling group find its reserves of forgiveness to administer to one another? King generalizes the problem with reference to Black Power's attitude toward whites, but the lesson may go deeper for any group as it moves into realms of struggle that invite suspicions and paranoia:

> I should have been reminded that disappointment produces despair and despair produces bitterness, and that the one thing certain about bitterness is its blindness. Bitterness has not the capacity to make the distinction between some and *all*. When some members of the dominant group, particularly those in power, are racist in attitude and practice, bitterness accuses the whole group. (King 1967: 26)

In sum, King argues that love enhances rationality. This will be true in thoughts about opponents and allies alike. Hatred muddies thought, love provides a clear pool for reflection.

In the heat of struggle, it is a staggering challenge to transform hate into love. Indeed, it is a heroic expectation, but King nevertheless judges that struggling groups owe it to themselves to regulate struggle through love.

King's effort to recover credibility for the logic of nonviolence moves from the psychology of the aggrieved to the ideology of the wider community. Nonviolence, says King, has a rare ability to define issues of conscience. As King would have it, nonviolent direct action invokes public demonstrations of suffering in order to reveal injustice. During such demonstrations, systematic structures of suffering are publicly confronted, the better to expose a common need to place the system under ethical control:

> The cause of a demonstration is the existence of some form of exploitation or oppression that has made it necessary for men of courage and good will to protest the evil. For example, a demonstration against de facto school segregation is based on the awareness that a child's mind is crippled by inadequate educational opportunities. The demonstrator agrees that it is better to suffer publicly for a short time to end the crippling evil of school segregation than to have generation after generation of children suffer in ignorance. (King 1967: 55–56)

The ability to raise ethical questions, assert their priority, and sustain their impact is important, especially in the face of structures famous for their ability to suppress ethical consciousness:

> In such a demonstration the point is made that the schools are inadequate. This is the evil one seeks to dramatize; anything else distracts from that point and interferes with the confrontation of the primary evil. Of course no one wants to suffer and be hurt. But it is more important to get at the cause than to be safe. It is better to shed a little blood from a blow on the head or a rock thrown by an angry mob than to have children by the thousands finishing high school who can only read at a sixth-grade level. (King 1967: 56)

To the prophets of rage, King poses the challenge: how will you engage the ethical? Thus, the discipline of the love ethic, which will occupy more and more of our concern, asserts that one must establish an ethical field of confrontation. Nonviolent direct action can do that, argues King. No other method works so well to pinpoint the fact that a system is evil. Violent tactics may announce that a structure is unbearable, but nonviolent tactics demonstrate the further fact that a structure is wrong. Without nonviolent direct action, there can be no "confrontation of the primary evil." The primary evil is not that segregation is unbearable but that segregation is unjust.

Armed racial struggle in the United States is a doubly faulty strategy, from King's point of view: it not only misses the point of liberation, but it also results in the weakest possible position, even given a militarist's point of view. "Now the plain, inexorable fact is that any attempt of the American Negro to overthrow his oppressor with violence will not work" (King 1967: 56). As long as one defines the enemy as the entire white population of America, one confronts "a well-armed, wealthy majority with a fanatical right wing that would delight in exterminating thousands of black men, women, and children" (King 1967: 57). In the decades since King made his assessment, the fanatical right wing has become even better equipped, with newer and more destructive arms, today augmented by high-tech communications.

Appropriating the terms of the race struggle in order to project the consequences of race war allows King to demonstrate the futility of escalating tensions along racial lines. To threaten whites *per se*, under contemporary conditions, is to conjure up an enemy of crushing power. Nor will it be helpful to recruit allies from the world's darker majority. "There is no colored nation, including China, that now shows even the potential of leading a violent revolution of color in any international proportions" (King 1967: 57). A race-hardened Black Power movement accentuates its isolation, then dares to entertain, literally, violent war with white America? This is an invitation to genocide at home, from which black America cannot expect to be saved by allies abroad. In the riots of 1965 and 1966, King sees confirmation of the futility of violent outbursts:

> There is something painfully sad about a riot. One sees screaming youngsters and angry adults fighting hopelessly and aimlessly against impossible odds. Deep down within them you perceive a longing for self-destruction, a suicidal longing. Occasionally Negroes contend that the 1965 Watts riot and the other riots in various cities represented effective civil rights action. But those who express this view always end up with stumbling words when asked what concrete gains have been made as a result. (King 1967: 57)

King finds no evidence that rioting has won "any concrete improvement such as have the organized protest demonstrations" (King 1967: 58). About the chances for overthrowing the government, King is positively fatalistic; armed forces of the United States will not be pried apart from their government:

> No internal revolution has ever succeeded in overthrowing a government by violence unless that government had already lost the allegiance and effective control of its armed forces. Anyone in his right mind knows that this will not happen in the United States. In a violent racial situation, the power structure has the local police, the state troopers, the national guard and finally the army to call on, all of which are predominantly white. (King 1967: 59)

Furthermore, writes King, any violent revolutionary minority, needs the support and sympathy of the passive majority. "It is perfectly clear that a violent revolution on the part of American blacks would find no sympathy and support from the white population and very little from the majority of Negroes themselves" (King 1967: 59). The very terms of a Black Power revolution in America relegate its prospects to a permanent shambles.

Having outlined the strategic, ethical, and psychological weaknesses of Black Power, King elaborates upon the importance of the ethical. For King, violence makes a poor appeal to conscience, and conscience is essential—not irrelevant—to social revolution, because "power and morality must go together, implementing, fulfilling and ennobling each other. In the quest for power I cannot by-pass the concern for morality" (King 1967: 59). In a remarkable reference to Anglo-Saxon history, King quotes Alfred the Great: " 'Power is never good unless he who has it is good' " (King 1967: 59). Nonviolent direct action offers a superior appeal to conscience because, among other things, nonviolent direct action refuses to accept violence as necessary to causes or persons. Thus, a righteous social change is already under way within the nonviolence movement. Already there is a change to nonviolent leadership. As Reinhold Niebuhr observed in concurrence with Du Bois, in our violence-riddled world we find masses maliciously equipped to rationalize brutal oppression as civilized progress. So long as such rationalizations rule public opinion, there will be no real overcoming to speak of, for black or white. Thus, nonviolent direct action "can save the white man as well as the Negro" (King 1967: 59).

BREAKING THE CYCLE OF FEAR

Still reeling from the bitterness of another kind of adversary—the kind he met in Chicago's white, ethnic neighborhoods—King returns to considerations of psychology—not the psychology of enraged victims but of fearful oppressors. King insists that white America suffers from a culture of fear:

Racial segregation is buttressed by such irrational fears as loss of preferred economic privilege, altered social status, intermarriage and adjustment to new situations. Through sleepless nights and haggard days numerous white people struggle pitifully to combat these fears. But how futile are all these remedies! Instead of eliminating fear, they instill deeper and more pathological fears. The white man, through his own efforts, through education and goodwill, through searching his conscience and through confronting the fact of integration, must do a great deal to free himself of these paralyzing fears. But to master fear he must also depend on the spirit the Negro generates toward him. Only through our adherence to nonviolence—which also means love in its strong and commanding sense—will the fear in the white community be mitigated. (King 1967: 59–60)

With attention to dynamics of psychology and power, nonviolent movements may employ love and shrewdness to break an oppressive cycle of fear. King defers to the words of James Baldwin, who, in an open letter to his nephew declares, "that we, with love, shall force our brothers to see themselves as they are, to cease fleeing from reality and begin to change it" (King 1967: 61).

Although King's arguments concern the specific problem of race relations in America, his advice offers insight into the general logic of nonviolence. The cycle of fear that drives the pistons of prejudice can only be reversed by those who know how to use power "creatively and not for revenge" (King 1967: 60):

The problem with hatred and violence is that they intensify the fears of the white majority, and leave them less ashamed of their prejudices toward Negroes. In the guilt and confusion confronting our society, violence only adds to the chaos. It deepens the brutality of the oppressor and increases the bitterness of the oppressed. Violence is the antithesis of creativity and wholeness. It destroys community and makes brotherhood impossible. (King 1967: 61)

Thus, the cycle of fear is a chaos to be calmed by a greater sense of fellowship or brotherhood—nothing less will suffice. As philosophy compels us to know ourselves, nonviolence would coerce others into knowing themselves as our fellow citizens. The knowledge of fellowship is not easy to produce, nor is the patience for this sort of revolution easy to muster; nevertheless, King insists upon it.

For King, fellowship, or empathy with one's opponent, must remain a living goal. For tactical reasons, this maxim is especially important in domestic conflicts. The American Civil War teaches us that internal wars do not easily heal over. Whereas one might well argue that a foreign invader can be beaten back in self-defense, one is not easily rid of enemies at home. Although King may allude to the ghetto as a domestic colony, he does not think the metaphor suggests lines of actual nationalistic conflict parallel to the case of a foreign invader, and he discourages Black Power also from pursuing such a line of reasoning. "The American Negro will be living tomorrow with the very people against whom he is struggling today" (King 1967: 62).

King's arguments for nonviolence stand at various rungs on a kind of ladder that ranges from material calculations to spiritual speculations. At the lower rungs of debate, King proves that nonviolence alone is feasible from a practical, even militarist, point of view. But these arguments do not exhaust the concept. With a Manichaean flourish, King illuminates a struggle for moral excellence in which nonviolence alone strives for true light. "Returning violence for violence multiplies violence, adding deeper darkness to a night already devoid of stars. Darkness cannot drive out darkness: only light can do that. Hate cannot drive out hate: only love can do that" (King 1967: 63). Thus, "the beauty of nonviolence is that in its own way and in its own time it seeks to break the chain reaction of evil" (King 1967: 63). This "majestic sense of spiritual power" adds moral excellence to the practical soundness of nonviolence; therefore, says King, "I will continue to follow the method" (King 1967: 63). And he pledges to argue for nonviolent direct action even if "every Negro in the United States turns to violence" (King 1967: 63).

Stepping down from the heights of his spiritual vision, King lingers with his doubts about the revolutionary validity of violence. His own investigation of structure reveals an addiction to violence that more violence can only feed. Nonviolence thus becomes a calculation of moral and scientific shrewdness. By exposing the violence of social inequality, one achieves precious moral high ground in a desperate war of conscience. By embracing terms of violent empowerment, one legitimates the very means of one's own subjugation. Reasoning from a shrewd consideration of the nature of structure, King concludes that violence is not revolutionary. "One of the greatest paradoxes of the Black Power movement is that it talks unceasingly about not imitating the values of white society, but in advocating violence it is imitating the worst, the most brutal and the most uncivilized value of American life" (King 1967: 64). Could there be racist imperialism without violence? Doesn't white America, in fact, fear its relinquishment of violence? How is more violence going to overcome what is most distinctively oppressive about white power? The Black Power flirtation with violence, by fueling white America's cycle of fear, can only aggravate the cycle of violence as it is internalized within the black ghetto. Rather than direct violence toward whites, King would channel "understandable anger" into the "healthy way" offered by "nonviolence" (King 1967: 64).

By now we have focused on some observations that enable us to understand why hatred is a temptation that King will not permit as policy. Following the advice of father and grandmother, echoed in the writings of Booker T. Washington, King will not stoop so low as to hate anyone, nor will anyone make him stoop to hate. These traditional hand-me-downs of folk wisdom again speak to deep concerns about psychological health. "Hate is just as injurious to the hater as it is to the hated. Like an unchecked cancer, hate corrodes the personality and eats away its vital unity" (King 1967: 64). Having witnessed the ugliness of hatred in the segregated South, King is loathe "to advise the Negro to sink to this miserable level" (King 1967: 65). Would we have the African American vanguard behaving like southern sheriffs with their dogs?

> Of course, you may say, this is not practical; life is a matter of getting even, of hitting back, of dog eat dog. Maybe in some distant Utopia, you say, that idea will work, but not in the hard, cold world in which we live. My only answer is that mankind has followed the so-called practical way for a long time now, and it

has led inexorably to deeper confusion and chaos. Time is cluttered with the wreckage of individuals and communities that surrendered to hatred and violence. For the salvation of our nation and the salvation of mankind, we must follow another way. This does not mean that we abandon our militant efforts. With every ounce of our energy we must continue to rid our nation of the incubus of racial injustice. But we need not in the process relinquish our privilege and obligation to love. (King 1967: 65)

King embraces a revolutionary challenge "to work out new concepts" and "set afoot a new man"; therefore, he is not willing "to imitate old concepts of violence" (King 1967: 66). "Violence has been the inseparable twin of materialism," in both its capitalist and communist forms (King 1967: 66):

Humanity is waiting for something other than blind imitation of the past. If we want truly to advance a step further, if we want to turn over a new leaf and really set a new man afoot, we must begin to turn mankind away from the long and desolate night of violence. May it not be that the new man the world needs is the nonviolent man? Longfellow said, "In this world a man must either be an anvil or a hammer." We must be hammers shaping a new society rather than anvils molded by the old. This not only will make us new men, but will give us a new kind of power. It will not be Lord Acton's image of power that tends to corrupt or absolute power that corrupts absolutely. It will be power infused with love and justice, that will change dark yesterdays into bright tomorrows, and lift us from the fatigue of despair to the buoyancy of hope. A dark, desperate, confused and sin-sick world waits for this new kind of man and this new kind of power. (King 1967: 66)

In a flourish of references to white European and American sources, King invites Black Power advocates to reach beyond white, Euro-American conceptions of violence and power in their thinking.

What King said to black America is the sort of advice most readily repeated today by white voices. But King spoke to white America. Especially after Chicago, King encouraged reflection on the prevalence of white racism, in order to see how "the white man's problem" may be understood as the origin of "the Negro problem" (King 1967: 67). And King insisted that racism had economic dimensions. "Since the institution of slavery was so important to the economic development of America, it had a profound impact in shaping the social-political-legal structure of the nation" (King 1967: 72). For economic reasons, "Black men, the creators of wealth of the New World, were stripped of all human and civil rights" (King 1967: 72). The cycle of fear that characterizes white psychology begins with the slave trade. Seeking to understand "the Negro problem," we are confronted with "the white man's problem," which in turn becomes the problem of rationalizing "a profitable system." Of this dynamic we have perhaps said enough.

Stipulating that white America is still structured upon the lie of racism, King judges two alternatives impossible: violent rebellion or passive waiting. Between these extremes is the possibility of "persistent pressure and agitation" (King 1967: 90). If white Americans sincerely want change, then King insists they also must be prepared for the tensions that will accompany reform:

> Nonviolent coercion always brings tension to the surface. This tension, however, must not be seen as destructive. There is a kind of tension that is both healthy and necessary for growth. Society needs nonviolent gadflies to bring its tensions into the open and force its citizens to confront the ugliness of their prejudices and the tragedy of their racism. (King 1967: 91)

King reminds the white liberal who accuses the nonviolent militant of creating "hatred and hostility" that these "hidden tensions" are already alive (King 1967: 91):

> Through the skills and discipline of direct action we reveal that there is a dangerous cancer of hatred and racism in our society. We did not cause the cancer; we merely exposed it. Only through this kind of exposure will the cancer ever be cured. The committed white liberal must see the need for powerful antidotes to combat the disease of racism. (King 1967: 91)

As King concludes his survey of white power, he reminds us: "The issue is injustice and immorality" (King 1967: 94). It is now time for King to address the "powerful antidotes" that will be needed.

SIX ASPECTS OF NONVIOLENT STRUGGLE

Following his general defense of nonviolent direct action, and having addressed its implications for black and white audiences, King situates the role of direct action into a broader process of liberation. As with previous writings, King's last monograph speaks of the nonviolent campaign as a four-step process of collecting information, formulating goals, negotiating for social reconstruction, and then taking action if negotiations need some spur to fruitful conclusion. Strictly speaking, direct action is the fourth step of this process. But in his last monograph, King makes it clear that nonviolent campaigns themselves must also be contextualized within a broader process of social change. It is still true for King that direct action should be preceded by systematic preparation, but he also wants to argue that such campaigns must also be embedded in a social process that prepares the ground and cultivates the seedlings of nonviolent efforts. Thus, campaigns of nonviolence, with their skillful use of direct action, can force laws onto the books, but without further direction, implementation may be spiritless and episodic. Furthermore, preparations for a nonviolent campaign presuppose social conditions that must be systematically nurtured for maximum empowerment.

In sum, King says that nonviolent campaigns are but one important aspect of struggle, but others are needed. In his systematic way, King outlines six aspects of a complete struggle: (1) "somebodyness," (2) "group identity," (3) "full and constructive use of the freedom we already have," (4) "powerful action programs," (5) "a continuing job of organization," and (6) "giving society a new sense of values" (King 1967: 122, 123, 126, 128, 132). King's analysis proposes a context for nonviolent direct action, which, as part of a dialectic of liberation, includes moments of self realization, group solidarity, personal achievement, mass confrontation, mass organization, and a transvaluation of values. Within this context, we see how nonviolent direct action is an organic element in a complex vision of social change, not an ultimate goal or panacea. I also think this model provides for a pluralistic appreciation of the various talents needed as society strives for justice—after all, we can't *all* be street leaders.

Just as the architecture of King's structural analysis has been crafted in relation to the fairly unyielding facts of social experience, so are his four steps and six aspects of nonviolent reconstruction proposed with experiences of struggle close at hand. It would be one thing to offer a wholly detached prescription, and it would be quite another thing to mutter platitudes about the need for empirical engagement. But, between these extremes of intellectual latitude, King offers general theories that may guide social change. His steps and principles thus reflect a philosophical pursuit of justice under conditions of "industrial democracy." King's theory accumulates lessons from the past in order to guide further inquiry. Here is love of wisdom at work.

As King reconstructed his philosophy of nonviolence in the wake of Chicago, he not only deepened his ontological analysis of the relationship between power and love, but he also worked out a comprehensive strategy for practical empowerment. Popular attention to King's ontological perspective is liable to generate the impression that he responded to new challenges with predictable reflexes—one more exhortation to love our enemies and to turn the other cheek. But it is our image of King that has become dogmatic. Challenged by Black Power and white backlash alike, King conceived an outline for comprehensive nonviolent liberation. This is where the philosophy of nonviolence refreshes its connection to the science of social change. King's six aspects of nonviolent reconstruction provide a means for taking inventory and organizing power along a broad front of struggle. As far as I can tell, this innovation in King's philosophy has been completely overlooked.

As we evaluate the six aspects of struggle proposed by King, two considerations seem especially important. First of all, King presents a specific checklist to test against the ongoing needs of liberation. Secondly, we find a pluralistic logic at work. With a specific checklist in mind, we may survey our resources for liberation to determine strengths or weaknesses. We may also evaluate the checklist itself,

adding or subtracting aspects in keeping with theoretical investigations. By employing a pluralistic logic, we also discourage divisive
thinking among potential allies. For King, each aspect has its distinctive feature, yet every aspect contributes to a comprehensive goal. As
much as possible, King's logic avoids dichotomies that would divide
comprehensive thinking. We have explored the dichotomy that is
often drawn between self-help and protest. Against the temptation to
pick any two aspects of liberation and set them against each other,
King's checklist encourages a vast coalition of talent--some specialized in self-help, others attending to public protest, and so on. In
characteristic fashion, King's six aspects of struggle exemplify a
philosophical approach that would guide practical conduct and provoke critical reflection.

In the first moment of struggle—the aspect of "somebodyness,"
the demoralized citizen overcomes "a disastrous sense of his own
worthlessness"—a "terrible feeling of being less than human" (King
1967: 122). Here King affirms the kind of movement that is emerging
under the slogan "Black is Beautiful." This kind of movement "asserts
for all to hear and see a majestic sense of his worth." Although King
is speaking to a black audience, the words may also be applied to other
aspiring groups in search of nonviolent social change. "We must no
longer allow the outer chains of an oppressive society to shackle our
minds. With courage and fearlessness we must set out daringly to
stabilize our egos. This alone will give us a confirmation of our roots
and a validation of our worth" (King 1967: 122–123). No longer
victim to white categories of identity, the African American is no
longer "duped into purchasing bleaching creams." Through "self-ac-
ceptance and self-appreciation" the black American leads the way
toward "opportunity to participate in the beauty of diversity." To
achieve such "self respect," King recommends courage—"the determination not to be overwhelmed by any object, that power of the
mind capable of sloughing off the thingification of the past" (King
1967: 123). King finds this courage of "somebodyness" abundant
among the traditions of black America; for instance, this is what gives
beauty to the songs of slaves.

In terms of social participation, King here lends worth to the
day-by-day activities of art and education as a broad social platform

for empowerment. Without these contributions in place, nothing happens. Thus, the process of justice does not marginalize cultural spaces. Quite the contrary, King is saying that some activities cannot be separated from the pursuit of happiness. Far from discounting these activities as irrelevant to the heat of social change, King provides foundations and criteria. Classrooms that do not slough off the thingification of the past are indeed fossils of spirit. Likewise with art. But to cultural forms that scratch away at our crusty shells, in search of new room to grow, King's logic of nonviolence gives primary pride of place.

After "somebodyness" King points to the second important step: "to work passionately for group identity" (King 1967: 123). This is the social realization of "somebodyness." The African American not only affirms her worth, but the worth of "his own kind." Despite petty conflicts, she recognizes that black Americans share interests; therefore, they can "unite around common goals" (King 1967: 124). King is not forgetting that many problems of black life are structurally imposed, nor that solutions will require the common energies of black and white. But he understands that black unity will be necessary to remove structural impositions and coerce whites into integration. "This form of group unity can do infinitely more to liberate the Negro than any action of individuals. We have been oppressed as a group and we must overcome that oppression as a group" (King 1967: 125). Struggling communities, including the black community in America, must continue to establish a sense of belonging among individuals who are not welcome on the larger scene. The overwhelming odds against this effort must somehow not deter its persistence. King himself noticed how his own children, when moved into the Chicago ghetto, became strange and uncontrollable to him. Under ghetto conditions, the call for more parental guidance at the individual level is perhaps well intentioned but also ludicrously inadequate as a response. King sent his own children back to Atlanta.

Here the public forms of culture are emphasized that allow common sharing, celebration, and negotiation of group identities. What this means in practice has become a central problem of the post-King era. Mostly the problem is posed by nervous liberals who find themselves increasingly marginalized from such forms of collective ethnic development. In large part, King anticipates this turn of events when he speaks about the unreliability of liberal support in an age that will question traditional cultural privileges enjoyed by liberal elites. He also worries that white America is not undertaking the sort of wholesale cultural revaluation that would be needed to sustain a healthy, new sense of what it means to be white and equal. White pride has ossified in identity movements that are not going to be eager partners in a new social order. In short, the cycle of fear has not been broken. With old, white collective identities disintegrating, special creativity is called forth. A new kind of courage is needed. What does it feel like to affirm one's own collective worth without attitudes of violence or superiority? Not until white liberals solve this problem for themselves will they be able to embrace energetic developments in other collectivities.

Building upon the needs of "somebodyness" and "group identity," there is a third aspect to King's program for nonviolent reconstruction: "We must make full and constructive use of the freedom we already possess" (King 1967: 126). Here King reminds his readers about African Americans who have, despite all external barriers, earned reputations for excellence and achievement. The African American can be somebody—"in spite of our lack of full freedom, we can make a contribution here and now" (King 1967: 127). This is true for stars as well as laborers. "All labor that uplifts humanity has dignity and worth and should be pursued with respect for excellence" (King 1967: 127–128).

With this admonition, King skates on thinnest ice. What does it mean to sweep streets with pride? Here is a sentiment that teeters between the profound and the plainly dangerous. Any other speaker would have some explaining to do. And it is tempting to read in these words a kind of weariness. But I think King's meaning can be reconstructed in a defensible way. He does not know as he writes that he will be called to assist Memphis garbage collectors, but the statement seems a perfect preparation. King does not wish to identify with the commonplace notion that there are some places for excellence and some places that excellence never visits. So, he wants to affirm the dignity of every useful act. The Memphis garbage collectors will wear signs that declare, "I am a man." Nevertheless, when King speaks of making the most of opportunity, he is not saying that everyone should be happy collecting garbage. The economic pressure to keep black America at the level of menial labor is a pressure worth fighting. Here again, King's vision outpaces our usual concepts of reality. And in the end we will be surprised to learn how radical that dream is. How far away we are from the day when the garbage collector comes home to his children and waves to his neighbor the brain surgeon, even as the brain surgeon is carrying his own garbage to the curb.

Having worked his way from individual dignity, to group unity, then to individual opportunities already available, only now does King call upon nonviolent campaigns to confront the collective structure of injustice in the larger oppressive society:

> We will be greatly misled if we feel that the problem will work itself out. Structures of evil do not crumble by passive waiting. If history teaches anything, it is that evil is recalcitrant and deter-mined, and never voluntarily relinquishes its hold short of an almost fanatical resistance. Evil must be attacked by a counteract-ing persistence, by the day-to-day assault of the battering rams of justice. (King 1967: 128)

If King's "third aspect," calling for individual effort within existing opportunities, sounds like the old Tuskegee doctrine, then his "fourth challenge," calling for mass demonstration, subsumes the truth of the former doctrine into a distinctive new whole. "I do not share the notion that Booker T. Washington was an Uncle Tom," says King, "Washington's error was that he underestimated the structures of evil" (King 1967: 129). In a struggle against oppression, individual efforts "pursued with respect for excellence" must be accompanied by collective "battering rams of justice." King picks up a feudal metaphor and swings it against a castle's door.

In this fourth moment of King's nonviolent project—the moment of direct action—a structure of evil is assaulted, and a system is coerced into change. In this moral equivalent of war, King returns to Manichaean metaphors: "In this generation the children of darkness are still shrewder than the children of light" (King 1967: 128). These ancient ontologies, perhaps adapted from the usage of contemporary white supremacists, soon give way, however, to modern techniques of power. Today's children of darkness "spend big money, to disseminate half-truths, to confuse the popular mind," while today's children of light "cautiously wait, patiently pray and timidly act" (King 1967: 128). The children of darkness use their time shrewdly, while the children of light do not. This relationship yields "a double destruction: the destructive violence of the bad people and the destructive silence of the good people" (King 1967: 128).

Prayer may have salutary effects, but one's patience must not rely on a superstitious notion that time, when left to the shrewd use of one's opponents, will miraculously produce some antidote to their effects. Shrewdness must be matched with shrewdness. Time must be seized during moral equivalents of war. Ethical appeals and persuasion will not be sufficient to bring about justice. "This does not mean that ethical appeals must not be made. It simply means that those appeals must be undergirded by some form of constructive social power. If the Negro does not add persistent pressure to his patient plea, he will end up empty-handed" (King 1967: 128–129). Although King has profound faith in the reality of God and the cosmic imperative of justice, they are not sufficient to overcome injustice. "So every ethical appeal to the white man must be accomplished by nonviolent pressure" (King 1967: 129). The lessons of history indicate that oppressed groups must "assume the primary responsibility" of making their citizenship "first class"; this is why "a powerful action program" is necessary (King 1967: 129). "With nonviolent resistance, we need not submit to any wrong, nor need we resort to violence in order to right a wrong" (King 1967: 130).

Furthermore, "the American racial revolution has been a revolution to 'get in' rather than to overthrow. . . . This goal itself indicates that a social change in America must be nonviolent. If one is in search of a better job, it does not help to burn down the factory" (King 1967: 130). Because mass nonviolent action addresses the need of such practical problems, it "will continue to be one of the most effective tactics of the freedom movements" (King 1967: 130). "But mass nonviolent demonstrations will not be enough" (King 1967: 131). As there were three aspects of social empowerment that had to be developed in preparation for nonviolent campaigns, there are two more aspects still in need of development to complete a social revolution. Nonviolent direct action thus confronts the context of structure (abundantly elaborated in earlier chapters), but it also fits into a complex vision of struggle that must be elaborated beyond the dimension of protest activity.

The penultimate aspect of King's nonviolent program is "organization." Such a recommendation is not novel. Douglass, Du Bois, and Randolph understood organization. The women who initiated the Montgomery bus boycott understood organization. With King, however, the role of organization is cast within a systematic logic of struggle. "More and more, the civil rights movement will have to engage in the task of organizing people into permanent groups to protect their interests and produce change in their behalf. This task is tedious, and lacks the drama of demonstrations, but it is necessary for meaningful results" (King 1967: 131). At this level, King is most insistent upon middle-class responsibility. The "haves" must join hands with the "have nots"; it is time for the middle class "to rise up from its stool of indifference, to retreat from its flight into unreality and to bring its full resources—its heart, its mind and its checkbook—to the aid of the less fortunate brother" (King 1967: 132). All of which brings us to the ultimate stage of nonviolent social change—the transvaluation of values.

The "final challenge" of nonviolent social change, then, is "to be ever mindful of enlarging the whole society, and giving it a new sense of values as we seek to solve our particular problem" (King 1967: 132):

> As we work to get rid of the economic strangulation that we face as a result of poverty, we must not overlook the fact that millions of Puerto Ricans, Mexican Americans, Indians and Appalachian whites are also poverty-stricken. Any serious war against poverty must of necessity include them. As we work to end the educational stagnation that we face as a result of inadequate segregated schools, we must not be unmindful of the fact, as Dr. James Conant has said, the whole public school system is using nineteenth-century educational methods in conditions of twentieth-century urbanization. (King 1967: 132–133)

In sum, there are a number of questions that remind us that "a radical restructuring" will be needed. If today's struggle is still organized along the color line by the de facto habits of history, King encourages a search for fresh coalitions. As confrontations reach across newfound lines of common interest, renewed conceptions of society emerge into view as viable ideals. Thus, the quest to widen alliances of struggle may result in a more expansive vision of social possibilities. "For the evils of racism, poverty and militarism to die, a new set of values must be born. Our economy must become more person-centered than property- and profit-centered. Our government must depend more on its moral power than on its military power" (King 1967: 133). Keeping this transvaluation of values in mind is the sixth aspect of King's answer to "The Dilemma of the Negro American."

Within the six aspects of social empowerment, King has provided space for contributions of many kinds. In the final aspect, we find a function for the intellectual. As values are reworked conceptually, scholars also have their work to do. But at this precious and risky level of social enterprise, King acknowledges that a specialized realm exists where the transvaluation of values is paramount to the development of justice. Thus, an ancient heritage of experience is in perpetual need of revaluation as ever new vistas of perspective emerge from the vanguards of experience. As the edges grow, the center moves, too. In this progressive dialectic of human effort, even divine inspirations may be heard anew. But we make no mistake about it—value reconstruction is important work, and it is labor-intensive.

AN EXPERIMENTAL TECHNIQUE

Having laid out a comprehensive method and defense of nonviolent social change, King admits that the tool of nonviolence is in an early stage of development. "Although our actions were bold and crowned with successes, they were substantially improvised and spontaneous" (King 1967: 137). As with any experimental technique, "groping through the wilderness finally must be replaced by a planned, organized and orderly march" (King 1967: 137). King concedes the charge of Black Power that nonviolence has not been shrewd enough: "our creativity and imagination were not employed in learning how to develop power" (King 1967: 137). And so King is ready to propose three "levers of power" that may be engaged through nonviolent techniques: "In our society power sources are sometimes obscure and indistinct. Yet they can always finally be traced to those forces we describe as ideological, economic and political" (King 1967: 138). As if King were not satisfied with the six principles of nonviolence outlined in his first movement book, *Stride toward Freedom*, or the four steps of the nonviolent campaign explicated in his second movement book, *Why We Can't Wait*, or even the six aspects of liberation outlined above, he now turns to the three levers of power.

The first lever of power is ideological, and since we know that racist ideology is supported by a network of deception, King argues that nonviolent protest is eminently able to provide a lever of clarification. As we know, King argues that nonviolent protest has the best chance of cutting through the rationalizations of injustice. In fact, he argues, nonviolent protest already has an outstanding record in this regard. "More white people learned more about the shame of America, and finally faced some aspects of it, during the years of nonviolent protest than during the century before. Nonviolent direct action will continue to be a significant source of power until it is made irrelevant by the presence of justice" (King 1967: 139). If the impact of the King years has been disappointing when compared to the expectations that were raised, those years of the civil rights movement nevertheless stimulated more racial progress than at any other time since the Civil War, and contributed to a decline in some explicit forms of prejudice.

The second lever of power is the economic lever, which African Americans hold as business owners, workers, and consumers. King encourages black capitalism in the spirit that he previously encouraged the full pursuit of opportunities now available. Black business provides "inspiration" and "resources" to develop the African American community (King 1967: 140). If King does not give up his macroeconomic critique of capitalism as a social system, neither does he discount the microeconomic importance of black businesses in an ongoing quest for power. But it is telling to note that King does not linger on this point; rather, he moves quickly to the needs of black labor. For the black worker, King encourages labor solidarity with whites and militant creativity in dealing with the racism of modern industry: "If manifestations of race prejudice were to erupt within an organized plant, it would set in motion many corrective forces" (King 1967: 140). As for consumers, King emphasizes that boycotts may be used as a powerful tool of integration in public accommodations, employment, and financing.

Regarding a nonviolent approach to the third lever, politics, King suggests voter registration, voter turnout, and the election of African American politicians who depend upon a genuine black base of power. "When our movement has partisan political personalities whose unity with their people is unshakable and whose independence is genuine, they will be treated in white political councils with the respect those who embody such powers deserve" (King 1967: 150). In addition, the nonviolence movement must master the art of alliance so that "the new consciousness of strength developed in a decade of stirring agitation can be utilized to channel constructive Negro activity into political life and eliminate the stagnation produced by an outdated and defensive paralysis" (King 1967: 154).

Having sketched a program for the accumulation of power through nonviolence along ideological, economic, and political lines, King returns to the tedious requirements of organization. "We shall have to have people tied together in a long-term relationship instead of evanescent enthusiasts who lose their experience, spirit and unity because they have no mechanism that directs them to new tasks" (King 1967: 159). And just as King's previous discussion of organization highlighted the need for middle-class engagement with issues of the masses, here King insists that organization leaders not become victim to "aloofness and absence of faith in their people" (King 1967: 160).

Poised for a nonviolent push into the future, King at last unveils the specific goal that will provide the organizing impetus for his next campaign—the abolition of poverty:

> This proposal is not a "civil rights" program, in the sense that term is currently used. The program would benefit all the poor, including two-thirds of them who are white. I hope that both Negro and white will act in coalition to effect this change, because

their combined strength will be necessary to overcome the fierce opposition we must realistically anticipate. (King 1967: 165)]

In preparation for the "Poor People's Campaign," King will involve himself in a labor dispute in behalf of the rights of city workers in Memphis, Tennessee. While there, "fierce opposition" will take his life, leaving the text of his last book to speak for the unfinished project ahead:

> The curse of poverty has no justification in our age. It is socially as cruel and blind as the practice of cannibalism at the dawn of civilization, when men ate each other because they had not yet learned to take food from the soil or to consume the abundant animal life around them. The time has come for us to civilize ourselves by the total, direct and immediate abolition of poverty. (King 1967: 166)

With these words, King concludes his analysis of domestic affairs.

The final chapter of King's last book is visionary. Like his famous dream, this chapter on "The World House" extends his analytical sketch to a global vision of nonviolent possibilities. Here we find the three broad categories of evil that must be confronted: poverty, racism, and war:

> Therefore I suggest that the philosophy and strategy of nonviolence become immediately a subject for study and for serious experimentation in every field of human conflict, by no means excluding the relations between nations. It is, after all, nation-states which make war, which have produced the weapons and threaten the survival of mankind and which are both genocidal and suicidal in character. (King 1967: 184)

A nonviolent approach does not isolate the evil of violence from its co-dependent evils of poverty and racism. Nor does nonviolence simply advocate that violence be stopped: "True nonviolence is more than the absence of violence. It is the persistent and determined application of peaceable power to offenses against the community—in this case the world community" (King 1967: 184).

Our review of the concept of nonviolent direct action has required that we situate the tactic within a complex logic of social
change, involving four-step campaigns and six aspects of struggle.
This process confronts three structural elements of race, class, or
violence by grasping three levers of economic, political, or ideological
power. And this process is experimental, not yet shrewd enough in its
ability to match tactics to structure. "People struggling from the
depths of society have not been equipped with the knowledge of the
science of social change"; hence, it will be necessary, for the moment,
to "subordinate programs to the studying of the levers of power"
(King 1967: 138).

In sum, King's philosophy of nonviolence lends content and
context to many other contemporary theories of justice. Working from
the premise that we live in a world of structural injustice, King not only
argues the universal merits of equality but also provides a general
account of the method most likely to reform actual conditions as we
find them. Intellectually, King will not condone nor apologize for
anything less than full equality in a milieu of fellowship or brotherhood.
Finding ourselves far short of that dream, King begins to work on the
procedural issues that arise as we seek democratic fulfillment. King's
logic of nonviolence is thus superbly matched to the challenge of his
age, even as it strives for relevance and elegance of expression.

While it has been argued that nonviolent direct action may be
severed from larger conceptions of truth and justice, such a disengagement would not help us to understand King's logic of nonviolence. Hence, this chapter insists upon a connection between questions of process and principles. Next, we will turn to King's own usage
of the word justice, in order to rehearse his explicit conception of this
necessary concept. But first, in keeping with our method in other
chapters, and to illuminate the context of King's philosophy, we pause
to consider the remarkable influence of Howard Thurman.

THURMAN'S VIEW OF JESUS

As we have seen, King's opening argument for nonviolent direct
action, was psychological—anger must be channeled into healthy

reconstructive confrontation. Perhaps the most elegant support on this point comes from a book with which King was very familiar. Thus, we turn to Howard Thurman's classic work, *Jesus and the Disinherited* (1949). By Thurman's own account, work on the thesis of his book began in 1935, about the time he was invited to chair a Methodist delegation to India (Thurman 1979: 219). Thurman declined the invitation, because "I did not want to go to India as an apologist for a segregated American Christianity" (Thurman 1979: 104). After being persuaded that he was not expected to be an apologist for American Christianity, Thurman accepted the appointment and commenced upon the journey.

Thurman's "first major engagement" in India was a lecture at Colombo. Following that lecture he was entertained by the chairman of the Law Club, who confronted Thurman with the very challenge that had nearly prevented him from making the trip in the first place. Said the chairman, "I think that an intelligent young Negro such as yourself, here in our country on behalf of a Christian enterprise, is a traitor to all of the darker peoples of the earth. How can you account for yourself being in this unfortunate and humiliating position?" (Thurman 1979: 114). Having anticipated the force of the challenge from the chairman of the Colombo Law Club, Thurman replied that he was not there to "bolster a declining Christian faith," nor was he there to "make converts" (Thurman 1979: 114). Thurman did not want to be mistaken for any missionary. Nevertheless, he argued, "the religion of Jesus in its true genius offers me a promising way to work through the conflicts of a disordered world. I make a careful distinction between Christianity and the religion of Jesus" (Thurman 1979: 114).

By 1948, Thurman had developed his thesis about the religion of Jesus into a "comprehensive study" that was first delivered as a series of lectures at Austin, Texas, then published in book form as *Jesus and the Disinherited* (Thurman 1979: 219). In this book, Thurman investigates the religion of Jesus as the achievement of a "true genius" who is born into the grip of an oppressive empire. As a Jew, and a poor Jew, Jesus was born with his back against the wall. Not far from where he is said to have lived, and around the time he lived there, Roman soldiers once leveled an entire town in retaliation against its rebellious citizens. Jesus, the carpenter, may have been called upon to resurrect new buildings from the wreckage.

Even with the "ethical quality" and "Godlike tone" of the tradition of Jewish prophets to draw upon, circumstances were hostile to any nurturing of the more divine qualities of human possibility. Nevertheless, Jesus was a "true genius":

> Here is one who was so conditioned and organized within himself that he became a perfect instrument for the embodiment of a set of ideals—ideals of such dramatic potency that they were capable of changing the calendar, rechanneling the thought of the world, and placing a new sense of the rhythm of life in a weary, nerve-snapped civilization. (Thurman 1949: 16)

Thurman's ontology presupposes an inner conditioning and organization that can be crafted to embody ideals of "dramatic potency." With the achievement of such "true genius," the person becomes a "perfect instrument" for a "new sense of the rhythm of life." Thus, the religion of Jesus calls attention to the powerful potential of inner organization—somebodyness—even under the assault of the most advanced and oppressive structures of the day. "His message focused on the urgency of a radical change in the inner attitude of the people. He recognized fully that out of the heart are the issues of life, that no external force, however great and overwhelming, can at long last destroy a people if it does not first win the victory of the spirit against them" (Thurman 1949: 21). Under assault from Rome, the Jewish people could choose to resist or not. But what were the chances of successful resistance in the face of Rome's terrible power? And what are the chances that a spirit of resistance can nevertheless thrive in the face of such oppression?

The religion of Jesus begins with the imperative that the spirit of resistance must live by means of some inner organization. "For the purposes of our discussion resistance is defined as the physical, overt expression of an inner attitude" (Thurman 1949: 26). The religion of Jesus is thus explored as a psychological project. How does one go about organizing one's spirit of resistance from within, as one faces ineluctable assault from without? "The basic fact is that Christianity as it was born in the mind of this Jewish teacher and thinker appears as a technique of survival for the oppressed" (Thurman 1949: 29). And this survival is spiritual, psychological—having what is sometimes called a "subjective" aspect. "Wherever his spirit appears, the oppressed gather fresh courage; for he announced the good news that fear, hypocrisy, and hatred, the three hounds of hell that track the trail of the disinherited, need have no dominion over them" (Thurman 1949: 29). We recall King's persistent attention to the psychologies of fear, deception, and hatred, as he sketched a complex development project for nonviolent social change. We also recall that King's opening argument for nonviolence concerned the need to address anger.

Anger, like the three hounds of hell, must be transformed—the inner state must be reorganized. At a deep level of meaning, this is a requirement for human dignity, hence a real requirement for survival. Jesus, like King and Thurman, "recognized with authentic realism that anyone who permits another to determine the quality of his inner life gives into the hands of the other the keys to his destiny" (Thurman 1949: 28). "Don't let anyone ever make you stoop so low as to hate them," admonished King's father and grandmother. King speaks out of this tradition of wisdom as he establishes his case for nonviolence upon psychological, or spiritual, grounds. For Thurman this approach reflects "authentic realism."

Thurman's elegant thesis needs no further elaboration here. It is sufficient to mark the general outline of his "authentic realism" as a quest for ontological survival. The human life is lived according to criteria of self-examination that cannot be ignored. Each of us lives with a tell-tale heart. What Thurman explicates is the precious integrity of self-direction. What King affirms is the need to keep this integrity central to our conceptions of liberation. In the moral equivalent of war, one can win material battles and lose spiritual wars. Successful revolutions can establish foundations more wicked than what came before. And so to the profound center of human activity King directly points as he works to clear paths for a revolutionary way. This sort of project may lend itself to elegant rhetorical flourish, and such rhetoric may indeed establish traditions of its own. But truth and beauty are no strangers, nor should we marvel that they work together so well.

As if King needed to be rescued from faint praise, I have argued in this chapter that his genius for nonviolent direct action speaks to a depth of philosophical sophistication not usually fathomed by detractors or admirers alike. The impression I get from most appreciations of King is that here was an admirable strategist and a marvelous speaker with a flair for motivating people to do difficult things. Yet, it is often assumed that the logical foundations of King's philosophy need not withstand the embarrassment of serious inquiry. In contrast to the received view, I have tried to show the numerous ways in which King was in pursuit of a systematic and coherent theory of justice.

If King was able to get people to do remarkable things, I think it was because he was able to actually convince people mentally, not just arouse their emotions. He was able to convince people that justice was as palpable as evil, and worthy of pursuit. In the aftermath of Chicago, however, doubts grew. And so King set about the business of convincing the world all over again. He gathered his arguments one more time. In the gathering process, his concepts were revalued and reconstructed for renewed debate. Freedom gave way to equality. Structure took a prominent role, and nonviolent direct action was recontextualized to meet new strategic requirements. But this undertaking was a thoroughly philosophical exercise in the sense that a systematic morality was also in the process of development. No gilded trappings accompanied King's concepts of love and justice. He meant it very seriously that such forms should inscribe the center of his logic of nonviolence.

Chapter 5

---•---

JUSTICE AND LOVE

The first duty of love is to produce love, to nourish it, to
extend the Kingdom of Heaven by teaching love to all men.
—JOSIAH ROYCE

OF ENDS AND MEANS

We have spent several chapters exploring questions of means. What are the means of perpetuating a status quo? Conversely, how do people with their backs against the wall gather the means for liberation? For King's logic of nonviolence, questions of means are intimately connected to questions of ends. Even on fields of struggle, where action confronts structure, King invokes values that should regulate the processes of inquiry and activity. Moreover, the very construction of fields of struggle is a task imbued with values that King would have us respect. Pursuing King's logic of nonviolence, we cannot ignore questions of means, nor can we privilege questions of ends. As principles call attention to facts, so do facts suggest imperatives to action. Within the realm of King's spirited inquiry, no false dichotomy between means and ends may sever philosophy from its ongoing concerns.

This chapter explores the concept of justice that regulates King's logic of nonviolence. As with each of the other concepts, our treatment of justice will require close attention to King's own usage.

Foundational to King's concept of justice is the imperative to love. For reasons suggested by Howard Thurman's "authentic realism"—in keeping with Broadus Butler's "humanicentric" mode of philosophy—all inquiries into justice shall be regulated by love. Where conceptions of justice fail to meet the test of love, King provides criticism and pursues reconstruction. In the history of philosophy, King's concept of justice arrives as a bold confrontation to the status quo. Following the method of Jesus, who was once pressed by "a certain teacher of the Law" to define the term neighbor, King tosses the question into the street. Whoever you meet there, on the dangerous road to Jericho—that is your neighbor. The parable of the Good Samaritan becomes a paradigm for the Good American. And various theories of justice are put to the test.

At first glance, King's outright call to love can hardly be taken seriously as a theory of justice—yet, this is the serious business that King would propose. To Black Power advocates and white liberals alike, King argues the imperative of love. It is love that awakens perception to injustice and love that gathers strength for liberation. Absent love, there is always room for one more bad-faith apology. As Robert Solomon (1990) suggests, a sense of justice depends upon a complex set of passions. King likewise pushes beyond liberal compassion into cosmic dimensions of love. If this direction is not fully charted by King, its consequences are nonetheless amply indicated. Beyond Black Power and white liberalism, King's theory of justice might serve to reenergize academic theory with new philosophical possibilities.

The concept of equality is invigorated by love. For audiences who do not yet proceed from the imperative of love, equality may be a problematic concept indeed. In such a case, King's quest for wisdom seeks to awaken a sensibility that is supralogical. Facts about inequality must be presented in a way that breaks the human spirit free from its prison of cool calculation. Even when faced with liberal sentimentality, a deeper caring must be invoked. But how is this to be done? From nineteenth-century London, two classic answers emerge that provide benchmarks for reflection. Charles Dickens, for example, engages a literary campaign, while Karl Marx organizes material revolution. In the first case, as with A Christmas Carol, the message of compassion is conveyed through imaginative manipulations of time and space. In the second case, as with The Communist Manifesto, the message is declared by way of revolutionary threat. In both examples, stubborn lack of compassion is confronted, and the bourgeoisie meet with consequences that provoke reflection. The figure of Tiny Tim at Christmas poses the same moral challenge echoed by Marx and Engels, namely: what values shall be honored here? If one is not awakened by three ghosts in the night, how about three shots at dawn? Or perhaps there is a middle way. King's logic of nonviolence seeks a middle way between ghosts and bullets. No superstitious idealism need apply, nor bloody materialism. Somewhere between A Christmas Carol and The Communist Manifesto, ethical coercion must be put to work in confrontation with those who do not care yet.

Viewed by the lights of love, nonviolent direct action is guerrilla theater of a special kind. Here the suffering body is offered up as an extraordinary plea for compassion. Whether in Gandhi-style hunger strikes, or public civil rights confrontations, nonviolent actions seek to establish new ground upon which reason and logic may proceed toward justice. Such actions provoke reflection on the consequences of an uncaring future, and hasten new awakenings of spirit. Without diminishing other things that can be said, nonviolent direct action attempts a kind of philosophical education upon the deeper issues of justice.

Although some may argue that justice is possible without love, King may not. The nonviolence campaign works upon this premise—that love must be recovered and recentered. This conception of justice anticipates an ethic of care developed in recent years by feminist scholars such as Nell Noddings (1984) and Carol Gilligan (1982). As Laurence Thomas once argued to me, King's philosophical importance revolves around this axis of "fellow feeling." Indeed, fellow feeling is a term that appears in King's last monograph precisely at the point where he criticizes the limitations of rule-bound conceptions of justice. Without modes of being that issue from "genuine fellow feeling" there can be no true peace nor justice. As Lawrence Blum (1994) has argued, following Iris Murdoch (1970), moral philosophy is impoverished when it turns away from love.

King criticizes the influential maximin principle that seeks to minimize differences between social groups. For King, this is faint morality that never grasps the imperative of love. Especially in his later years, as he pursues a guaranteed national income to maximize the minimum standard of living, King nevertheless maintains a theoretical high ground. Just as King once pursued desegregation without embracing it as his highest aspiration, so King later calls for a national minimum income. But King's theoretical framework is not exhausted by his reformist practice. Even as King pursues a guaranteed minimum income as one step toward justice, his concept of justice is not satisfied short of equality. In terms that confront what is most readily received today, King suggests that we do not honor the principle of respect for all persons so long as we define justice in terms that would merely minimize social disparities. When love serves as the arbiter of justice, inequalities are not minimized—they are abolished. The outlook proposed by love chooses equality as a principle because the principle of equality offers the severest test that one can pose. Thus, the principle of equality does not fall from the sky but rather proceeds directly from the heart.

As King unfolds his concept of justice in preparation for a Poor People's Campaign, his first definition is negative: "the absence of brutality and unregenerate evil is not the presence of justice" (King 1967: 4). Here King speaks to those who find questions of justice less urgent after the campaigns of Birmingham and Selma. He wants it known that America's contradictions have been barely meliorated, that the world's racist structure has been hardly touched:

> The majority of white Americans consider themselves sincerely committed to justice for the Negro. They believe that American society is essentially hospitable to fair play and to steady growth toward a middle-class Utopia embodying racial harmony. But unfortunately this is a fantasy of self-deception and comfortable vanity. (King 1967: 5)

Even today, white America does not yet acknowledge the persistence of structural inequality. An ideological cloaking device still operates to cover heaps of misery as "just desserts." Under such an account of justice, individuals and groups are judged to cause their own misery, the better to rationalize not caring. By means of such structural blinders, sympathy is systematically disengaged.

King introduces his concept of justice as a challenge to the fundamental lack of sympathy that underlies America's color line. If white Americans were secretly "uneasy with injustice," and if they cared for their fellow citizens, then they would rise up and change conditions. Instead, when faced with the pervasive and persistent injustice of the color line, they are "unwilling yet to pay a significant price to eradicate it" (King 1967: 11). Negations pile up as King's concept of justice confronts white America. Despite King's attention to psychological realism, the civil rights movement had not produced widespread commitments to justice. While King asserts that a partial victory has been achieved, all the factions well understand that justice has not arrived.

In the aftermath of Chicago, King chooses his words with care. "To lightly dismiss a success because it does not usher in a complete order of justice is to fail to comprehend the process of achieving full victory. It underestimates the value of confrontation and dissolves the confidence born of a partial victory by which new efforts are powered" (King 1967: 12–13). Here King joins with Black Power advocates in affirming that a struggle for justice is *still raging*. In this limited regard, King is more sympathetic to Black Power's militancy than to white liberalism's utter complacency. Furthermore, King asserts that nonviolence is the method best suited to ignite further confrontation with injustice. To a country that would condemn rioters for their spontaneous outbursts, King warns that fundamental responsibilities are indeed at issue, but they might be better placed elsewhere: "Social justice and progress are the absolute guarantors of riot prevention" (King 1967: 21–22). If King cannot condone riots, neither can he fail to indicate mitigating circumstances that might temper a rush to judgment and direct criticism in intelligent directions.

In keeping with his claim of partial victory, and still seeking to communicate hope for the logic of nonviolence, King argues to advocates of Black Power that the civil rights movement has tapped some reliable reservoirs of white commitment. Referring back to the preceding summer King notes: "I reminded them of the dedicated whites who had suffered, bled and died in the cause of racial justice, and suggested that to reject white participation now would be a shameful repudiation of all for which they had sacrificed" (King 1967: 28). But King is not able to turn back the bitterness that grows with each new day of the Meredith march in the summer of 1966. The movement splits into factions. "News stories now centered not on the injustices of Mississippi, but on the apparent ideological division in the civil rights movement" (King 1967: 32). In fact, when news media herald the martyrdom of white civil rights workers, advocates of Black Power see confirmation of their own alienation. "Their frustration is further fed by the fact that even when blacks and whites die together in the cause of justice, the death of the white person gets more attention and concern than the death of the black person" (King 1967: 34). From the perspective of Black Power, the eager and sporadic dramatization of white martyrdom, compared with the daily discounting of black struggle, only seems to confirm the uselessness of white martyrdom in converting the basic values of white America. Nonviolent martyrdom does not seem to be making its costly point on either side of the color line.

Throughout this give-and-take with Black Power, King focuses the central question on matters of justice. Whatever the sins of the white media may be, white martyrs are nevertheless dying in service to justice. Similarly, if Black Power somehow falls short of providing a satisfactory plan of action, there is something about the slogan that contributes to our understanding of what justice really is. Thus, the Black Power faction is making an important point about the material requirements of justice: "In this sense power is not only desirable but necessary in order to implement the demands of love and justice" (King 1967: 37). What bothers King is the connotation that "Black Power" brings to a movement for justice. The Black Power slogan mimics the cry of "White Power" and thus conveys a spirit of terrorism, domination, and exclusion. Shouts of "White Power" announce the very corruption that King is seeking to avoid in his logic of nonviolence. Thus, the Black Power slogan taunts its opponents by suggesting that the methods of "White Power" provide a worthy standard for struggle. Black Power thus invokes a terrible threat of retribution at the level of brute force. It sounds bold, but also reckless and desperate. King objects to the slogan and argues that true liberation requires the establishment of a new plateau of value. "Power at its best is love implementing the demands of justice. Justice at its best is love correcting everything that stands against love" (King 1967: 37). Appealing to the centrality of love, King proceeds with his analysis of justice, providing critical outlines for his logic of nonviolence.

BRINGING LOVE TO BLACK POWER

If Black Power means to have true power (that is, meeting the test of rigorous ontological reflection) then King is suggesting some important philosophical considerations for the new movement. Above all, King warns, avoid the popular course of modern thought that divorces power from love. In the active call for power, King encourages us not to accept passively a conception of power in which "love is identified with a resignation of power and power with a denial of love" (King 1967: 37). From King's point of view, the error of separating power from love has been tragically compounded by Christian thinkers who, in divorcing their ethereal Platonic version of love from their temporal struggles for power, left themselves open to Nietzsche's withering attacks. As Nietzsche rejects the "Christian" concept of love, Christians reject the "Nietzschean" will to power. All this mutual rejection is unfortunate in King's view, because the two concepts are not really "polar opposites" but necessary co-conceptions of ethical development. "What is needed is a realization that power without love is reckless and abusive and that love without power is sentimental and anemic" (King 1967: 37). Because Black Power and White Power perpetuate the separation of these principles, neither offers a satisfactory solution. "It is precisely this collision of immoral power with powerless morality which constitutes the major crisis of our times" (King 1967: 37). A realistic approach to power must pay respect to the foundational requirements of love. "In his struggle for racial justice, the Negro must seek to transform his condition of powerlessness into creative and positive power" (King 1967: 37).

King will join with Black Power advocates in stressing the need to pool black capital and bloc votes. And King will join with Nietzsche in emphasizing the need to reject all slavelike psychologies. But King sees in each of these approaches a tendency toward exaggerated analysis that falsifies a need for absolute and total rejection of one's opponents. The case is exacerbated by gross perversions of power and a legacy of deep revulsion:

> It is in the context of the slave tradition that some of the ideologues of the Black Power movement call for the need to develop new and indigenous codes of justice for the ghettos, so that blacks may move entirely away from their former masters' "standards of good conduct." Those in the Black Power movement who contend that blacks should cut themselves off from every level of dependence upon whites for advice, money or other help are obviously reacting against the slave pattern of "perfect dependence" upon their masters. (King 1967: 40)

A cycle of revulsion is being perpetuated when black liberation refuses to consider white allies. Approaching the same problem from a different angle, King says that revolution has too often been based on "hope and hate" (King 1967: 44):

> The hope was expressed in the rising expectation of freedom and justice. The hate was an expression of bitterness toward the perpetrators of the old order. It was the hate that made revolutions bloody and violent. What was new about Mahatma Gandhi's movement in India was that he mounted a revolution on hope and love, hope and nonviolence. This same new emphasis characterized the civil rights movement in our country dating from the Montgomery bus boycott of 1956 to the Selma movement of 1965. We maintained the hope while transforming the hate of traditional revolutions into positive nonviolent power. As long as the hope was fulfilled there was little questioning of nonviolence. But when the hopes were blasted, when people came to see that in spite of progress their conditions were still insufferable, when they looked out and saw more poverty, more school segregation and more slums, despair began to set in. (King 1967: 44–45)

As despair causes hate and dissipates creative energy, King would reconstruct the psychology of Black Power following the model of Gandhi.

Instead of "hope and hate" energizing a fractious revolution of rejection, King proposes "hope and love." King's tribute to Gandhi is genuine and deserved; but as Lerone Bennett, Jr. (1964), reminds us, King read Thurman during the bus boycott, too. From whatever source such convictions may come, King is an "authentic realist" in matters of spirit and psychology. The difference between love and hate, like the difference between courage and fear, hope and despair, is as real as the difference between a chisel and no chisel at all. "Today's despair," writes King, "is a poor tool to carve out tomorrow's justice" (King 1967: 48).

Because the legitimate questions of any revolution turn upon issues of justice, because there can be no lasting separate solution, King insists upon an inclusive method of revolution rather than an exclusive one. "Black Power alone is no more insurance against social injustice than white power" (King 1967: 49). "In short, the Negro's problem cannot be solved unless the whole of American society takes a new turn toward greater economic justice" (King 1967: 50). Furthermore, King sees no reason to exclude "a substantial group" of people "who have demonstrated a will to fight side by side with the Negro against injustice" (King 1967: 51). "Since we are Americans the solution to our problem will not come through seeking to build a separate black nation within a nation, but by finding that creative minority of the concerned from the ofttimes apathetic majority, and together moving toward that colorless power that we all need for security and justice" (King 1967: 54). Taken in isolation, each of the above arguments surrounding the use of Black Power seems chiefly concerned with immediate questions of tactical procedure. When we notice in retrospect, however, that each argument is centered around terms of justice, then we glimpse the philosophical nature of King's evaluation. King's theory of justice would regulate revolutionary struggle in the direction of more inclusive participation, even if there is little evidence of support from whites.

King's theory of justice thus gives support to his integrationist principle of revolution and reflects the material condition of the black citizen in the United States: "In the struggle for national independence one can talk about liberation now and integration later, but in the struggle for racial justice in a multiracial society where the oppressor and the oppressed are both 'at home,' liberation must come through integration" (King 1967: 62). All of which brings King to conclude the question of Black Power with rhetorical questions: "May it not be that the new man the world needs is the nonviolent man?"—and a "new kind of power"? King's vision is dreamy because it asserts values that have rarely been put into action. "It will be power infused with love and justice, that will change dark yesterdays into bright tomorrows, and lift us from the fatigue of despair to the buoyancy of hope. A dark, desperate, confused and sin-sick world waits for this new kind of man and this new kind of power" (King 1967: 66). Not only is this a shrewd response to racist structures, but it is sound ethical ground upon which individual spirits may begin to build relationships to ensure a just community.

If integration was a public value of some prestige during King's day, then we must acknowledge that subsequent history has tarnished that shiny symbol. Not only has white resistance dimmed the hopes that were once focused on integration, but black intellectuals have also warned of the term's limited value. Following the criticism of Harold Cruse, for example, the value of integration would seem to deserve critical refinement (Cruse 1987: 241). We have seen how King never embraced the pure rationalism of Bunche's theory of oppression. In other words, black group identity is something cherished by King, even as he works to formulate ties with other exploited groups. This group reality becomes problematic, however, depending upon the way in which integration is used as a value. If, as in Bunche's sense, integration means the atomization of the black group into white neighborhoods or schools, then integration is nothing more than assimilation, and we meet several serious objections from Cruse and others. If integration means the pluralistic group sharing of a common economy, regulated by Alain Locke's notions of tolerance and reciprocity, then we have what I think is a more defensible concept (Harris 1989: 49). If King was not explicit about this dispute between Bunche and Cruse, I think the evidence indicates that King proceeded in the pluralistic direction indicated by Cruse and prefigured by the lifework of A. Philip Randolph.

BRINGING JUSTICE TO LIBERALISM

Having contrasted his own theory of justice with the separatism of Black Power, King next turns to address the phenomenon of white backlash and the responsibility of white liberals. As usual, King begins with an observation: "There never has been a solid, unified and determined thrust to make justice a reality for Afro-Americans" (King 1967: 68). The ambivalence of white America, with its brutal contradictions, seems bound to a logic of backlash with respect to black achievements. This is a structural fact. On the side of democracy, there have been many white people who have, "through a deep moral compulsion, fought long and hard for racial justice" (King 1967: 69). But the typical history of racial justice administered by white America has more often resembled the Emancipation Proclamation, in that:

> It was like freeing a man who had been unjustly imprisoned for years, and on discovering his innocence sending him out with no bus fare to get home, no suit to cover his body, no financial compensation to atone for his long years of incarceration and to help him get a sound footing in society; sending him out with only the assertion: "Now you are free." What greater injustice could society perpetuate? (King 1967: 79)

The so-called emancipation of the slave brings with it no real commitment to freedom. The so-called enactment of civil rights legislation does little to cure the diseased body politic of racial injustice.

From King's point of view, we still diagnose a "high blood pressure of creeds and an anemia of deeds." This is a centuries-old characteristic of white backlash. "This tendency of the nation to take one step forward on the question of racial justice and then to take a step backward is still the pattern" (King 1967: 80). The failure to make substantial efforts toward racial justice is especially telling when one considers the "success" of the United States: "With all of her dazzling achievements and stupendous material strides, America has maintained its strange ambivalence on the question of racial justice" (King 1967: 82–83). After all that has been done, this moral choice still awaits a choosing. King quotes Myrdal's description of the resulting time-worn dilemma:

> The Negro problem is not only America's greatest failure but also America's incomparably great opportunity for the future. If America should follow its own deepest convictions, its well-being at home would be increased directly. At the same time America's prestige and power abroad would rise immensely. The century-old dream of American patriots, that America should give to the entire world its own freedoms and its own faith, would come true. America can demonstrate that justice, equality and cooperation are possible between white and colored people. . . . *America is free to choose whether the Negro shall remain her liability or become her opportunity.* (King 1967: 84–85; emphasis in Myrdal's original)

King illustrates the patience of his approach to White Power by quoting Gunnar Myrdal's 20-year-old book (1944). Furthermore, King reiterates for White Power what he has argued before for Black Power—that real power increases only along lines of justice. "The failure to pursue justice is not only a moral default. Without it social tensions will grow and the turbulence in the streets will persist despite disapproval or repressive action. Even more, a withered sense of justice in an expanding society leads to the corruption of the lives of all Americans" (King 1967: 85). Insistently, King recasts oppressive power in terms of a common corruption that diminishes *everyone's* humanity. Injustice concerns every person imaginable.

As King found it necessary to argue the importance of love for Black Power, he also argues the importance of justice for the white liberal. But this feature of King's thought has been too often ignored. As Black Power suggested the danger of shrewdness gone cold, so white liberalism exemplifies the trouble with sentimental rationality gone soft: "Many blatant forms of injustice could not exist without the acquiescence of white liberals" (King 1967: 89). And so the white liberal must be awakened out of his dogmatic slumber to join in the shrewd business of liberation. "When evil men conspire to preserve an unjust status quo, good men must unite to bring about the birth of a society undergirded by justice" (King 1967: 89):

> The white liberal must see that the Negro needs not only love but also justice. It is not enough to say, "We love the Negroes, we have many Negro friends." They must demand justice for Negroes. Love that does not satisfy justice is no love at all. It is merely a sentimental affection, little more than what one would have for a pet. Love at its best is justice concretized. (King 1967: 90)

In this address to white liberals, King submits a definition of justice that embodies "love at its best." The philosophical stratagem is apparent. Beginning with a common ground of assumption—that the liberal loves black America, perhaps even individual black Americans—King seeks to organize the assumption for its most fruitful development.

In the wake of widespread liberal retreat, King warns liberals that their declarations of love have missed the point of what is required. "He who contends that he 'used to love the Negro, but . . . ' did not truly love him in the beginning, because his love was conditioned upon the Negroes' limited demands for justice" (King 1967: 90). Having hinted at an imperative favoring unconditional love, King moves on to define his conception of absolute justice. Here is the full paragraph:

> The white liberal must affirm that absolute justice for the Negro simply means, in the Aristotelian sense, that the Negro must have "his due." There is nothing abstract about this. It is as concrete as having a good job, a good education, a decent house and a share of power. It is, however, important to understand that giving a man his due may often mean giving him special treatment. I am aware of the fact that this has been a troublesome concept for many liberals, since it conflicts with their traditional ideal of equal opportunity and equal treatment of people according to their individual merits. But this is a day which demands new thinking and the re-evaluation of old concepts. A society that has done something special *against* the Negro for hundreds of years must

now do something special for him, in order to equip him to
compete on a just and equal basis. (King 1967: 90)

In sum, arguing from the standpoint of justice founded upon love, King
asks white liberals to endorse full employment, universal education,
decent housing, and democracy. Moreover, he would challenge liberals
to show solidarity through support of affirmative action. As much as
this would seem to follow from an Aristotelian sense of justice, the
liberal doctrine of fair play is strangely unable to cope with any of these
collective structures. Perhaps a concept of justice tested by the value of
equality, awakened to structural inequality, and founded upon an
imperative of love can meet the need for "new thinking" that will carry
the white liberal back into alliance with civil rights.

More often than not, white liberalism constructs its theories for
frictionless conditions. But King's nonviolence cannot be constructed
nor appreciated by such criteria. For King's nonviolence, conflict and
friction are presupposed. If, as King claims, nonviolent direct action
instigated no riots, it did seem to cause trouble. By such reckoning,
King was causing trouble when he was assassinated in Memphis. And
he was organizing a massive trouble-causing campaign called the Poor
People's Campaign, aimed at Washington, DC. But, as we know, King
would argue that the real trouble was present already. Nonviolent
direct action merely transformed the trouble into a form capable of
intelligent control.

To white liberals, King argued that fundamental assumptions
would have to be reviewed and reconstructed. The sorts of difficulties
confronted by nonviolence cannot be rationalized out of existence. If
liberals plan to be any help, they will have to learn what it means to
wade into troubled waters. "The white liberal must rid himself of the
notion that there can be a tensionless transition from the old order
of injustice to the new order of justice" (King 1967: 90). In short,
King is announcing that liberal theory cannot do the work that justice
requires. As I say, this is a charge that has not received the serious
attention that it deserves.

For King, the challenging days ahead would require unprece-
dented commitments from the white liberal: "The white liberal must
escalate his support for the struggle for racial justice rather than

de-escalate it" (King 1967: 91). "Jews," for instance, "have identified with Negroes voluntarily in the freedom movement, motivated by their religious and cultural commitment to justice" (King 1967: 92). Perhaps the Jewish prophetic tradition had something to say to white liberals. But the tension-charged days of Black Power caused lasting damage to the black–Jewish alliance and signaled a rupture that was difficult for liberals to cross, or even to want to cross. As Black Power encouraged the retreat of white liberals, King admonished both sides to focus on the issue: "The issue is injustice and immorality. This was the issue before shouts of 'Black Power' came into being and this will be the issue when the shouts die down" (King 1967: 94). In the meantime—if justice is actually the issue—white liberals should be willing to face down any attempts to exile them from the issues. This was strong advice from King, urging white allies to fight the good fight despite Black Power's rejection. Yet how many liberals have studied this challenge? Most directly, this admonition warns white America that justice demands their alliance with the forces of black liberation, even when white participation is rejected by prominent black leaders. To turn away because one has been asked to turn away is for King no worthy excuse.

The common cause of justice provides King with a guiding light that must be followed, no matter what the source of discouragement. White liberals rejected by black leaders may find resources within King to argue the importance of the larger issues. Whether black leaders want white help or not, concerned white citizens can argue that real problems remain to be addressed. Injustice has consequences for homes and families:

> The Negro father became resigned to hopelessness, and he communicated this to his children. Some men, unable to contain the emotional storms, struck out at those who would be least likely to destroy them. They beat their wives and their children in order to protest a social injustice, and the tragedy was that none of them understood why the violence exploded. (King 1967: 107)

As black Americans seek to control the "removable causes" of their most desperate conditions, King encourages renewed focus on the broad context of injustice that affects the community's most intimate relationships. The problems of black family life must not be attributed to "innate weaknesses" that in turn may be used to "justify further neglect" (King 1967: 109). Instead, it must be insisted, "America owes a debt of justice which it has only begun to pay. If it loses the will to finish or slackens in its determination, history will recall its crimes and the country that would be great will lack the most indispensable element of greatness—justice" (King 1967: 109).

One overriding concern should be emphasized at this point. From the beginning of King's last monograph, he is intent on showing how white backlash forms the context for Black Power. It is the already limited commitment of whites and their wavering ways that contribute to the frustrations of black leadership. If whites want to use Black Power as their best excuse to turn away from the movement, then King suggests the rationalization is self serving. Whites close to the movement who feel betrayed are asked to do some hard thinking about the predicament, especially toward the very real racism that lingers in their own neighborhoods. Although King does not go so far as to prescribe antiracism campaigns, it would be fair to suggest that there are plenty of options for work available to white citizens—if justice, not the mere assuaging of guilt, is the motivation.

In any event, the torment of the black family must be returned to the context of the "personal torment" fostered by the American status quo. The former will not be resolved without reconstruction of the latter. And this is work for blacks and whites to share. "After 348 years racial injustice is still the Negro's burden and America's shame" (King 1967: 120). It is the dilemma of black America that, in the face of continued backlash, its citizens must continue to work impossible feats of overcoming. "With a dynamic will, we must transform our minus into a plus, and move on aggressively through storms of injustice and the jostling winds of daily handicaps, toward the beaconing lights of fulfillment" (King 1967: 120). Hence, King's six-stage program of nonviolent social change, which we reviewed in the preceding chapter, includes the call to "unite around powerful action programs to eradicate the last vestiges of racial injustice" (King 1967: 128).

King's call for action is also extended to middle-class blacks who "have forgotten their roots and are more concerned about 'conspicuous consumption' than about the cause of justice" (King 1967: 131). As the civil rights movement has infused a "new sense of values" into American institutions, it has "contributed infinitely more to the nation than the eradication of racial injustice" (King 1967: 133). By displacing the assumptions of the color line, the civil rights movement has encouraged a larger reconstruction of values "more person-centered than property- and profit-centered" (King 1967: 133). Applying a new sense of values to society at large, calling for universal income or employment, King argues that "positive psychological changes inevitably will result from widespread economic security. . . . Personal conflicts between husband, wife and children will diminish when the unjust measurement of human worth on a scale of dollars is eliminated" (King 1967: 164). Here the larger project of justice exceeds the terms of integration and opens the way for a revolution of values. Middle classes are not exempted from the risky break with American materialism, and are encouraged to explore the new values that might emerge from a renewed pursuit of justice.

In his vision of the "World House" King elaborates upon the larger question of values: "The good and just society is neither the thesis of capitalism nor the antithesis of Communism, but a socially conscious democracy which reconciles the truths of individualism and collectivism" (King 1967: 187). King's philosophy seeks to inscribe new categories of democratic fulfillment that cannot be satisfied by present activity. "A true revolution of value will soon cause us to question the fairness and justice of many of our past and present policies" (King 1967: 187). With these pointers, King elaborates a list of structures that must soon be judged unjust: glaring contrasts of poverty and wealth, automation that displaces workers as it maintains profits, capitalists who extract profits from other continents with no concern for their social betterment, Western arrogance, war, and the "conflict" in Vietnam. These things, says King, "cannot be reconciled with wisdom, justice, and love" (King 1967: 188).

King's final appeal is to America. The "richest and most powerful nation in the world, can well lead the way" in the revolution of values that must come (King 1967: 188). "There is nothing to keep us from remolding a recalcitrant status quo with bruised hands until we have fashioned it into a brotherhood" (King 1967: 189). With "affirmative action," says King, we must seek to remove "conditions of poverty, insecurity and injustice" (King 1967: 189). "These are revolutionary times. All over the globe men are revolting against old systems of exploitation and oppression, and out of the wombs of a frail world new systems of justice and equality are being born" (King 1967: 189). Yet, because of "comfort, complacency, a morbid fear of Communism and our proneness to adjust to injustice, the Western nations that initiated so much of the revolutionary spirit of the modern world have now become the arch antirevolutionaries" (King 1967: 190). America can recapture its revolutionary spirit and declare its eternal opposition to "poverty, racism and militarism" (King 1967: 190). With this "powerful commitment" Americans shall challenge "the status quo and unjust mores" (King 1967: 190).

KING'S WORLD HOUSE
OF TOUGH-MINDED LOVE

In the history of civil rights, it is commonplace to announce that King's death marked the end of an era, but in the broader life of the mind a logic of nonviolence was just beginning to make its way into the world. No doubt, the intellectual achievement was presaged by Gandhi. But the logic of nonviolence is no merely intellectual pursuit, and its force must be discovered in a special kind of disciplined activity, not to be mistaken for a baton that is passed during a relay race. This book has attempted to outline a neglected dimension of King's logic of nonviolence by showing how the maxims of such logic are borne by a heritage of African American struggle. King's logic of nonviolence is not the only heritage presented by African American struggle, and it does not exhaust even the few historical figures who have been presented here. More important to this book than any arguments about where to locate the African American tradition is the attempt to demonstrate how King's vision—indeed, nourished by a heritage of African American struggle—illuminates contours of philosophy neglected by contemporary theories of justice. With King, equality is reinvigorated, not diluted; structural injustice is exposed, not ignored; justice is pursued with explicit attention to process, not confined to any static array of concepts. In these concluding remarks, I want to explore King's vision of justice as it culminates in his call for a revolution of values. More than a brassy, rhetorical flourish, King's revolution of values challenges our theories of justice to synthesize the concepts of struggle and love.

In the final analysis, said King, the genuine revolution of values now calls upon each nation to "develop an overriding loyalty to mankind as a whole in order to preserve the best in their individual societies" (King 1967: 190):

> This call for a world-wide fellowship that lifts neighborly concern beyond one's tribe, race, class and nation is in reality a call for an all-embracing and unconditional love for all men. This often misunderstood and misinterpreted concept has now become an absolute necessity for the survival of man. When I speak of love, I am speaking of that force which all the great religions have seen as the supreme unifying principle of life. Love is the key that unlocks the door which leads to ultimate reality. (King 1967: 190)

King's logic of nonviolence seeks to address a global human crisis by positing a general theory of justice that is grounded in love and struggle. Although King appeals to the authority of religious tradition, his logic is regulated by systematic, critical reflection upon the normative challenge of justice in our age.

As Thurman eulogized in the wake of King's death: "Always he spoke from within the context of his religious experience, giving voice to an ethical insight which sprang out of his profound brooding over the meaning of his Judeo-Christian heritage. And this indeed was his great contribution to our times" (Thurman 1979: 223). Although others had been working along the same lines, King's contribution was nevertheless distinctive: "He was able to put at the center of his own personal religious experience a searching ethical awareness. Thus organized religion as we know it in our society found itself with its back against the wall" (Thurman 1979: 223).

King effected a transformation that analysis cannot deny, and this transformation worked because King's principles were closely adhered to for the complex work at hand: "To condemn him, to reject him, was to reject the ethical insight of the faith it [the organized church] proclaimed. And this was new" (Thurman 1979: 223). Proclaiming, with the Book of John, that love is the key to ultimate reality, King shattered all double-truths that would separate metaphysical investigation from social change. Thurman's eulogy continues: "Racial prejudice, segregation, discrimination were not regarded by him as merely un-American, undemocratic, but as mortal sin against God. For those who are religious it awakens guilt; for those who are merely superstitious it inspires fear. And it was this fear that pulled the trigger of the assassin's gun that took his life" (Thurman 1979: 223). "Along the way of life," writes King, "someone must have sense enough and morality enough to cut off the chain of hate. This can only be done by projecting the ethic of love to the center of our lives" (King 1958: 104). When unremitting violence grips a situation, as in the "lyncherdom" of Southern segregation, only an "ethic" that proceeds from "the center of our lives" has hope of cutting that chain of hate.

If cutting the chain of hate liberates creative resistance, then the "strength to love" has profound survival value for one's self. This is how one has "sense enough" to cut the chain of hate. To also have "morality enough" to cut the chain of hate requires an engagement with love's imperatives and unyielding concern for others. King was always appealing to good sense, arguing that shrewdness provided necessary reasons for following the nonviolent path. But King was also arguing that his principles of justice rested on less contingent, if more precarious, foundations.

King's own compassion was not altogether selfless. He, too, had been assaulted by the segregated South, and he felt the sting of racist imperialism as an intimate torment. After decades of consideration, King reached the conclusion that these pains must never abandon what makes them possible—a sense of love for one's self. For this, a sense of pain is essential. And when self-love is asserted against the pain of oppression, the thing most difficult to grasp is love for the other. This is why, I think, King titled one of his books *Strength to Love*. The strenuous nature of this love is indicated by its reciprocal challenge, to love self and other. Clearly, King does not invent this imperative principle, but he puts it to rigorous and novel use, especially when we see how it is a necessary component of his concept of justice.

Even if the forces of violence could prove their shrewdness in overthrowing some forms of injustice, King would still reserve the right to insist upon the "morality" of nonviolence. There is an "internal violence of spirit" that slips into existence with even the most skillful act of violence. "The nonviolent resister," on the other hand, "not only refuses to shoot his opponent but he also refuses to hate him" (King 1958: 103). Since hatred is an ally to violence, and violence is largely the purview of the status quo, the "oppressed people of the world" cannot afford to intensify hatred, and so nonviolence makes "sense" (King 1958: 104).

Ironically, this kind of reasoning makes most "sense" from the point of view of the struggling or oppressed; thus, "morality" must be introduced into the reasoning of the oppressor. To the master's moral code, as it were, King suggests that only love can lead one to sufficient conditions of justice. King's distinction between "sense" and "morality" serves to reinforce their ethical interdependence in a world of conflict. Justice is the common conception that seeks to bind all parties to ethical action.

Morality, as Nietzsche warned, is undergoing a historic transvaluation at the hands of the masses. From Nietzsche's point of view, the ascendant morality looked too much like revenge, and its advocates seemed to be motivated by pity. King would also take warning from such developments. For King, the transvaluation of struggle depends upon a centering of the habits of love within a commitment that cannot be otherwise "determined." The nonviolent resister is thus liberated from a chain of revenge, and achieves a freedom of spirit that is no longer pitiful for its determined dependence upon structured forces. As with Thurman, resistance is said to begin with the projection of an inner attitude that cannot have been created in the interest of the status quo. The principle of liberation, as opposed to the principle of domination or that of that of revenge, proceeds from the groundwork of an ethic of love. Thus, liberation and love share necessary connections.

"In speaking of love at this point," writes King, "we are not referring to some sentimental or affectionate emotion. It would be nonsense to urge men to love their oppressors in an affectionate sense" (King 1958: 104). Above all, the concept of love that King invokes in the context of nonviolent struggle is bound by a reflective engagement with justice. That is why King turns to "a love which is expressed in the Greek word *agape*" (King 1958: 104). "*Agape* means understanding, redeeming good will for all men. It is an overflowing love which is purely spontaneous, unmotivated, groundless, and creative. It is not set in motion by any quality or function of its object. It is the love of God operating in the human heart" (King 1958: 104). The *agape* type of love seeks what is best for another, renouncing any empirical judgments of the other's "quality or function" that might limit love's creativity. Indeed, *agape* would seem to require a radical veil of ignorance to screen out any calculus of "just desserts." Not even the vaguest distinction between doctor and janitor would be relevant for this love of justice. It is *humanicentric*.

JESUS IN JAIL IN TEXAS

Du Bois captured the morality of this "love of God for man" in his short story "Jesus Christ in Texas." The setting is a Waco jail yard, where Jesus questions the jailer regarding the activities that have been planned for the inmates—"will it be good for them?" It seems a ludicrous question to ask. *Who cares* if the day's program will be good for the prisoners? What "quality or function" of a prisoner obligates anyone to care? Yet, this is what I think King means when he speaks of the radical "love of God operating in the human heart":

> *Agape* is disinterested love. It is a love in which the individual seeks not his own good, but the good of his neighbor (I Cor. 10:24). *Agape* does not begin by discriminating between worthy and unworthy people, or any qualities people possess. It begins by loving others *for their own sakes*. It is an entirely "neighbor-regarding concern for others," which discovers the neighbor in every man it meets. Therefore, *agape* makes no distinction between friend and enemy; it is directed toward both. If one loves an individual

merely on account of his friendliness, he loves him for the sake of the benefits to be gained from the friendship, rather than for the friend's own sake. Consequently, the best way to assure oneself that Love is disinterested is to have love for the enemy-neighbor from whom you can expect no good in return, but only hostility and persecution. (King 1958: 104–105)

One seeks directly the good of another for the sake of another—"it springs from the *need* of the other person—his need for belonging to the best in the human family" (King 1958: 105).

King's logic calls for a conception of love that cannot be reduced to terms of enlightened self-interest. There is no contract that binds the other to any obligation whatsoever. Yet, this quality of love demands liberation for all—in other words, justice. "Since the white man's personality is greatly distorted by segregation, and his soul is greatly scarred, he needs the love of the Negro. The Negro must love the white man, because the white man needs his love to remove his tensions, insecurities, and fears" (King 1958: 105). Thus, the cycle of fear is broken in service to self and other. "*Agape* is a willingness to go to any length to restore community. It doesn't stop at the first mile, but it goes the second mile to restore community. It is a willingness to forgive, not seven times, but seventy times seven to restore community" (King 1958: 105). This astounding requirement must rest upon *enormous* reserves of patience.

And it is at this juncture that the religious dimension comes into view, because it seems absurd to think that any individual could muster such patience in service to such a love. A mystery is implied. King's term for this mystery is Holy Spirit, or "the continuing community creating reality that moves through history" (King 1958: 106). This "love of God" that sustains liberation through its dark hours defines the essence of reality, so that "he who works against community is working against the whole of creation" (King 1958: 106). To dissipate community is to create a lie, whereas to work in behalf of community is to sustain a truth:

It is true that there are devout believers in nonviolence who find it difficult to believe in a personal God. But even these persons

believe in the existence of some creative force that works for
universal wholeness. Whether we call it an unconscious process,
an impersonal Brahman, or a Personal Being of matchless power
and infinite love, there is a creative force in this universe that
works to bring the disconnected aspects of reality into a harmonious whole. (King 1958: 106–107)

King's commitment to the love ethic is situated within a challenging
metaphysics of exhausting ethical commitment. If Christian terms are
used, King also makes it clear that such terms do not exhaust the
mysteries that are implied. Whatever terms one may use, replenish-
ment of the exhausted individual calls into play a mysterious process.
"Man by his own power can never cast evil from the world. The
humanist's hope is an illusion, based on too great an optimism
concerning the inherent goodness of human nature" (King 1963:
129).

If King believes in an ontological dimension deeper than any sum
of personal commitments, he does not assign to this dimension any
simple agency that can be relied upon to combat injustice. "No
prodigious thunderbolt from heaven will blast away evil" (King 1963:
132). If the world of commitment flourishes in a larger reality of love,
the larger reality does not obviate the need for commitment. "Rather,
both man and God, made one in a marvelous unity of purpose
through an overflowing love as the free gift of himself on the part of
God and by perfect obedience and receptivity on the part of man, can
transform the old into the new and drive out the deadly cancer of
sin" (King 1963: 134).

This unity requires constituents that are both individual human
commitments and more. "The principle which opens the door for
God to work through man is faith" (King 1963: 134). While the
"mind's faith" may be directed toward a theory, "the heart's faith is
centered in a Person" (King 1963: 134). King's theory of justice thus
points to an attitude that depends upon a reality not reducible to
oneself, which draws upon a personality that exceeds oneself, and
which is directed toward an object that is not oneself. "Man filled
with God and God operating through man bring unbelievable
changes in our individual and social lives" (King 1963: 135).

Thus, our philosophical investigations, centered upon King's theory of justice, lead us to the hypothesis that the depersonalization of injustice may be resisted, because there is a sense of personality that seems to exceed the limitations of any oppressive circumstance. The "inflowing" of this personality is a phenomenon that King treats in one of his published sermons:

> To say that this God is personal is not to make him a finite object besides other objects or attribute to him the limitations of human personality; it is to take what is finest and noblest in our consciousness and affirm its perfect existence in him. It is certainly true that human personality is limited, but personality as such involves no necessary limitations. It means simply self-consciousness and self-direction. So in the truest sense of the word, God is a living God. In him there is feeling and will, responsive to the deepest yearnings of the human heart: this God both evokes and answers prayer. (King 1963: 155)

As "Holy Spirit" is King's term for the mystery that makes community possible, "God" is King's term for the perfect possibilities of self-direction. "God is able to give us the interior resources to confront the trials and difficulties of life. . . . He is able to give us the inner equilibrium to stand tall amid the trials and burdens of life. He is able to provide inner peace amid outer storms" (King 1963: 111). With the experience of God, King finds "the quiet assurance of an inner voice, saying, 'Stand up for righteousness, stand up for truth. God will be at your side forever' " (King 1963: 113).

If we seem to have sailed far beyond the reach of our academic concerns, our deeper understanding of King requires such an excursion, at least briefly. And this is because King's theory of justice carries him into the violence of the status quo so deeply that the ethical lines of theory give way to metaphysical speculations about ultimate reality. In so doing, King anticipates, through his own experience, how a theory of justice must sooner or later confront death. And for King, "the fear of death, nonbeing, and nothingness, expressed in existential anxiety, may be cured only by a positive religious faith" (King 1963: 123).

One does not *argue* King away from this position; rather, one *demonstrates* that the fear of death can be conquered by other means, for the fear of death is meant to be paralyzing whenever the claims of justice threaten the structure of the status quo. How one prepares for the occasional bombing is not a question to be disconnected from any real engagement with a theory of justice that is grounded in the process of struggle:

> A positive religious faith does not offer an illusion that we shall be exempt from pain and suffering, nor does it imbue us with the idea that life is a drama of unalloyed comfort and untroubled ease. Rather, it instills us with the inner equilibrium needed to face strains, burdens, and fears that inevitably come, and assures us that the universe is trustworthy and that God is concerned.
>
> Irreligion, on the other hand, would have us believe that we are orphans cast into the terrifying immensities of space in a universe that is without purpose or intelligence. Such a view drains courage and exhausts the energies of men. (King 1963: 123)

A theory of justice that requires persistent nonviolence against structures of stubborn violence is not a complete theory until it grapples with the reality of death, for this is what such a theory risks. That courage and energy have to be mustered in the face of death becomes a practical requirement. In this regard, King is not to be faulted when he makes his theory of justice complete. By following King into these excursions, we do not end up outside of the bounds of philosophy.

As much as possible I have tried to explicate King's philosophy of nonviolence on nonreligious grounds, but we confront the limits of such an approach. Can King's appreciation for infinite reserves of personality be secularized into a kind of common faith divorced from any particular concepts of God? Here hangs a tenuous but sturdy thread that attaches philosophy to theology, and this thread was of interest to King since his seminary days. It is this thread that connects questions of religion to science, which thread King did not want to sever. If the secular reader feels betrayed by King's attachment to this thread, let her ask the following questions. Is there some feature of experience that allows us to affirm a kind of infinite reserve of personality upon which we may throw ourselves at times of utter risk? Is there some secular avenue to the commitment for justice that confirms the infinite worth of personality such that we refuse to participate in the violation of its integrity, even at risk of death? There may be other ways to approach this problem than from the specific revelations of Christian theology. In fact, I think King's pluralism commits him to insist that there are other ways. Nevertheless, *some specific commitment is demanded* from each reflective nonviolent practitioner because the circumstances of nonviolent engagement will pose these questions in such a fundamental way that they *must be* answered.

The above considerations also lend warning to the limits of Gene Sharp's (1973) invaluable investigations into the methods of nonviolent action. True, the catalog of nonviolent resources can be pursued in explicit disengagement from the religious contexts in which they are often found. But at some point a real person takes a real risk, and here the issue of past effectiveness does not contain the issue of future risk. If nonviolence is to be *practiced* under risky circumstances, there are some commitments that cannot be fully motivated by a calculus of cause and effect. Spare us the zealot who shows little regard for her own life, but spare us also the calculating strategist who neglects the existential moment of risk. King's appeal to terms of Holy Spirit or God indicates the moment when one confronts death but chooses, nevertheless, *not to turn back*. In the end, even the philosopher Socrates pledged a sacrifice to the temple of Asclepius as his last dying words.

A PHILOSOPHY OF LIBERATION?

In the preceding pages I have explicated King's philosophy of nonviolence using four concepts—equality, structure, nonviolent direct action, and justice—that I consider crucial to a systematic understanding of King's mature thought. I have introduced each term with close attention to King's usage, then I have constructed a genealogy that would help us to understand each concept in the context of African American critical theory. Taken together, for the purposes of this reconstruction, King and his sources may be seen to constitute a Heroic Age of American Philosophy.

This study makes a genuine contribution to our understanding of King, especially as we seek to understand how his philosophy of nonviolence may be developed from the concrete experiences of the struggle for African American liberation. This treatment emphasizes a philosophy of liberation rather than a theology of liberation, and I think this emphasis provides fertile ground for critical examination and development of King's contributions to philosophy. If we cannot deny King's religious faith, neither can we understand King as simply deducing his complex logic of nonviolence from that faith.

What has emerged from this study is a logic of nonviolence that grapples with fact, even as it seeks loyalty to principle. This logic culminates in a complex and distinctive theory of justice, grounded in struggle and love. Because of this grounding, King's theory of justice must confront the risk of death and must explore the reserves of power that would sustain such a commitment. Ultimately, King must appeal to something that exceeds human control, but only after he has exhausted the reserves of intelligent human energy. If, as is widely assumed, King's struggle for justice is grounded in his religious faith, this study serves to show how, conversely, King's religious faith is grounded in his struggle for justice. The relationship between faith and struggle in King's philosophy presents an intellectual challenge that is not sufficiently appreciated. Perhaps the general relationship is best illuminated by the words of Angela Davis:

> In other words, it is true indeed that real wants, real needs, and real desires can be transformed into impotent wish-dreams via the process of religion, especially if things appear to be utterly hopeless in this world. But it is also true that these dreams can revert to their original state—as real wishes, real needs to change the existing social reality. It is possible to redirect these wish-dreams to the here and now. (Harris 1983: 135)

This study seeks to weigh in the evidence for terms of struggle, because contemporary analysis of King tends to emphasize terms of faith. Furthermore, this study seeks to show how terms of faith may be articulated almost completely in terms of justice. The result of this work, I hope, will be to reinvigorate debate about King's distinctive contribution to a theory of justice.

Having completed an explication of King's philosophy of non-violence, I wish to conclude by suggesting how the results of this investigation might affect our concept of philosophy. The first feature we note about the concept of philosophy explicated here is its participation in a history of dialogue. In order to practice philosophy we must be immersed in conversation—not necessarily conversation as we find it, but conversation as we reconstruct it. And the conversation reconstructed in support of King's philosophy of nonviolence has been marked by a color line.

With deliberate effort, I have chosen African American thinkers, and I have outlined a speculative conversation that accentuates the facts of a racist milieu. Douglass, Du Bois, Randolph, Bunche, Thurman, and King are all interpreted through their attempts to bring intelligence to bear upon the persistent experience of racism. As much as possible, I have asked what, specifically, do particular black voices have to say in contribution to a philosophy of nonviolence. This approach calls forth a fierce debate in which we are all called to account for the influence of one or another's skin color.

What fascination, for instance, do white scholars have in what black scholars think? When King was coming up through seminary and graduate school, the answer to the question was painfully obvious: none at all. Even today, the answer is usually as embarrassing as that. If philosophy is known for its conversations, then American philosophy must still be known for its color line. There are entire curricula that still (when all is said and done) have not entertained the opinion of a single black voice. As King said in his final book, it is still necessary to refute the idea that racism is an isolated feature of our experience (King 1967: 83). For this reason, it is important that scholars indeed reverse their discrimination. This essay shows by example how one may take inherited categories of exclusion and turn them into critical categories of inclusion. And doing just that more often might ultimately begin to affect our conception of philosophy. Finding the ineluctable logic of prejudice still assaulting our experience, we strive for integration. And this, I submit, is the wider meaning of affirmative action.

Plato tells us that philosophy is the art of dying, that a philosopher is a gadfly to the state and a midwife to knowledge. King reminds us that, before Plato, there were Jewish prophets, and that, before them, there were African viziers. In his recently published seminary papers, King makes it clear what he believed to be the contribution of African thought. "I think I can be safe in saying that the composing of proverbs were begun in Egypt," writes King in the seminary. "One of the first and, to many, the greatest proverb writers to appear on the Egyptian scene was Ptahotep. . . . It was the greatness of Ptahotep's proverbs that led Breasted to say, 'these maxims of Ptahotep constitute the earliest formulation of right conduct to be found in any literature'" (Carson 1992: 175). For King, Ptahotep was the one black voice that could not be denied admission to the curriculum. Neither could the seminary ignore the Egyptian cult of Isis.

If King was a master in his reconstruction of a racist curriculum, both in the seminary and at graduate school, then we do not fully understand King if we take that same curriculum as marking the apex of his philosophical advancement. During his notorious excursions in plagiarism, King was smuggling in contemporary black thinkers without a trace. Thus, Thurman, for one, never gets the credit he deserves. King was justified in claiming that a new sense of dignity was liberated during the civil rights movement. He was also justified in warning that Black Power could go too far and that white liberalism could be too self-interested. Today, we find the same predicament with respect to Afrocentrism. A new sense of dignity is certainly being created when students wear T-shirts that declare that "World history begins with African history." While, obviously, it is possible to go too far, common liberal criticisms of Afrocentrism have a shrillness of tone that is both defensive and selfish.

To this debate, white scholarship owes more than sound bites. White scholarship is white because no one has yet taken the trouble to integrate its curricula beyond white voices. And frankly, white scholarship looks worse than smug when all it can do is argue that Ptahotep's skin color is irrelevant. Ptahotep's skin color is exceedingly relevant to some students. So long as syllabus after syllabus continues to ignore black voices, some students will have good reason to take Ptahotep's skin color as an exceedingly relevant fact. And so this essay has taken skin color as an exceedingly relevant fact. And yet, it is possible to go too far. If we want to understand King, we cannot be separatist, even if we celebrate enormous contributions from Africa. As I argued at the beginning of this study, King's thought will not be nationalized. This study has embraced a kind of nationalism for a reason, but the obvious limits of nationalism are central to King's philosophy.

If this study explores King's African American heritage, the purpose of developing such a genealogy must remain provisional. We have not begun to ask, for instance, how King and the African American tradition reflect modern Western political discourse. As this project begins to integrate philosophy, the importance of such questions can only be acknowledged here. It is little remarked that soon after the Montgomery bus boycott King traveled to Ghana to celebrate its day of independence from Great Britain. Taylor Branch notes that New York reporters who covered the American delegation's departure from New York took a special interest in King, slighting Ralph Bunche and A. Philip Randolph in the process (Branch 1988: 214). With this delegation (and Vice President Richard Nixon, as well), King watched from a throng at midnight in Accra as a British flag was lowered and an African flag—of Marcus Garvey's favorite colors—was raised. Our understanding of King's attitudes toward African traditions and influences is abetted by his relative silence on these issues. This essay allows us to speculate, however, that, in this instance at least, a largely philosophical delegation was paying homage to its ongoing conversation with Africa.

One of King's seminary teachers collected translations of ancient texts from Africa, from which we may read the instruction of Ptahotep, from Egypt's Fifth Dynasty, circa 2450 B.C.:

> Let not thy heart be puffed-up because of thy knowledge; be not confident because thou art a wise man. Take counsel with the ignorant as well as the wise. The (full) limits of skill cannot be attained, and there is no skilled man equipped to his (full) advantage. Good speech is more hidden than the emerald, but it

may be found with maidservants at the grindstones. (Pritchard 1958: 234)

King was fond of quoting jewels of wisdom that he personally encountered. There was the woman in Montgomery who turned away from segregated buses, saying, "My feets is tired, but my soul is rested." And then there was the girl in Birmingham whose sign shrieked, "Feedom!" This is good speech, out of hearts that have not been puffed up, confirming Ptahotep's observation that philosophy may be best informed by a plain style. As Richard Lischer studied King's sermons, he reported that he heard "the same voice, that of an older man, speaking from the congregation. In those places in the sermon where King is analyzing contemporary problems in light of the Bible, the man regularly intones, 'Make it plain' " (Lischer 1989: 176). That was the voice of King's father. Thanks to his elders, a tradition of plain speaking is brought to bear upon King's style of philosophy with emphatic authority.

If philosophy—especially a philosophy of justice—may be comfortable with grindstones and plain talk, it also has its great halls where philosophers talk to one another, oftentimes not so plainly. King was relatively impatient with such spaces, even though he was qualified to walk there. Philosophy for the sake of philosophy had limited appeal to King. This tells us something about King, and it suggests something about philosophy as we find it. This essay owes its chief importance to the fact that, by today's light, it is not obvious that King's nonviolence can be an important philosophical conception. As philosophers talk to one another, however, King does have something to contribute, even as he lingers at the door of their great hall.

During the course of this essay, we have envisioned King within a great hall of African American philosophy. But we cannot imagine that King and his African American sources could simply replace other traditional figures in the repose of a resplendent, detached academy. That would be a strange metaphor for the philosophy of Douglass, Du Bois, Randolph, Bunche, Mays, Thurman, King, Daddy King, or the vizier Ptahotep. Thus, to the extent that we imagine philosophical conversation confined to moments of repose, our conception of philosophy is unsettled. Perhaps these viziers stand at the Lincoln

Memorial, between marches, choosing the site for their next campaign. Perhaps they meet at the Mississippi, or on the Georgia coast, in retreat.

Whatever grand hall or green shore that might be envisioned for a new academy of nonviolence, it will not be the *summum bonum* of philosophy, because these conversations are undertaken in service to further work, action, and campaigns for liberation. Thus, the maids at the grindstones and, indeed, stonecutters, also participate in nontrivial ways. For the new academy, the struggle of philosophy will be sustained in the streets, and in the pluralism of the street's demands. This is not to say that philosophy can ever be divorced from its moments of solitude or repose. There were times when King himself retreated to the forests of contemplation. In taking King seriously as a philosopher, however, we find that detachment from the streets cannot be regarded as a universal criterion for what counts as philosophy.

If our vision of philosophy begins with Plato's Academy, this visionary experiment reveals how King reaches further back than Plato for the earliest sources of his wisdom. When King looked for formulations of right conduct, he turned to traditions older than Aristotle's *Ethics*. These remarks suggest that King's philosophical importance is but dimly realizable today. Philosophy has yet to grow in the two directions of past and future suggested by King. In fact, the importance of the philosophy of nonviolence was barely known to King himself. Certainly King had explicit hopes that nonviolence could be extended to the labor struggle (via Chávez). But how could King have anticipated that nonviolence would lend support to feminist developments in the ethics of care (via Noddings and Gilligan). How could King see that the triple evils of structure would be expanded to a fourth, sexism, or a fifth, homophobia (via Davis and West). King did not see how the organizing principles of nonviolence could give way to ecological struggles at home and abroad (Greenpeace, Kelley). King could not have guessed, any better than the rest of us, that the tyranny of Soviet-bloc communism would deconstruct in a nonviolent moment, leaving everyone on the planet concerned with the amelioration of the suffering caused by homophobic, sexist, and racist imperialism—and suggesting in a dramatic way how the proletarian revolution has been superseded by nonviolent mass actions.

King did know, however, that nonviolence was a challenge to liberalism. King did try to warn that liberalism (whether contract or utilitarian) was trapped within its own preconceived assumptions of fair play, unable to deal with the fact that collective inequality is both pervasive and in need of affirmative action. King did try to warn that we go to hell when we maximize the minimum, minimize the maximum, and rationalize contemporary inequality as a market necessity. Furthermore, King argued in ways that suggest an inconsistency between a principle of equal respect and maximin distribution. Without illusions of some frictionless veil of ignorance, King encouraged us to prepare for the coercive mass actions that will be necessary to overcome structures of injustice. And King did predict that mass nonviolent action would continue to find new ways of working wonders. As the specialized reader will surely note, these considerations lend value to King's work as a philosopher among philosophers.

Any of the above propositions may be enlarged upon as we argue King's place among philosophers. What interests me most at this point, however, is King's contribution to American philosophy, especially America's nonviolence and its pragmatism. The case for American nonviolence is succinctly stated by Staughton Lynd (1966) in his introduction to Nonviolence in America: A Documentary History:

> It is often supposed that nonviolence is a philosophy conceived by Gandhi and Tolstoy, and recently imported into the United States by Martin Luther King, Jr. The fact is that a distinctive American tradition of nonviolence runs back to the seventeenth century. Thoreau's influence on Gandhi is well-known. Tolstoy, too, was indebted to American predecessors. In "A Message to the American People," written in 1901, Tolstoy stated that "Garrison, Parker, Emerson, Ballou, and Thoreau . . . specially influenced me." Three years later Tolstoy wrote that "Garrison was the first to proclaim this principle [of nonresistance to evil] as a rule for the organization of man's life." There is good ground for arguing that the Christian pacifism of the radical Reformation was kept alive from about 1650 to 1850 primarily by Americans; and that, in view of the cumulative impact of Penn and Woolman, Garrison

and Thoreau, William James and Jane Addams, and now Martin Luther King, Jr., America has more often been teacher than student in the history of the nonviolent idea. (Lynd 1966: xv–xvi)

As we have shown in the course of this essay, "the nonviolent idea" as developed by King certainly refers us to a distinctive African American tradition. We have also seen how "nonresistance to evil" has been transformed by King into "nonviolent confrontation with structural evil." What does it mean that we have a duty to love our neighbor? Who counts as a neighbor anyway? When confronted with this sort of query, Jesus does not fly into abstractions that are hard to understand. Instead, as King reminds us, Jesus tells a story, and throws us onto a dangerous curve in the Jericho road. If the story is not difficult to understand, it may nevertheless be difficult to emulate.

Early in his career King asked the question "What is man?" He answered by saying that humans are material and spiritual, that the material part is not to be condemned after the manner of religious fundamentalists—only the willful misuse of material goods is to be condemned. But furthermore, and to the point of our illustration, humans are divine in the sense that they are made in the image of God. This means, in fact, that humans have the capacity for intellect. Nothing less than intelligence is the feature that makes humans most divine and that indicates that we are made in the image of God. And certainly King was no stranger to passionate intelligence.

EPILOGUE FOR A TOUGH MIND

Every year I am presented with an undergraduate paper on Malcolm and Martin that reflects a prevailing belief that Malcolm was active and effective while Martin was passive and ineffective. I usually write something like this in response: "Indeed, Malcolm was a great person, but there is no need to boost Malcolm by disseminating disinformation about Martin." Passive? Ineffective? How quickly history gets transmuted and inverted, so that "circumstances appear upside down as in a *camera obscura*" (Marx 47).

What happened to the Martin once known as "the most dangerous and effective Negro leader in the country"? (Fairclough 1987: 155). The answer, I think, is that his memory has been swallowed up by a liberal conception of love. If all we remember about Martin today is that he was nonviolent because he insisted upon love, and if all we know about love is the sentimental liberal interpretation, then we naturally conclude that the King of love must have been passive and ineffective. On our way to this conclusion we must not remember how King "rocked the land like rolling thunder" (Kristofferson 1986), nor must we know anything about King's remarkable concept of love. In other words, we must be overcome by a soft-minded approach to King.

As King says, "Let us consider, first, the need for a tough mind, characterized by incisive thinking, realistic appraisal, and decisive judgment" (King 1963: 10). King's sermon "A Tough Mind and a Tender Heart" begins with the philosophical claim that "life at its best is a creative synthesis of opposites in fruitful harmony" (King 1963: 9). The sermon argues first for a tough mind, second for a soft heart. The order of things is important here. This is the first sermon published in King's 1963 collection, Strength to Love. And so the first argument made in this book of sermons is an argument for tough-mindedness: "The shape of the world today does not permit us the luxury of softmindedness" (King 1963: 13).

Soft-mindedness, for King, is "a prevalent tendency" that arises out of human "gullibility" and is manifest in our culture of adver-tisement. "Advertisers have long since learned that most people are softminded, and they capitalize on this susceptibility with skillful and effective slogans" (King 1963: 10). The soft-minded individual is prone to superstition, fear of change, religious stagnation, a dichot-omy between science and religion, fascism, and race prejudice (King 1963: 10–12):

> The softminded man always fears change. He feels security in the status quo, and he has an almost morbid fear of the new. For him, the greatest pain is the pain of a new idea. An elderly segregationist in the South is reported to have said, "I have come to see now that desegregation is inevitable. But I pray God that it will not take place until after I die." The softminded person always wants to

freeze the moment and hold life in the gripping yoke of sameness. (King 1963: 11)

Thus the soft-minded individual is passive and ineffective whenever change is needed. The sermon goes on to talk about the need for a tender heart, but, however tender a heart may be, it must nevertheless live in "fruitful harmony" with a tough mind. Having a tender heart, in other words, is no excuse for being either passive or ineffective. For very good reasons the tough mind must not only oppose segregation but also seek the means for change.

King's remarkable sermon was published in 1963, the year of the great Birmingham campaign. Taylor Branch has recently given us a vivid picture of that campaign, but his words are still mismatched against the incessant image of screaming firehoses or the lingering echo of James Foreman's passionate declaration that Birmingham was a betrayal. Thus, the prevailing image teaches us that, because King was a soft-hearted man, he subjected hundreds of people to brutal victimization and sold out to the timetable of the downtown business district. After all those people got hurt, King agreed to 60 more days of segregation and then ate steak for breakfast. Dare we refer to Birmingham as evidence that King was tough-minded, active, or effective?

For starters, we might recall that Birmingham is still the only great example of the Americanization of Gandhi's maxim to "Fill the jails!" On D-Day, May 2, 1963, six-year-old children shouted their age and jumped into paddy wagons (Branch 1988: 757). Two days later, police commissioner Bull Connor, shouting, "Dammit! Turn on the hoses," was only swallowed up by silence (Branch 1988, 767). When the city later jailed King, he tried to hold himself hostage, refusing bail until the demonstrators were released. But King in jail was a fact too hot for the White House to handle, and he was quickly rescued (Branch 1988: 786). By this time, the crisis of Birmingham had become so intense that the vaults of Chase Manhattan Bank were opened after hours, at the request of Nelson Rockefeller, so that bundles of cash could be hustled off to Birmingham to pay everyone's bail (Branch 1988: 789). These are just a few reminders of how passive, ineffective, and soft-minded King was. Tough-minded King was out to break the back of Southern segregation in the same city that bore Angela Davis and swept her up to Dynamite Hill so that she might grow up where bombs go off in the night. Perhaps we forget that "Bombingham" was the most unlikely territory one could choose for a nonviolent confrontation—and that, nevertheless, thousands rushed into battle, ages six to sixty.

These observations help us to appreciate what King meant when he talked about love, so that we can understand in what ways King's battalions were motivated by love. If *agape* love is creative in its concern for others, it is restless in its pursuit of justice. The Birmingham campaign was, first, a tough-minded effort to vindicate the centennial of the Emancipation Proclamation. After 100 years of mostly Jim Crow laws and traditions, King's campaign would force desegregation upon the downtown business district of Birmingham and prove the point that a new reality was dawning for all of, and the good of, the nation. And sure enough, an infamous century of segregation ended right there, though not without one final, despotic bombing. The children of Birmingham had won the new century. Four of them paid with their lives. Those were tough-minded kids.

Today there is a lone statue in Kelley Ingram Park that stands in representation of that revolutionary campaign. And a new generation makes its pilgrimage to 16th Street. The day I went, there were four guys in the park, about my age, so they were nine years old in 1963. We talked briefly. And, although the gulf between us was enormous, we shared the common feeling that something liberating had happened there. Even as Kelley Ingram Park commemorates a campaign that was *regulated* by love, I think today's pilgrims are more interested in the liberating confrontation that is more widely publicized and recognized. In this sense, I do not think liberation movements are *motivated* by love for their oppressors. Pilgrims don't come to Kelley Ingram Park to celebrate their tolerance for oppression.

In this epilogue about King's concept of love, I have been focusing on the aspect of the tough mind. And so there are liberals who may object that, since I am not talking about a soft heart, I haven't begun to talk about King's concept of love. But this is just the point I am trying to make about King's concept of love. First King talks about the shrewdness of the serpent, *then* he talks about the harmlessness of the dove.

As Malcolm X's martyrdom began to awaken masses of people to his message, especially with publication of The Autobiography with Alex Haley in 1965, and as brutality continued to batter the nonviolent movement, King's love ethic became vulnerable to criticism that it wasn't tough enough to face the realities of white power. Even the eminent psychologist Kenneth B. Clark argued that King could not expect the masses of black Americans to "love their oppressors" (Clark 1985: 9). In the 1985 introduction to interviews that he had conducted with Martin, Malcolm, and Baldwin, Professor Clark wrote:

> While my relationship with Martin was at all times friendly, and while I agreed from the beginning with his position on Vietnam, our views did not always coincide. For example, I frequently discussed with him the question of the extent to which he could expect blacks in America, who were oppressed, to be able to muster the ability "to love their oppressors." I would argue that this placed an additional burden on the masses of Negroes. It required a level of maturity and sophistication that I, as a psychologist, did not believe most human beings had. Martin would respond to these concerns by explaining the philosophical meaning of his concept of love. Essentially, he felt, love meant not being dehumanized by oppression, but, rather, seeking to tap the humanity and conscience of the oppressor. (Clark 1985: 9–10)

Thus, we conclude our investigation of King's logic of nonviolence with this brief reexamination of his philosophy of love.

In his 1963 sermon, King concludes his treatment of the need for tough-mindedness by warning that "a nation or a civilization that continues to produce softminded men purchases its own spiritual death on an installment plan" (King 1963: 13). Indeed we are awash in such installment plans today. And King's words continue to tell us that tough-mindedness alone, not fuzzy faith, is going to enable us to avert our own spiritual death. "But we must not stop with the cultivation of a tough mind," preaches King. "The gospel also demands a tender heart" (King 1963: 13). Thus, King begins his argument for a tender heart by arguing the general case. Whether one is a nonviolent activist or not, King insists that love is a human necessity. With a hard heart, we never truly love, we lack capacity for compassion, we never see people as people but as objects and cogs, terminal points in the distribution of goods and services (King 1963: 13):

> The rich fool was condemned not because he was not tough-minded, but rather because he was not tenderhearted. Life for him was a mirror in which he saw only himself, and not a window through which he saw other selves. Dives went to hell, not because he was wealthy, but because he was not tenderhearted enough to see Lazarus and because he made no attempt to bridge the gulf between himself and his brother. (King 1963: 14)

Now there is a cynical moment in every struggle for liberation when we want to stop trying to bridge the gulf. Either we are dismayed by our opponents or, yes, we are disillusioned by our friends. When it seems that either implacable party no longer cares to bridge the gulf of oppression, we ask ourselves, "What's the use? Why try?" Many such moments must be overcome during the long preparation that precedes any dramatic movement such as Birmingham. And paradoxically, King suggests to us that these hard-bitten moments of cynicism cannot be overcome by tough-mindedness alone. After all, the gulf of oppression is a realm of battered souls, and if we stop feeling compassion for that pain of oppression, then we are succumbing to the gulf, and this leaves us in no position to render the best efforts we may make.

And this is where history left King himself, courageously refusing to succumb to the gulf of oppression, although neither liberal America nor Black Power were any longer interested in bridging the gulf that still divided our nation. In those last years of his life, King argued to both sides of the gulf that they must not surrender the strength of love. To Black Power and liberal America alike, King argued they could not bracket their hearts from fellow citizens, nor could they cease to exercise the toughest rigors of their own minds. Against the division of oppression, one first asserts the wholeness of one's individual personality. Instead of mirrors, one seeks windows. And yet this is not what has happened. Cornel West is one voice that today picks up where King left off, encouraging citizens to reestablish communication in a spirit of common undertaking, encouraging us, in other words, to look for one another across the habitual gulf of the color line.

Meanwhile, King has been swallowed up by Jonah's great whale, and it is time we liberated his memory from a liberal blubberous conception of love. In other words it is time for American liberalism to look for King through real windows, not mirrors of its own making. And for all the things this might mean, I would like to look at King as he prepares to mount the great Birmingham campaign in April 1963. Numerous voices of moderation advise him to take it easy, because there is a new administration in town. Albert Boutwell has just defeated Bull Connor in a tenacious runoff election for mayor, and the Birmingham *News* appears on the stands, "its front page bright with a color drawing showing a golden sun rising over the city. It was captioned: 'New Day Dawns for Birmingham' " (King 1964: 59).

> For all the optimism expressed in the press and elsewhere, we were convinced that Albert Boutwell was, in Fred Shuttlesworth's apt phrase, "just a dignified Bull Connor." We knew that the former state senator and lieutenant governor had been the principal author of Alabama's Pupil Placement Law, and was a consistent supporter of segregationist views. His statement a few days after the election that "we citizens of Birmingham respect and understand one another" showed that he understood nothing about two-fifths of Birmingham's citizens, to whom even polite segregation was no respect. (King 1964: 59)

Does King's love ethic require him to be gullible to our culture of advertising? Does King's love ethic settle for docile patience where there is still no justice? Does King's love ethic require him to dismiss the historical behavior patterns of his opponents so that they might be portrayed in a flattering fashion? Does King's love ethic require him to turn both cheeks and head home, leave a battle that he need not encounter, and retire to a quiet life of intimate pleasure?

Today we are awash with new administrations at all levels of our complex institutional world. And King's ethic of love requires that we look through real windows using tough minds, that we not pander to the pandering of the press, that we insist upon justice, and, no, docile patience is not enough—with nice guys we just might finish last—flattery is not helpful, and we do not turn cheeks and run when the facts show that we are, indeed, once again, faced with "just a dignified Bull Connor." Because, if that's what we've got today, then we've all been hiding out too long. If we seek justice within a World House, then, with King, we will resume a tough-minded investigation into the levers of power and protest so that we may exercise our liberty to full effect. In any case, we are not allowed to rest in any self-satisfied, cynical knowledge that the world will get what's coming. King's logic of nonviolence requires us to care a great deal more than that.

Finally, it must be admitted that King's logic of nonviolence has been too quickly appropriated by liberal friends of the status quo, in order to talk "sense" to would-be militants. This patronizing use of nonviolence serves to discredit King's philosophy by deploying it as a means of social control. As we know, King argued both the "sense" and the "morality" of nonviolence. Thus, liberal friends of the status quo conveniently ignore the part of King's argument that urges risk and sacrifice among the privileged classes. Thus, the sooner that philosophy elevates the theory of justice outlined by King's logic of nonviolence, the sooner "morality" will be thrown into the crisis announced by King's revolution of values and the sooner a creative tension of change will come to pervade our institutions. Meanwhile, the true requirements of a nonviolent future will not be fully satisfied so long as the "sense" of nonviolence is simply preached to the masses while theories of justice carefully calculated to insulate the "morality" of the status quo hold sway.

Appendix

A CHRONOLOGY
OF EVENTS

1955–1956, MONTGOMERY, ALABAMA—Following the arrest of Rosa Parks, who refuses to give up her bus seat to a white person, black citizens of Montgomery organize a year-long boycott of the city bus system. Martin Luther King, Jr., a new pastor in town, is selected to serve as president of the boycott committee.

1957, ATLANTA, GEORGIA—At King's invitation, about sixty black pastors convene to organize the Southern Christian Leadership Conference. Under King's leadership, the SCLC will provide an organizational base for nonviolent pursuit of civil rights.

1961–1962, ALBANY, GEORGIA—King and the SCLC are invited to join an ongoing campaign for desegregation, but months of effort result in a stalemate.

1963, BIRMINGHAM, ALABAMA—King and the SCLC join with Reverend Fred Shuttlesworth and the Alabama Christian Movement for Human Rights to confront segregation in downtown facilities. Schoolchildren join the movement to fill the jails, and the movement wins its demands. The campaign is widely credited for galvanizing political support for the Civil Rights Act of 1964.

1965, SELMA, ALABAMA—King and the SCLC, along with the Student Nonviolent Coordinating Committee, undertake a three-month campaign

---

Note. For more details, see Fairclough, 1987.

for voting rights. The campaign culminates in a march from Selma to the state capitol in Montgomery. Meanwhile, President Lyndon B. Johnson introduces the Voting Rights Act in Congress after a nationally televised appeal.

1966, CHICAGO, ILLINOIS—King and the SCLC join the Chicago Freedom Movement and mount a campaign for open housing. Dramatic marches through white suburbs are halted when King accepts an agreement brokered by Mayor Richard Daley.

1968, MEMPHIS, TENNESSEE—King and the SCLC march in support of a strike by city sanitation workers.

1968, WASHINGTON, DC—King and the SCLC plan a summer campaign of disobedience in the nation's capital to secure national legislation that would abolish poverty, either by means of a minimum income or full employment.

BIBLIOGRAPHY

Anderson, Jervis. 1973. *A Philip Randolph: A Biographical Portrait.* New York: Harcourt Brace Jovanovich.

Ansbro, John J. 1982. *Martin Luther King, Jr.: The Making of a Mind.* Maryknoll, NY: Orbis.

Appiah, Anthony. 1992. *In My Father's House: Africa in the Philosophy of Color.* New York: Oxford University Press.

Asante, Molefi Kete. 1980. *Afrocentricity.* Trenton, NJ: Africa World Press.

———. 1987. *The Afrocentric Idea.* Philadelphia: Temple University Press.

———. 1990. *Kemet, Afrocentricity, and Knowledge.* Trenton, NJ: Africa World Press.

Baldwin, Lewis V. 1991. *There Is a Balm in Gilead: The Cultural Roots of Martin Luther King, Jr.* Minneapolis: Fortress.

Bennett, Lerone, Jr. 1964. *What Manner of Man: A Biography of Martin Luther King, Jr.* Chicago: Johnson.

Blum, Lawrence. 1994. *Moral Perception and Particularity.* Cambridge, UK: Cambridge University Press.

Branch, Taylor. 1988. *Parting the Waters: America in the King Years.* New York: Simon and Schuster.

Bunche, Ralph Johnson. 1936. *A World View of Race.* Port Washington, NY: Kennikat Press, 1968.

Butler, Broadus. 1983. "Frederick Douglass: American Philosopher." In *Philosophy Born of Struggle* (Ed. Leonard Harris). Dubuque, IA: Kendall-Hunt.

Carson, Clayborne. 1992. *The Papers of Martin Luther King, Jr.* (Vol. 1). Berkeley: University of California.

———. 1994. *The Papers of Martin Luther King, Jr.* (Vol. 2). Berkeley: University of California.

Castell, Alburey, Donald M. Borchert, and Arthur Zucker. 1994. *An Introduction to Modern Philosophy: Examining the Human Condition.* New York: Macmillan.

Clark, Kenneth B. 1985. *King, Malcolm, Baldwin: Three Interviews.* Middletown, CT: Wesleyan University Press.

Cone, James H. 1984. "Martin Luther King, Jr., Black Theology—Black Church." *Theology Today* 40.4 (January): 409–420.

———. 1991. *Martin and Malcolm and America: A Dream or a Nightmare.* Maryknoll, NY: Orbis.

Cook, Anthony E. 1990. "Beyond Critical Legal Studies: The Reconstructive Theology of Dr. Martin Luther King, Jr." *Harvard Law Review* 103 (March): 985–1044.

Cruse, Harold. 1967. *The Crisis of the Negro Intellectual.* New York: Morrow.

———. 1987. *Plural but Equal.* New York: Morrow.

Davis, Angela. 1985. "Peace Is a Sisters' Issue, Too: Afro-American Women and the Campaign against Nuclear Arms." In *Women, Culture, and Politics.* New York: Vintage, 1990.

Dewey, John. 1934. "The Human Abode of the Religious Function." In *The Later Works: Vol. 9. A Common Faith.* Carbondale, IL: Southern Illinois University Press, 1989.

———. 1938. "The Needed Reform of Logic." In *The Later Works: Vol. 12. Logic: The Theory of Inquiry.* Carbondale, IL: Southern Illinois University Press, 1986.

Douglass, Frederick. 1845. *Narrative of the Life of Frederick Douglass* (Ed. Benjamin Quarles). Cambridge, MA: Harvard University Press, 1960.

———. 1852. "The Meaning of the Fourth of July for the Negro." In *The Life and Writings of Frederick Douglass* (Vol. 2, pp. 181–204, Ed. Philip Foner). New York: International Publishers, 1950.

Du Bois, W. E. B. 1898–1917. *Atlanta University Publications* (Proceedings of the Annual Conference for the Study of Negro Problems) (20 vols.). Atlanta: Atlanta University Press.

———. 1899. *The Philadelphia Negro: A Social Study* (Introduction by Herbert Aptheker). Milwood, NY: Kraus-Thomson, 1973.

———. 1903. *The Souls of Black Folk.* New York: Penguin, 1969.

———. 1910–1940. *The Crisis: A Record of the Darker Races* (Vols. 1–47). New York: Negro Universities Press, 1969.

———. 1968. *The Autobiography of W. E. B. Du Bois: A Soliloquy on Viewing My Life from the Last Decade of Its First Century* (Ed. Herbert Aptheker). New York: International Publishers.

Fairclough, Adam. 1987. *To Redeem the Soul of America: The Southern Christian Leadership Conference and Martin Luther King, Jr.* Athens, GA: University of Georgia Press.

Farmer, James. 1942. "Provisional Plans for Brotherhood Mobilization." In *Lay Bare the Heart* (pp. 355–360). New York: Plume, 1985.

Fletcher, Joseph. 1966. "Love Decides There and Then." In *Situation Ethics: The New Morality* (pp. 134–145). Philadelphia: Westminister.

Fluker, Walter E. 1990. "They Looked for a City: A Comparison of the Idea of Community in Howard Thurman and Martin Luther King, Jr." [Special issue]. *Journal of Religious Ethics* 18.2 (Fall): 33–55.

Forman, James. 1985. "Betrayal in Birmingham." In The Making of Black Revolution-
    aries (pp. 311–316). Washington, DC: Open Hand.
Garrow, David J. 1986. Bearing the Cross: Martin Luther King, Jr., and the Southern Christian
    Leadership Conference. New York: William Morrow.
Genovese, Eugene D. 1992, May 11. "Pilgrim's Progress" [Review of MLK, Jr.,
    Papers, Vol. 1]. New Republic, pp. 33–40.
Gilligan, Carol. 1982. In a Different Voice: Psychological Theory and Women's Development.
    Cambridge, MA: Harvard University Press.
Hallman, Max O. 1995. Expanding Philosophical Horizons: A Nontraditional Philosophy
    Reader. Belmont, CA: Wadsworth.
Harris, Leonard. 1983. Philosophy Born of Struggle: Anthology of Afro-American Philosophy
    from 1917. Dubuque, IA: Kendall-Hunt.
———. 1989. The Philosophy of Alain Locke: Harlem Renaissance and Beyond. Philadelphia:
    Temple.
———. 1995. "'Believe It or Not' or the Ku Klux Klan and American Philosophy
    Exposed." Proceedings of the American Philosophical Association 86.5 (May): 133–
    137.
Hickman, Larry A. 1990. John Dewey's Pragmatic Technology. Bloomington: Indiana
    University Press.
James, William. 1910. "The Moral Equivalent of War." In The Writings of William
    James: A Comprehensive Edition (pp. 660–671, Ed. John J. McDermott). Chicago:
    University of Chicago Press, 1977.
Journal of Religious Ethics Fall 1990 [Special issue on King].
Kazemek, Francis E. 1988. "The Fierce Urgency of Now: Honoring the Life of
    Martin Luther King, Jr., in and out of the Classroom." Journal of Education
    170.1: 66–76.
Kearns, Kell. 1988. In Remembrance of Martin (Produced by Lori Kearns and Dave
    Marquis, 60 min.). Alexandria, VA: PBS Video.
Kessler, Gary E. 1995. Voices of Wisdom: A Multicultural Philosophy Reader. Belmont, CA:
    Wadsworth.
King, Martin Luther, Jr. 1958. Stride toward Freedom: The Montgomery Story. San
    Francisco: Harper and Row.
———. 1959. The Measure of a Man. Philadelphia: Christian Education Press.
———. 1963. Strength to Love. Philadelphia: Fortress, 1989.
———. 1964. Why We Can't Wait. New York: Mentor.
———. 1967. Where Do We Go from Here: Chaos or Community? Boston: Beacon.
———. 1968. The Trumpet of Conscience. San Francisco: Harper and Row.
King, Martin Luther, Sr., with Clayton Riley. 1980. Daddy King: An Autobiography.
    New York: William Morrow.
Kondrashov, Stanislav. 1981. The Life and Death of Martin Luther King, Jr. (Trans. Keith
    Hammond). Moscow: Progress Publishers, 1984.
Lerner, Michael, and Cornel West. 1995. Jews and Blacks: Let the Healing Begin. New
    York: Grosset/Putnam.

Lewis, David L. 1970. *King: A Critical Biography.* New York: Praeger.

————. 1993. *W. E. B. Du Bois: Biography of a Race.* New York: Henry Holt.

Lischer, Richard. 1989. "The Word That Moves: The Preaching of Martin Luther King, Jr." *Theology Today* 46.2 (July): 169–182.

————. 1995. *The Preacher King: Martin Luther King, Jr., and the Word that Moved America.* New York: Oxford University Press.

Lynd, Staughton. 1966. *Nonviolence in America: A Documentary History.* Indianapolis: Bobbs-Merrill.

Malcolm X, with Alex Haley. 1965. *The Autobiography of Malcolm X.* New York: Ballantine.

Marable, Manning. 1987. "King's Last Years: 1966–1968—From Civil Rights to Social Transformation." In *Fulfill the Dream* (Ed. Howard Richards and Cassie Schwerner). Richmond, IN: Earlham College, 1988.

————. 1990. "The Legacy of Martin Luther King, Jr." In *Crisis of Color and Democracy: Essays on Race, Class, and Power.* Monroe, MN: Common Courage Press, 1992.

Marty, Martin E. 1989. "Martin Luther King: The Preacher as Virtuoso." *Christian Century* (April 5): 348–350.

Marx, Karl, and Frederick Engels. 1970. *The German Ideology* (Ed. C. J. Arthur). New York: International Publishers.

Mays, Benjamin. 1938. *The Negro's God.* New York: Negro Universities Press, 1969.

Miller, Keith D. 1992. *Voice of Deliverance: The Language of Martin Luther King, Jr., and Its Sources.* New York: Free Press.

Murdoch, Iris. 1970. *The Sovereignty of Good.* London: Routledge and Kegan Paul.

Myrdal, Gunnar. 1944. *An American Dilemma: The Negro Problem and Modern Democracy.* New York: Harper.

Noddings, Nell. 1984. *Caring.* Berkeley: University of California Press.

Oates, Stephen B. 1982. *Let the Trumpet Sound: The Life of Dr. Martin Luther King, Jr.* New York: Mentor.

Peirce, Charles S. 1878. "How to Make Our Ideas Clear." In *Charles S. Peirce: Selected Writings* (Ed. Philip P. Wiener). New York: Dover, 1966.

Pettigrew, Thomas F. 1964. *A Profile of the Negro American.* Princeton: Van Nostrand.

Pfeffer, Paula F. 1990. *A. Philip Randolph: Pioneer of the Civil Rights Movement.* Baton Rouge: Louisiana State University Press.

Pritchard, James B. 1958. *The Ancient Near East: An Anthology of Texts and Pictures.* Princeton: Princeton University Press.

Ralph, James. 1993. *Northern Protest: Martin Luther King, Jr., Chicago, and the Civil Rights Movement.* Cambridge, MA: Harvard University Press.

Randall, Margaret. 1983. [Interview of Fernando Cardenal]. In *Christians in the Nicaraguan Revolution* (Trans. Mariana Valverde). Vancouver, BC: New Star.

Randolph, A. Philip. 1917. *The Messenger: New Opinion of the New World—World's Greatest Negro Monthly* (Ed. Randolph and Chandler Owen). New York: Negro Universities Press, 1969.

Reddick, Lawrence D. 1959. *Crusader without Violence: A Biography of Martin Luther King,* Jr. New York: Harper.

Royce, Josiah. 1918. *The Problem of Christianity* (Introduction by John E. Smith). Chicago: University of Chicago Press, 1968.

Rustin, Bayard. 1987. "A. Philip Randolph." *Yale Review* 76 (Spring): 418–427.

Santayana, George. 1986. *Persons and Places: Fragments of Autobiography* (Ed. William G. Holzberger and Herman J. Saatkamp, Jr.). Cambridge, MA: MIT Press.

Senghor, Leopold Sedar. 1965. *Prose and Poetry* (Trans. John Reed and Clive Wake). London: Heineman.

Sharp, Gene. 1973. *The Politics of Nonviolent Action* (3 vols.). Boston: Sargent.

Smith, Ervin. 1981. *The Ethics of Martin Luther King, Jr.* (Bibliographical essay by Janine Anderson Sawada, Studies in American Religion, Vol. 2). New York: Edwin Mellen Press.

Smith, Kenneth L. 1989. "The Radicalization of Martin Luther King, Jr.: The Last Three Years." *Journal of Ecumenical Studies* 26 (Spring): 270–288.

Smith, Kenneth L., and Ira G. Zepp, Jr. 1986. *Search for the Beloved Community: The Thinking of Martin Luther King, Jr.* Lanham, MD: University Press of America.

Soccio, Douglas J. 1995. *Archetypes of Wisdom: An Introduction to Philosophy.* Belmont, CA: Wadsworth.

Solomon, Robert. 1990. *A Passion for Justice: Emotions and the Origins of the Social Contract.* Reading, MA: Addison-Wesley.

Thomas, Laurence. 1993. *Vessels of Evil: American Slavery and the Holocaust.* Philadelpia: Temple University Press.

Thurman, Howard. 1949. *Jesus and the Disinherited.* Richmond, IN.: Friends United Press, 1981.

———. 1979. *With Head and Heart: The Autobiography of Howard Thurman.* New York: Harcourt Brace Jovanovich.

Walton, Hanes, Jr. 1971. *The Political Philosophy of Martin Luther King, Jr.* (Introduction by Samuel Du Bois Cook). Westport, CT: Greenwood.

Ward, Douglas Turner. 1966. *Day of Absence.* In *Two Plays.* New York: Third Press.

Washington, James Melvin (Ed.). 1986. *A Testament of Hope: The Essential Writings of Martin Luther King, Jr.* San Francisco: Harper and Row.

West, Cornel. 1989. *The American Evasion of Philosophy: A Genealogy of Pragmatism.* Madison: University of Wisconsin Press.

Woolfolk, George. 1981. "W. R. Banks: Public College Educator." In *Black Leaders: Texans for their Times* (Ed. Alwyn Barr and Robert A. Calvert). Austin: Texas State Historical Association.

INDEX

Action, King's concept of, 147
African American intellectual tradition
  in American academy, 213–215, 216–217
  concept of equality, 41–44
  economic justice, 133
  exponents of, 3, 5–8, 213
  as humanicentric, 41–43, 44
  King in, 3, 5–8, 18, 19–20, 202–203, 215–
    216, 219
  nommo, 19
  nonviolence in, 92, 202–203
  progressive nationalism in, 141–142
  structural analysis in, 49–50, 64–65
Afrocentrism, 214
Agriculture, 120–121
Allen, Geri, xv
Ansbro, John, 14, 18, 229
Asante, Molefe, 14, 19, 229

Backlash, 195–196, 200
Black Power movements, 13, 51
  black–white coalitions and, 199, 200
  conceptual basis, 140
  dialectical analysis, 58–59
  King and, 28–29, 153–154, 189–195
  motivation for, 56
  as nationalist movement, 141–142
  nonviolent direct action and, 139–140
  strategic weaknesses, 161–162
Bunche, Ralph Johnson, 49–50, 194
  in African American intellectual tradition, 3,
    5, 130
  Du Bois and, 130, 136
  on intensity of race prejudice, 136–137
  international perspective, 125–126
  on international significance of African
    American liberation, 133–134
  on meaning of equality, 127–129
  on perpetuation of racism, 132–133
  professional accomplishments, 125

  race-class analysis, 97–98, 129–132
  on racial justice, 126–127
  on racist imperialism, 134–136
Butler, Broadus, xv, 6, 19, 41–44, 186, 229

Capitalism
  African American cooperative economy, 82–
    84
  imperialism in, 134–136
  implications of mass production, 92–93
  King on, 2–3, 100
  laissez-faire principle, 108–109
  obstacles to social reform, 107–108
  race relations in, 92–93, 97
  Randolph on, 118–119
  in structural analysis of racism, 88–89, 104–
    105, 118–119
  suppression of agitators, 111–113
  transnational, 109
Chicago, King's experiences in, 25–26, 78, 80,
    152–153
Christianity
  concepts of power and love in, 191
  Douglass's condemnation of, 38–39
  Marxism and, 100
  struggle for equality and, 34–35
  See also Religious faith/practice
Clark, Kenneth, 223, 230
Class analysis
  black aristocracy, 122
  black petty bourgeoisie, 79
  Bunche's, 7
  Du Bois' study of black Philadelphia, 69–79
  intensity of race prejudice, 137
  international struggle, 136, 137, 138
  King's, 7
  middle-class participation in social reform,
    77–78, 79–80, 175, 200–201
  Randolph's, 7, 107–113
  salience of, 7–8

in structural analysis of American racism, 57–
58, 59–60, 97–98, 104–105, 116–117,
138–143
supremacist tradition, 128–129, 130
systems vs. personalities in, 58
Coalitions
interracial, black power movement and, 199,
200
in logic of nonviolence, 98–99
for social change, 175–176
for structural change, 62–63
Cook, Anthony E., 20, 230
Cruse, Harold, 194–195

Davis, Angela, 6, 19, 52, 53, 80, 212, 217,
222, 230
Death, philosophical implications of, 209–210
Deconstructive critical thought, 20
Deductive reasoning, 16, 35
Douglass, Frederick
in African American intellectual tradition, 3,
5, 6, 42
evidence of structural analysis, 64–65
Independence Day speech, 25, 36–38
intellectual method, 39–40
King on, 36
similarities to King, 23–25
Du Bois, W. E. B.
in African American intellectual tradition, 3,
5, 6–7, 125
Bunche and, 130, 136–137
centrality of color line, 46, 47, 68, 80–89,
138–139
class consciousness, 122
on closed black economy, 82–84
on collective responsibility, 66–67
contribution of, as social scientist, 130
elitist formulations of, 81–82
intellectual project, 67–69
King and, 49, 50
on labor question, 89–91
love ethic, 206–207
as petty bourgeois, 79–80
Randolph and, 101–107, 113–121, 124
on social agitation, 85–86
socialist thought, 91, 139
structural analysis, 65–80, 95–96
on Teutonic civilization, 65–66, 67, 122
on World War I, 91–92, 101–103

Economic analysis
African American cooperative economy, 81–84
cycle of racial oppression, 133
Du Bois' study of black Philadelphia, 69–79
ideological component of exploitation, 116–
117
implications of mass production, 92–93
in industrial democracy, 124
in logic of nonviolence, 139
power of African American community, 177–
178

racial component of exploitation, 140–141,
167
structural basis of American racism, 55–56,
57, 59–61
Economic issues. See Class analysis
Education, nonviolent direct action and, 146–
147
Enlightenment concepts, 127
Equality
in African American intellectual tradition, 41–
44
in American thought, 25, 26–27, 30–31, 44
centrality of, in liberation struggle, 32–34
characteristics of struggle for, 150
collective value, 34
commitment of American social groups to,
31–32, 34–35
definition of, 27–28, 35, 39–40
foundationalist conceptualization, 35, 40
freedom and, 34
hypocrisy in practice, 142
in King's philosophy, 17, 44–45
in logic of nonviolence, 29–30, 32–33
love ethic and, 186–187
race in conceptualizations of, 129–130
social–political conceptualizations, 127–129
timeliness of King's philosophy, 40–41

Farrakhan, Lewis, 141–142
Fear
in American culture, 162–163
as basis of racism, 17
of death, 209–210
Feminism, xii, 99, 187, 217
Fluker, Walter, 8, 14, 231
Freedom
equality and, 17, 34
individualistic conceptualization, 34

Gandhi, Mohandas, 34–35, 149
Gender issues, feminization of black ghettos, 73
Gilligan, Carol, 187, 217, 231

Harris, Leonard, v–viii, xv, 8, 14, 19, 43, 44,
194, 212, 231
Hatred, 164–165, 192–193
Hickman, Larry, xv, xvi, 52, 231
Humanicentric tradition, 41–44, 206
Hypocrisy, 142

Idealism, 144
Individual responsibility
in American intellectual tradition, 65–66
collective responsibility vs., 58, 61
Du Bois' analysis, 66–67
structural analysis of racism, 51
Integration, 194–195
Intentionality in racist behavior, 51
International perspective
after World War I, 114–116
Bunche's intellectual orientation, 125–126

International perspective (cont.)
  class struggle, 136–138
  King's, 179
  lynching in, 123
  progressive nationalist movements and, 141–
    142
  racist imperialism, 134–135
  Randolph's project, 122–123
  significance of African American liberation,
    133–134
  transnational capitalism, 109

Jackson, Jesse, 148
Jesus Christ, 151–155, 181–183
Judaism, 199
Justice
  American structure, 188–189
  as basis for social reform, 120, 196–197
  Black Power movement and, 189–190, 193
  King's conceptualization, 8, 150–151, 185–
    186, 196–198
  in logic of nonviolence, 147
  love and, 186–187
  racial inequality and, 60–61
  social change and, 193–194

King, Coretta Scott, xiv
King, Martin Luther, Jr., life of, 145
  assassination, 142–143
  civil rights campaigns, 148–149, 221–222,
    227–228
  early exposures to racism, 10, 204
  failures of civil rights movement, 158
  goals of civil rights movement, 178–179
  higher education, 17–18
  historical context, 10–11
  as petty bourgeois, 79–80
  published works, 12
  successes of nonviolent movement, 13, 154–
    155
King, Martin Luther, Jr., philosophy of
  in African American intellectual tradition, 3,
    5–8, 18, 19–20, 202–203, 215–216, 219
  black group identity in, 194–195
  Black Power movement and, 139–140, 141,
    153–154, 189–195
  on capitalism, 100
  class analysis, 98
  concept of equality, 25–36, 39–40, 44–45
  concept of justice, 8, 150–151, 185–186,
    196–198
  conceptualization of color line, 47
  contemporary analyses of, 14–21, 219–226
  of cycle of fear in America, 154, 161–168
  defense of nonviolent direct action, 155–162
  Douglass's intellectual method and, 39–40
  early scholarship, 214, 215–216
  on economic dimensions of racism, 167
  ethic of love, 204–209, 221–224
  idealism, 144
  influences on, 11–12, 18
  international perspective in, 179

  language of, 3, 13–14
  legacy of, 1–4, 9–10, 143, 150, 184, 217–
    218
  Marxist content, 99–100
  means and ends in, 185
  moral basis, 205
  originality of, 4–5, 203–204
  as philosophy of liberation, 211–219
  practical advantages of nonviolence, 164
  process orientation, 150
  race–class relations, 138–143
  religious basis, 9, 17–18, 207–211, 212
  on responsibilities of white liberalism, 195–
    202, 218
  revolution of values in, 9, 201–202, 203–204
  social action in, 145–146, 147–148
  social context for liberation struggle, 168–169
  structural analysis, 47–48, 49, 52–64
  Thurman and, 145–146, 151–155
  tough-mindedness of, 219–226
  urban context, 121
  work ethic, 172–173

Labor movement
  King on, 177–178
  race and, 83–84, 89–91, 104–105
  strike of African American labor, 123
Law, American racism and, 56
Lerner, Michael, 19, 53, 99, 232
"Letter from Birmingham Jail," 53–54
  philosophical content, 11–12
  targets of, 24, 31
Liberalism
  current challenges for, 225
  in liberation struggle, 195–202, 218
  as obstacle to liberation, 31–32, 196–197
Logic of nonviolence
  African American intellectual tradition, 92,
    202–203
  allies in struggle, 98–99
  as analytical system, 147, 149
  basis in structural analysis, 51–52, 60–62
  collective self-interest in, 140–141
  concept of justice in, 147
  economic context, 139
  ethic of love in, 52, 157–160, 187
  hatred and, 164–165
  intellectual challenges to, 5
  interrelationship of struggles, 48, 52–53, 175
  moral basis, 205
  philosophical basis, 144–145, 146
  practical advantages, 164
  rejected by African American community, 25–
    26, 29
  as subject of philosophy, 217
  urban context, 121
  See also Nonviolent direct action
Love ethic
  concept of equality and, 186–187
  concept of justice and, 186–187
  criticism of King's thought on, 16–17
  Du Bois', 206–207

King's, 204–209, 221–224
in logic of nonviolence, 52, 157–160
power relations and, 191
with structural analysis, 51, 93–94
toughness in, 220–222, 223–224
vs. minimization of social inequalities, 187–
188
Lynching, 117–118, 123

Malcolm X, 27
Marable, Manning, 20, 232
March on Washington, 101
Marxist thought
American socialist movement, 110–111
Du Bois', 91, 139
King's thought and, 2–3, 20–22, 99–100
Randolph's socialist affiliations, 110–111
structural analysis, 49
See also Class analysis
Mass media, 87–88
Meredith, James, 139–140
Military service, 96

Nationalism
international labor and, 83–84
as liberation movements, 126
progressive, 141–142
Nietzschean philosophy, 191–192, 205
Nobel Peace Prize, 13, 49, 125
Noddings, Nell, 187, 217, 233
Nommo, 19
Nonviolent direct action
achievements of, in civil rights movement,
154–155
after King assassination, 142–143, 149–150
to break cycle of fear, 163–164
class-race issues, 139
community context, 159–160
as component of complete struggle, 168–
170, 180
conceptual bases, 146, 148
conditions for implementation, 170–176
declining influence of, in King Years, 13,
139–140, 156, 192–193
education and, 146–147
emergence of, in King Years, 12–13
equality as goal of, 29–30, 32–33
as experimental technique, 176–177
goals of, 8
King's philosophy, 155–162
levels of power in, 177–180
mechanism of change, 187
as militancy, 155–156
moment of direct action, 173–174
organization for, 175, 178–179
religious/spiritual component, 63–64, 157–
158, 211
significance of King's Chicago experience,
152–153
strategic implementation, 147–149, 168,
174–175
subsequent developments, 217

suffering entailed by, 157
See also Logic of nonviolence

Operation Breadbasket, 148
Organizing, 175, 178–179

Philadelphia, Du Bois' structural analysis of,
69–78
Postmodernism, 149
Power relations
economic, 177–178
economic power of African American community, 177–178
love ethic and, 191
political contexts, 178
Prophetic pragmatism, 19–20
Ptahotep, 11, 18, 214–216

Race relations
as basis for sociopolitical analysis, 129–130
black nationalism and, 141–142
in capitalist mass production, 92–93
class analysis, 57–58, 59–60, 97–98, 116–
117, 138–143
as focus of Black power movement, 140
justice in, 193–194
King's concept of equality, 33–34
labor movement and, 83–84, 89–91, 104–
105, 117–120
military service and, 96
for radical reform, 121–122
salience of, in social analysis, 6–7, 8, 80–89
strategies for social change, 160–161
structural analysis, 49–50, 96–97, 125
white liberalism, 195–202
white participation in civil rights movement,
189–190
See also Racism
Racism
in American philosophical method, 44–45
American socialism and, 110–111
arbitrariness of, 130–131
black support for, 61–62
concept of equality and, 127–130
cycle of oppression, 132–133
determinants of intensity, 137
Du Bois' study of black Philadelphia, 69–78
economic context, 140–141, 167
fear as basis of, 17, 162–168
imperialist practice, 134–136
intentionality, 51
international perspective, 126–127
King's early experiences with, 10
media-supported, 87–88
rationalization for, 46–47
as social concept, 131–132
structural analysis, 47–48, 53–64, 69, 86–89
violent vs. nonviolent tactics against, 165–167
Randolph, A. Philip
in African American intellectual tradition, 3,
5, 125
on capitalism, 118–119

Randolph, A. Philip (*cont.*)
  career as activist, 101
  Du Bois and, 101–107, 113–121, 124
  intellectual project, 97
  internationalism of, 122–123
  King and, 49, 95, 100–101
  on lynching, 117–118
  race–class analysis, 107–113, 116–121
  on role of church in social reform, 106
  socialist affiliations, 110–111
  on World War I, 104
Relativism, 34, 40
Religious faith/practice
  conception of supreme being, 64
  Jesus as ethical model, 151–155, 181–183
  Judaism, 199
  King's, 9, 17–18
  in King's philosophy, 207–211, 212
  in nonviolent direct action, 63–64, 157–158
  as obstacle to empowerment, 132
  role of church in social reform, 106
  structural change and, 63, 64
  See also Christianity

Segregation, 11
Self-concept
  African American, 194
  African Americans, 171–172
  for liberation struggle, 170–172, 182–183
  work ethic, 172–173
Self-defense, 123–124
Smith, Ervin, 14, 17, 233
Smith, Kenneth, 14, 17–21, 234
Social change
  advantages of nonviolent approach, King on, 155–156, 161–162
  African Americans as vanguard of, 120, 133–134
  agents of, 62–63
  agrarian, 120–121
  American social groups committed to, 31–32, 34–35
  based on concept of equality, 142
  class relations for, 136
  coalitions for, 175–176
  concept of justice in, 193–194
  Du Bois on, 85–86
  goals for black anti-capitalists, 121–122, 124
  holistic approach, 168–169
  for human rights above property rights, 117–118
  impediments in capitalism, 107–108
  implications of structural analysis, 59, 62–63
  justice as basis for, 120, 196–197
  King's optimism, 30–31
  King's philosophy and action, 145–146, 147–148
  local ordinances for inhibiting organization, 111–112
  middle-class contribution, 77–78, 175, 200–201

  moment of direct action, 173–174
  nationalist movements and, 126
  organization for, 175
  prospects for violent revolution, 161–162
  as revolution of values, 9, 201–202, 203–204
  role of white liberalism in, 195–202, 218
  self-attitude for, 170–172
  social organization for, 76
  structural obstacles to civil rights movement, 56–57
  systems model, 58
  theological dimension, 63–64
  value reconstruction for, 176
  violence for, 105–106
  white backlash, 195–196, 200
  work ethic for, 172–173
Structural analysis
  African American intellectual tradition, 49–50, 64–65
  basis of logic of nonviolence in, 51–52
  of black institutions, 61–62
  of Black Power movement, 58–59
  collective vs. individual responsibility, 51, 58, 61, 66–67
  color line in, 49–50, 69, 96–97
  Du Bois', 65–80, 95–96
  experiential account of racism for, 53–56
  goals, 48–49
  ideological component of exploitation, 116–117
  justice in America, 188–189
  meaning of, 47
  pluralism of liberation struggles in, 48, 52–53, 93, 99
  race–class interaction, 57–58, 59–60, 125
  racist imperialist model, 47–48, 49, 134–135
  structural change, 59, 62–63

Thomas, Laurence, xv, 99, 187, 234
Thurman, Howard
  in African American intellectual tradition, 3, 5
  on King, 203–204
  King and, 8, 18, 145–146, 151
  life of, 145, 181
  philosophical project, 181–183

Vietnam War, 20–21
Violence
  as agent of liberation, 105–106
  docility of victims, 132
  as inappropriate for revolution, 165–166
  King on, 154, 161–162, 163, 164–165
  self-defense, 123–124
  social relations and, 66

Walton, Hanes, 14–18, 157, 234
West, Cornel, 14, 19, 20, 44, 53, 111, 141, 217, 224, 234
World War I, 91–92, 101–103, 104

Zepp, Ira, 14, 17, 18, 234